Daily Wisdom for Men

2017 Devotional
Collection

© 2016 by Barbour Publishing, Inc.

Print ISBN 978-1-63409-904-2
Special edition ISBNs: 978-1-68322-002-2; 978-1-68322-003-9

eBook Editions:
Adobe Digital Edition (.epub) 978-1-68322-040-4
Kindle and MobiPocket Edition (.prc) 978-1-68322-041-1

Published by Barbour Books, an imprint of Barbour Publishing, Inc., P.O. Box 719, Uhrichsville, Ohio 44683, www.barbourbooks.com

Our mission is to publish and distribute inspirational products offering exceptional value and biblical encouragement to the masses.

Member of the
Evangelical Christian
Publishers Association

Printed in China.

Daily
Wisdom
for Men

2017 Devotional
Collection

BARBOUR BOOKS
An Imprint of Barbour Publishing, Inc.

HAPPY NEW YEAR

*The path of the righteous is like the morning sun,
shining ever brighter till the full light of day.*
PROVERBS 4:18 NIV

Today is the first day of a brand-new year. The last year may have been a wonderful time of prosperity and of God fulfilling promises. . .or it may have been marked by unexpected setbacks and baffling problems. Or perhaps it was a mixture of the two. So you're facing this coming year with eager expectation and perhaps a little concern. What will the coming months bring?

Your way may seem unclear at first, but if you stay close to God, living in His presence, you'll share in His Spirit and His holiness. You may not feel all that enlightened or righteous much of the time, but as long as you're seeking the Lord and doing your best to obey Him, He will hear and answer your prayers, guide you, and protect you and your family.

Then, slowly but surely, just as the initial glow of light in the sky at dawn gives way to the full light of day, the sun will rise and God's blessing will be made manifest in your life. It may take a while, and you may have to walk cautiously at first, feeling your way in semidarkness. But God has promised to be with you, so He will be.

The Bible says that Jesus, God's Son, is "the true Light which gives light to every man coming into the world" (John 1:9 NKJV). Walk according to His truth and you won't be in darkness.

BUILDING WITH GOD

Commit your actions to the LORD, and your plans will succeed.
PROVERBS 16:3 NLT

You may be involved in a complex project that has many unsettled issues surrounding it, and you might not know how to resolve them. Or its chances of succeeding might be slim. You're racking your brain, and your thoughts are all over the place. But have you committed the project—lock, stock, and barrel—to God? That's the way to gain peace and clarity. If you commit what you're involved in to God, He will see to it that your plans succeed.

The devil often fights what men of God are doing, so you need divine assistance to bring your works to completion. A solid Bible promise states, "Commit everything you do to the LORD. Trust him, and he will help you" (Psalm 37:5 NLT). He'll help you, that is, if the project was His will to begin with.

On the other end of the spectrum, however, the Bible warns, "Except the LORD build the house, they labour in vain that build it" (Psalm 127:1 KJV). Too many men are spinning their wheels trying to accomplish something, but they didn't check it out with God first to get His stamp of approval. So their labor is potentially in vain. Whether they're building a house or whatever they're trying to accomplish, it won't succeed, or it won't last.

Before you embark on a project, big or small, humbly lay it before God's feet and be sure to get His blessing and authorization before you sink time and energy into it.

WISE INVESTMENTS

Lay up for yourselves treasures in heaven.
MATTHEW 6:20 KJV

On this day in 1959, fifty-eight years ago, Alaska was admitted as the forty-ninth US state. When Secretary of State William Seward bought this vast northern territory from the Russians back in 1867, many Americans considered it a waste of money, calling it "Seward's Icebox." In hindsight, however, it was an extremely wise investment. For a mere $7.2 million ($121 million in today's dollars), 586,412 square miles were added to the nation.

Investing in the future always costs money, and it often seems at the time that you can ill afford it. And frankly, some things you *don't* need. Not yet, at least. For example, if you can get by with your present tools and business machines, you should. "If it ain't broke, don't fix it"—and don't squander your money on a new one.

But when it comes to vital things like health insurance, if you think you can get by without it and save yourself a few dollars, you usually find your wallet smarting you in the end. Similarly, it's unwise to neglect investing in your eternal future. Jesus advises all Christians to invest in heavenly treasure. You do that by having faith in Him, living a godly life, giving generously, and doing good to all men.

Typically, when you invest in your future eternal life in heaven, worldly people will speak disparagingly and insist that you're wasting your time. That's because they have no vision for the future. Like Seward's critics, they don't recognize a truly wise investment when they see one.

WORKING FOR A WAGE

In all labor there is profit, but idle chatter leads only to poverty.
PROVERBS 14:23 NKJV

Many men are dissatisfied with their jobs. You, too, may wonder from time to time whether you're in the right career. This is especially true if you're beginning to experience burnout at your workplace, or if you're in a profession where the markets are drying up. But more often than not, it's the day-to-day monotony of your job that eats away at your contentment. Either that, or you're working for a boss you can't stand.

The Bible puts things in perspective by reminding you that "in all labor there is profit." Your hourly wage might not be high, and it might not be your dream job, but if it's paying work, it's better than nothing—at least until you can find something more rewarding. Paul advised Christians, "Use your hands for good hard work" (Ephesians 4:28 NLT). While we would all rather be working smart, *not* hard, working hard is scriptural.

"Our people have to learn to be diligent in their work so that all necessities are met . . .and they don't end up with nothing to show for their lives" (Titus 3:14 MSG). You must not only apply yourself to your work, but you must keep at it faithfully, day after day, month after month.

Although ultimately you'll only be fully content when you're doing what God designed you for, you can find a measure of contentment even in imperfect situations. You can do this by working "heartily, as to the Lord, and not unto men" (Colossians 3:23 KJV).

LOVE DOES NO HARM

Love does no harm to a neighbor;
therefore love is the fulfillment of the law.
ROMANS 13:10 NKJV

The five books of Moses contained the law of God, and the overwhelming majority of these laws were intended to promote the well-being of the Israelites' fellow men and to bring about justice and restitution for those who had been wronged. They boiled down to this simple precept: Do no harm to your neighbor.

Since this was the whole point of the law, Paul explained that if you loved your neighbor you'd automatically fulfill the law, because you'd avoid harming him. Thus, you are to allow your life to be ruled by God's love. How do you do this? Simple. Yield to His Spirit, because "God is love" and "the love of God has been poured out in our hearts by the Holy Spirit" (1 John 4:8; Romans 5:5 NKJV).

As a man, you may feel that you must be rough and tough; you can't let anyone push you around; you must be assertive in business dealings and never show weakness. Loving others and being gentle may seem soft and weak by comparison.

Not so. You can be gentle to the weak, yet still be tough when you need to be. You can be assertive in business dealings, and adding love to the mix simply makes you honest and fair. You can act justly toward others without letting anyone push you around. Loving others takes courage and strength, and it proves you're a true man of God.

HAVING AN EPIPHANY

May you experience the love of Christ,
though it is too great to understand fully.
EPHESIANS 3:19 NLT

To experience an epiphany (from the Greek *epiphaneia*, "manifestation, striking appearance") means to have a sudden spiritual realization that allows you to grasp a profound truth or understand a mystery from a new perspective.

Epiphany, observed today, is also known as "Three Kings Day" because traditionally this was when the infant Jesus was revealed to the wise men, who are often referred to as "three kings" in Christmas hymns (Matthew 2:1–11). This fulfilled the prophecy that "the Gentiles shall come to thy light, and kings to the brightness of thy rising" (Isaiah 60:3 KJV).

Two thousand years have passed since that day, but we *all* still need an epiphany of Christ. Like the wise men, we must all come to His light and have a revelation of who He is. Ignatius of Loyola taught that Christians should cultivate an ardent love for Jesus by deeply contemplating Him. This good practice also draws you into union with Christ. In *The Spiritual Exercises* 104, Loyola prayed, "Lord, grant that I may see thee more clearly, love thee more dearly, follow thee more nearly."

You need to experience Christ's love, even though it's too great to ever fully comprehend. This needn't be limited to a sudden, dramatic experience—although those are desirable. What's needed most of all is to make a deliberate, daily commitment to Jesus, and to experience a continual lifelong series of epiphanies of Christ and His love for you. The Bible says, "They looked unto him, and were lightened" (Psalm 34:5 KJV).

LIVING FOR GOD

So then, each of us will give an account of ourselves to God.
ROMANS 14:12 NIV

"We must all stand before Christ to be judged. We will each receive whatever we deserve for the good or evil we have done" (2 Corinthians 5:10 NLT). There will be no hiding anything from Him in that day. "He will bring our darkest secrets to light and will reveal our private motives. Then God will give to each one whatever praise is due" (1 Corinthians 4:5 NLT).

This is not the condemnation of the unsaved at the end of time (Revelation 20:11–15). Rather, this event is the Judgment Seat of Christ, which happens shortly after His second coming. At this time, only Christians appear before Jesus; no one is being sent to hell. They have all been purchased with the blood of the Lamb, and their names are inscribed in the Book of Life.

The purpose of this accounting is to reward believers for the good they have done. But they will also suffer loss for sinful deeds. First Corinthians 3:11–15 is clear that although the people being judged shall be spared themselves, any selfish works will be burned up. Knowing this ought to spur you to do your best for Christ now. You don't want to enter heaven and live there forever with little or no reward.

Jesus repeatedly promised that God would reward faithful, diligent service for Him and also warned that we would be called to give an account for idle words and idle lives (Matthew 12:36; James 4:17). It matters very much how you live. So live for God!

SEEKING GOD EARLY

O God, thou art my God; early will I seek thee: my soul thirsteth
for thee . . .in a dry and thirsty land, where no water is.
PSALM 63:1 KJV

Though it may be difficult to believe at the time, there are benefits to experiencing a difficult life with numerous setbacks and problems. For one thing, it forces you to draw close to God, because you're painfully aware that you're unable to resolve your problems yourself. So you cry out to Him to help you. That is, in fact, one of the main reasons God *allows* you to experience difficulties.

As you grow older, there's a God-designed tendency for you to gain a more spiritual focus on matters. Jesus said it all along: "Seek ye first the kingdom of God, and his righteousness; and all these things shall be added unto you" (Matthew 6:33 KJV). However, when you're young and full of energy and plans, you often push ahead under your own steam. But a lifetime of difficulties has a way of loosening your grip on material things.

Many men make little time for prayer, apart from shooting off a quick cry to God in the morning or during emergencies. But you don't need to wait till you're old to get a deeper perspective. You can pray even in your youth, "Teach us to realize the brevity of life, so that we may grow in wisdom" (Psalm 90:12 NLT).

This world is like a dry and thirsty land without water. The sooner you realize that the things of earth don't truly satisfy, the sooner you'll focus on God.

HOPE IN THE LORD

*Unrelenting disappointment leaves you heartsick,
but a sudden good break can turn life around.*
PROVERBS 13:12 MSG

Although difficulties are woven into the very fabric of life and many are designed by God to draw you close to Him, He also knows that a constant onslaught of problems can frustrate you and cause you to give up in despair. That's why He frequently sends relief in answer to your prayers.

Sometimes you can get by without the whole problem being solved immediately. But you desperately need a glimmer of hope to know that God is with you and that He will eventually work everything out. So you pray, "Send me a sign of your favor" (Psalm 86:17 NLT). This is very scriptural.

But how can you know that God even *desires* to do good to you? Because He promises this repeatedly in His Word—stating clearly that He will supply what you need, bring peace to troubled situations, and relieve intense pressure. When an unknown psalmist was downhearted and discouraged, he prayed, "I wait for the LORD, my soul waits, and in His word I do hope" (Psalm 130:5 NKJV). He put his faith in God's promises.

God knows that unrelenting problems and testing can dishearten you. And He loves you and thinks upon you, even when He seems most distant. If you pray for it and look for it, He will not only send you a sign of His favor—to give you hope—but as dawn breaks after a long, dark night, He will send His full cavalry charging in to rescue you.

HUSBANDS AND WIVES

There is neither Jew nor Greek. . .there is neither
male nor female: for ye are all one in Christ Jesus.
GALATIANS 3:28 KJV

The Declaration of Independence states "that all men are created equal, that they are endowed by their Creator with certain unalienable rights. . ." We understand that when it states "all men" that it means "mankind"; it is self-evident that women have unalienable rights before God as well.

These rights include, among other things, the right to vote. Yet it wasn't until January 10, 1878—139 years ago to the day—that Senator Sargent introduced a bill in Congress to grant women this right. And it didn't become a reality for another forty-one years; in 1929, the Nineteenth Amendment to the Constitution was ratified, granting women's suffrage.

The Bible shows the attitude that men should have toward women when it says, "You husbands must give honor to your wives. Treat your wife with understanding as you live together. She may be weaker than you are, but she is your equal partner in God's gift of new life. Treat her as you should so your prayers will not be hindered" (1 Peter 3:7 NLT).

If your prayers are frequently being hindered, you might want to check your heart and make sure that you're honoring your wife and treating her as you should. She isn't always right, any more than you are, but listen to her counsel, even as Manoah listened to his wife (Judges 13:21–23). Chances are good you'll be blessed and even learn something.

GOD PROTECTS YOU

The Lord is faithful, and he will strengthen
you and protect you from the evil one.
2 THESSALONIANS 3:3 NIV

God can strengthen you so that you can resist the onslaughts of the devil. These can be dark, negative thoughts, sexual temptation, waves of paralyzing fear, accidents, inexplicable illnesses, and many other kinds of attacks. Fortunately, you don't need to depend on your own strength to withstand these calamities. God has promised to supply strength.

Jesus instructed believers to pray, "'Our Father in heaven. . .deliver us from the evil one'" (Matthew 6:9, 13 NIV). Since Jesus commanded us to pray for this, we can certainly expect that this is a prayer that God will hear and answer. Jesus also told His Father, "My prayer is. . .that you protect them from the evil one" (John 17:15 NIV). It's reassuring to know that Jesus is backing your prayers up, praying along with you, entreating the Father to protect you.

And will God be faithful to respond? Yes, He will. As Paul stated, "The Lord is *faithful*, and he *will* strengthen you and protect you from the evil one" (2 Thessalonians 3:3 NIV, emphasis added).

Of course, you need to put forth some effort as well. As the famous description of our spiritual armor in Ephesians 6 says, you need to stand your ground, hold firmly to your shield of faith, and steadfastly resist the devil. This can be a difficult battle, but know that God is overshadowing you, infusing your spirit with strength, and—if you remain steadfast and continue believing—He will make you victorious.

GAINING WEALTH GOD'S WAY

*Dishonest money dwindles away, but whoever gathers
money little by little makes it grow.*
PROVERBS 13:11 NIV

According to many people, the way to get ahead financially is to make false claims on your income tax, to overcharge for goods or services, and to cut corners on quality whenever you can. But people find out after a while if you're dishonest, and your business will suffer as a result.

God's way to financial prosperity is to gather money honestly little by little and diligently set it aside in a savings account. If you start early enough, you'll eventually earn compound interest. There are no shortcuts, no maps leading to pirate treasure, and no leprechauns guiding you to a pot of gold. And if you're counting on winning the lottery, forget it.

If you gain enough money, you can earn even more by investing it. Jesus taught the importance of investments in the parable of the talents (Matthew 25:14-30). In His story, when a master entrusted each of his servants with a sum of money, the first two went out and invested it, earning double and even five times what they had started with.

And Solomon pointed out the best way to build your retirement savings, saying, "Take a lesson from the ants, you lazybones. Learn from their ways and become wise! Though they have no. . .ruler to make them work, they labor hard all summer, gathering food for the winter" (Proverbs 6:6-8 NLT).

As with most things in life, being faithful day after day is the best way to build a successful life, career, and savings account.

SURROUNDED BY TROUBLE

"In this godless world you will continue to experience difficulties.
But take heart! I've conquered the world."
JOHN 16:33 MSG

The fact that today is Friday the Thirteenth puts many superstitious people on edge. They're constantly looking over their shoulders, expecting "bad luck" to strike. They worry that on days like this, there's a greater chance of accidents, misfortune, and loss. While that's nothing more than a quirky fallacy, the fact is that "'man is born to trouble as surely as sparks fly upward'" (Job 5:7 NIV).

In fact, Jesus Himself promised that "in this world you will have trouble" (John 16:33 NIV). He literally guaranteed it. And it's just as likely to happen on one day as the next, regardless of whether it's a Friday on the thirteenth day of the month or not.

Many serious problems are caused by the unrelenting attacks of our spiritual enemy. In his hymn "A Mighty Fortress Is Our God," Martin Luther wrote that "our ancient foe doth seek to work us woe," but God is our helper "amid the flood of mortal ills." He ends with this triumphant declaration: "And though this world, with devils filled, should threaten to undo us, we will not fear, for God hath willed His truth to triumph through us."

So despite all your troubles, take heart! Jesus has overcome the world, and despite every problem that Satan throws your way, God will eventually cause you to triumph. You may end up with a few scratches and dents, but God will come through. He won't abandon you.

CARING FOR OTHERS

Don't look out only for your own interests,
but take an interest in others, too.
PHILIPPIANS 2:4 NLT

When the Bible says "take an interest in others," it's referring to *all* other people. This includes your wife, children, relatives, workmates, acquaintances, and total strangers—anyone who's not the person looking back at you in the mirror. God understands that you'll naturally look out for yourself and take care of business that's important to you. You have to. That's your responsibility. But this verse reminds you that you're also your brother's keeper.

Take your children, for example. Because they're children, they think as children and act like children (1 Corinthians 13:11). And they're also interested in the things that interest most children—things that long ago ceased to interest *you*. But since you love them, you make an effort to engage with them. This includes taking the time to listen to their jokes, as well as pausing to sympathize with their sorrows.

The Bible says, "Be willing to associate with people of low position" (Romans 12:16 NIV). This includes cousins who have made little of themselves and whose interests seem boring and mundane to you. It includes an elderly relative who seems to be a relic of a bygone century. To associate with them, you have to let go of the idea that your time is too valuable or that the rewards aren't worth the trouble.

Many people aren't willing to put forth the effort to care for others. But there are indeed great rewards for doing so.

DON'T LOSE YOUR NERVE

The children of Ephraim, being armed and carrying bows,
turned back in the day of battle.
PSALM 78:9 NKJV

The writer of Psalm 78 describes a situation where the men of Israel had been called to battle, so they assembled their armies and marched forth, armed with swords and shields and carrying bows and quivers full of arrows. But when the tribe of Ephraim saw the enemy, they turned back and headed home. Why was that? Although they had trained for war and were well armed, they lost their nerve. They didn't believe that God was with them.

This applies to challenges in modern life as well. You could be fully trained in your profession and have all the tools you need, but if a situation seems overwhelming, you may throw up your hands in defeat before you even start. It might be that you got out of the wrong side of bed that morning. But more often it's because of an attitude you've entertained for years.

One time when Moses doubted that he could do what God had commanded him, the Lord asked, "What is that in your hand?" Moses answered, "A rod" (Exodus 4:2 NKJV). It didn't seem like much, but God proceeded to do astounding miracles when Moses held it up. Even so, when large bills are looming and you have limited cash. . .you may simply need to get your eyes on your potential for earning the extra funds.

Never underestimate your ability to do what God asks you to do. When He is with you, you can do amazing things.

Martin Luther King Jr. Day

LOVE YOUR ENEMIES

"If anyone slaps you on the right cheek,
turn to them the other cheek also."
MATTHEW 5:39 NIV

Today is the day we celebrate the life of a great American and one of the last century's most outstanding orators. Martin Luther King Jr. was born on January 15, 1929, in Atlanta, Georgia, and grew up during an era of racial injustice when African Americans were segregated from the larger society, were barred from many establishments and organizations, and suffered countless racial indignities.

Slaves had been declared free by the Emancipation Proclamation in 1863, yet for most black men and women, true freedom and equality were still an elusive dream.

Martin Luther King Jr. rose to become the leading civil rights advocate of modern times. He spoke eloquently and movingly and motivated millions of black Americans, and many white Americans, to march to bring about change. Dr. King stressed nonviolent methods, for which he received the Nobel Peace Prize in 1964. He was assassinated on April 4, 1968. Much has changed for the better since then, but there remains work to be done.

We must never forget that Dr. King found the courage and inspiration for his life's work in his Christian faith. He was motivated by Jesus' commands to "love your neighbor" and "love your enemies" (Matthew 19:19; 5:44 NIV). Jesus' statement to "turn. . .the other cheek" (Matthew 5:39 NIV) inspired his nonviolent civil disobedience.

So as we ask ourselves what we can do to honor Dr. King's memory and continue the work he left unfinished, it is to our Christian faith that we must look for guidance.

CRYING AND LAUGHING

To every thing there is a season, and a time to every purpose under the heaven. . .A time to weep, and a time to laugh.
ECCLESIASTES 3:1, 4 KJV

You may be persuaded that grown men shouldn't cry, but as you look through the pages of the Bible, you see again and again that men of God weren't afraid to make themselves vulnerable by showing their emotions. From Jacob and Esau weeping as they embraced, to King David publicly lamenting his son Absalom, Bible men often wept.

And they just as frequently laughed and enjoyed humorous situations. They even had a proverb: "A feast is *made* for laughter" (Ecclesiastes 10:19 KJV, emphasis added), so you can be sure that they looked forward to times when they would cut loose and laugh heartily.

Whether you laugh and cry in public or hold it in stoically, the literal meaning of these passages from Ecclesiastes 3 is that during the course of your life, you can expect seasons of both sorrow and joy, times that would be enough to make a grown man cry as well as others that cause him to burst into uncontrollable laughter.

Many men wish that they could have *only* happy times, an "abundant life" where they never experience stress, hardship, or sorrow. They quote verses, claiming that they promise unending prosperity and happiness. But this is an unrealistic expectation that sets them up for a hard landing.

Thank God for the happy times. Enjoy them to the full. Know that you will also experience times of sorrow, too—but remember that you won't have to walk through them alone.

GIVING GENEROUSLY AND WISELY

Give freely and spontaneously. Don't have a stingy heart.
*The way you handle matters like this triggers G*OD*, your God's,*
blessing in everything you do, all your work and ventures.
DEUTERONOMY 15:10 MSG

Often it seems contrary to sound reason to give "freely and spontaneously."
Aren't you supposed to follow a well-thought-out budget and not deviate
from it with impulse purchases? Yes, you are. But God makes a difference
between selfish personal expenditures and unselfish giving to the needy.
And He promises to bless you for your generosity.

A word of caution, however: Some people can be just as irresponsible
in giving as they can be in impulse buying. They have so *much* empathy that,
without thinking things through, they would give away their car or drain
their bank account. Remember, "wisdom brings success" (Ecclesiastes 10:10
NKJV). Or as *The Message* says, "Use your head." And bear in mind: you are
to care for your family first and foremost (Matthew 15:5–6; 1 Timothy 5:8).

But there are times to follow your heart instead of your head—and
that's when God's Spirit is speaking to you. The New King James Version
states clearly, "You shall surely give to him, and your heart should not be
grieved when you give" (Deuteronomy 15:10). If you *know* that God wants
you to give, then absolutely, give—even if your natural mind tries to hold
you back, grieving over giving away any hard-earned cash.

However, if you have reasonable doubts about whether it's wise to give at
this time, then don't. "Whatever is not from faith is sin" (Romans 14:23 NKJV).

SERVICE WITH A SMILE

Whatever your hand finds to do, do it with your might.
ECCLESIASTES 9:10 NKJV

The business world has appropriated many Christian principles simply because it knows that giving excellent customer service is good for its bottom line. That's why businesses use Bible principles in slogans such as "We're not satisfied until you are" and "We go the extra mile." Jesus was the One who said, "'Whoever compels you to go one mile, go with him two'" (Matthew 5:41 NKJV), yet it sometimes seems like commerce has grasped the value of this principle better than Christians.

In Paul's day, there were many slaves in the Roman Empire, and he gave them the following advice when doing their work:

> *Obey your earthly masters in everything; and do it, not only when their eye is on you and to curry their favor, but with sincerity of heart and reverence for the Lord. Whatever you do, work at it with all your heart, as working for the Lord, not for human masters.*
> (Colossians 3:22–23 NIV)

This is excellent advice for Christian employees today as well. Do an honest day's work for an honest day's pay, and do it cheerfully.

You may work for a business that prides itself in excellent service—in fact, "service with a smile." They may even advise you to smile *all* the time. The message they want you to send to your customers is that this isn't just a sale, but that you genuinely care about them. These are Christian principles, so you should not only practice them while on the job, but in your personal life as well.

INAUGURATION DAY

I urge. . .that petitions, prayers, intercession and thanksgiving be made for all people—for kings and all those in authority, that we may live peaceful and quiet lives.
1 TIMOTHY 2:1–2 NIV

Today, the person who won the election for the office of president of the United States is being inaugurated. (To "inaugurate" means to formally admit someone to public office.) At noon, the president-elect will take the oath of office at the west front of the Capitol Building, then give a speech. A member of the clergy will pray a public prayer, dedicating the new president. After a congressional luncheon, the president will walk down Pennsylvania Avenue to the White House.

Depending on who won the election, this will either be a time of new beginnings or a continuation of many of the same policies that marked the last four years. Depending on whom you voted for, you'll either find this day exciting and hopeful or discouraging and sad.

But whoever begins his or her term today, you're called upon to pray for him or her. . .even if you voted for the other person. It's in your own interest. After all, the new president's decisions will determine whether you live a peaceful life or not, and whether you prosper or not. As Jeremiah told the Jews living in Babylon, "'Seek the peace and prosperity of the city to which I have carried you into exile. Pray to the LORD for it, because if it prospers, you too will prosper'" (Jeremiah 29:7 NIV).

So take some time today to pray for the new president to make wise decisions.

SAY SOMETHING

Everyone enjoys a fitting reply;
it is wonderful to say the right thing at the right time!
PROVERBS 15:23 NLT

Some people have such great empathy for others and read people so well that they habitually know the right thing to say at the right time. On top of this, they're very communicative; they can so easily give advice to family and friends or say something comforting to encourage others when they're down. And have you noticed how many of these people happen to be *women*?

But what if you're not a mind reader, especially when it comes to people's mysterious emotions? And what if you're not that communicative? What if, like so many other men, you're the strong, silent type?

Solomon wrote, "The heartfelt counsel of a friend is as sweet as perfume" (Proverbs 27:9 NLT), and he was talking to men as much as to women. Note that this counsel is effective because it's "heartfelt." It comes from the heart. As long as what you say is caring and authentic, it doesn't matter if it lacks eloquence. The most important thing is that the person you're speaking to knows that you deeply *care* for him or her.

Even if you're the quiet type, you can still say something, no matter how awkwardly or haltingly you express yourself. So what if you can't read a person's emotions? You can find out where they're at by gently asking. They may not always reveal the full picture, but again, they'll know that you love them. You can say the right thing at the right time even if you stumble all over yourself saying it.

TRUE AND REASONABLE FAITH

*Always be prepared to give an answer to everyone who asks
you to give the reason for the hope that you have.*
1 PETER 3:15 NIV

Many Christian men know very little about their faith. If asked to give a reason why they believe in Jesus, they don't know what to answer. About all they can say is "I just do." Responses like that won't convince anyone, and it indicates that they haven't given careful thought to the matter.

However, the same person may give *very* careful thought to his business plans and decisions. After all, a great deal of money and many months of his life is riding on them being right. Yet much *more* is riding on whether his faith is true or not. And Christianity, because it is firmly rooted in actual history, not mere myths, can stand up to close scrutiny.

When the Roman governor, Festus, protested that Paul was out of his mind for believing in Jesus, Paul replied, "'I am not insane. . .What I am saying is true and reasonable'" (Acts 26:25 NIV). The Christian faith is not only true, it is also reasonable. It makes sense.

If you're too busy to study the matter yourself, you should avail yourself of the excellent resources that are available—books by Christian writers such as Josh McDowell, Lee Strobel, and J. Warner Wallace. Their books contain multitudes of good reasons to believe.

Make up your mind to investigate the foundations of your faith. Then you can be a more effective witness for Jesus.

LIVING WHAT YOU UNDERSTAND

To him who knows to do good and does not do it, to him it is sin.
JAMES 4:17 NKJV

There are sins of omission as well as sins of commission. How often do men fail to do something good out of lethargy, procrastination, or simply a lack of concern? Solomon instructed, "Do not withhold good from those to whom it is due, when it is in the power of your hand to do so" (Proverbs 3:27 NKJV). As we see in the next verse, he was talking about giving generously to people when you just don't feel like it.

There are many complex situations where you won't *know* the correct thing to do. In hindsight, yes, you may see clearly what you should've done, but if you simply don't know at the time what you should do, you won't be held accountable. But most of the Bible's important teachings are very plain and simple. There's little that's puzzling about them. The problem, however, is that they can be difficult to obey.

Mark Twain said, "It ain't those parts of the Bible that I can't understand that bother me, it is the parts that I do understand." Whatever context Twain meant this in, it's very relevant here. For example, most Christians are deeply bothered by Jesus' command "Love your enemies" (Matthew 5:44 NKJV). They reason that He couldn't really have meant that literally. So they withhold love and forgiveness from people they don't like.

Once you understand clearly what you ought to do, however, it's a sin if you don't follow through and do it.

THE MAD GOLD RUSH

"Wisdom is more valuable than gold and crystal."
JOB 28:17 NLT

The California Gold Rush began exactly 169 years ago today, on January 24, 1848, when James Marshall found gold at Sutter's Mill in California. The next year, 1849, some three hundred thousand "forty-niners" rushed to California in hopes of striking it rich. It sounds exciting, but this was a dark period in America's history. A *few* people became rich, but at what price?

By 1855, the madness ended, after revealing human beings at their greediest, most fallen state. Some 4,200 people had been murdered, 5,300 miners had starved or died without medicine, 1,400 people had committed suicide, 1,700 had gone insane, and 120,000 Native Americans had been wiped out.

You might have had the idea that rough-and-tumble events like the gold rush are what built our country and made it great. But the credit belongs elsewhere. During this same time, many Bible-believing pioneers traveled across America to claim a farm and begin patiently working the soil. For them, contentment and the wisdom of God were the greatest riches.

Still, for many men, all of *life* is still one big gold rush. Millions get excited about an enormous lottery jackpot. Millions more pursue other get-rich-quick schemes. "Greedy people try to get rich quick but don't realize they're headed for poverty" (Proverbs 28:22 NLT). Today, just like back in the gold rush days, unselfishness, hard work, and patience turn out to be truly wise in the long run.

Beware gold fever! "The love of money is a root of all kinds of evil" (1 Timothy 6:10 NKJV).

WORKPLACE HUMOR

Nor should there be obscenity, foolish talk or coarse joking,
which are out of place, but rather thanksgiving.
EPHESIANS 5:4 NIV

If you work in a professional environment or a business that constantly interacts with the public, the language you hear on a daily basis is apt to be clean and courteous. But there are many trades (particularly all-male workplaces) where cursing and off-color humor are common—particularly if certain coworkers are outspoken unbelievers who habitually use graphic curse words and find crude sexual jokes funny.

While you don't want to come across as a straitlaced old fogey, it's important that you don't encourage their behavior. If you go along with their jokes, laughing politely to avoid offending them, they'll be emboldened to keep going. It's best to let them know up front that this is not your type of humor. There are ways to do this without giving offense. You can simply consistently refrain from smiling at their jokes. They'll get the point that you don't find them funny.

Of course, you have little control over their reaction. Some men will take the cue and turn down the volume around you. Others may mock you for being "puritanical" and speak disparagingly of Christianity. Don't be surprised. Peter says, "You have spent enough time in the past doing what pagans choose to do. . . . They are surprised that you do not join them in their reckless, wild living, and they heap abuse on you" (1 Peter 4:3-4 NIV).

Whatever others around you do, continue to follow Christ with a clear conscience.

GOD'S ENDGAME

My son, do not despise the chastening of the Lord,
nor detest His correction; for whom the Lord loves He corrects,
just as a father the son in whom he delights.
PROVERBS 3:11–12 NKJV

If God constantly sends hardship, financial problems, or health issues into your life, you can begin to get mentally exhausted. You may even think that He allows you to experience grief because He hates you. But the opposite is true. The Lord chastens you because He *loves* you. He especially delights in you and rejoices to see you do your best—and He knows that you only truly excel under pressure.

The Lord says, "'The people I love, I call to account—prod and correct and guide so that they'll live at their best'" (Revelation 3:19 MSG). It's no fun being repeatedly called to account for your actions and decisions. It's frustrating when the boss calls you to his office once again to account for a mistake you made and asks, "Why did you do that?"

At times, you wish God would just let your sloppy behavior slide. And if He didn't care for you as much as He does, He just might do that. But He has a purpose in continually correcting you. He's refining you, and He invites you to actively join the process. Paul wrote, "Those who cleanse themselves. . .will be instruments for special purposes, made holy, useful to the Master and prepared to do any good work" (2 Timothy 2:21 NIV).

God seeks to make you into a better person, capable of great things. Are you okay with that?

FIGHT LIKE MEN

Keep your eyes open, hold tight to your convictions, give it all you've got, be resolute, and love without stopping.
1 CORINTHIANS 16:13–14 MSG

Are you facing an aggressive, belligerent enemy in some area of your personal life? Is one of your children going through a crisis that demands much of your time and energy? Are financial problems putting you at risk of losing your home? These and many other serious challenges test your resolve and show what you're made of.

When Nehemiah and his men were surrounded by enemies who threatened to overwhelm them, he encouraged them, saying, "'Don't be afraid of the enemy! Remember the Lord, who is great and glorious, and fight for your brothers, your sons, your daughters, your wives, and your homes!'" (Nehemiah 4:14 NLT). Or as David instructed his son Solomon when he was about to face great challenges, "'Take courage and be a man'" (1 Kings 2:2 NLT).

You're already used to dealing with a certain level of problems and difficulties in your daily life. But sometimes problems go on and on and become very serious threats. At that point, they can seem so overwhelming, so impossible to deal with, that you feel like simply throwing up your hands in despair and saying, "I give up!" But that is precisely the point when you need to be resolute. Have courage and don't give up the fight.

Certain things are well worth fighting for and giving all you've got. That's how you win battles and withstand the onslaughts of the enemy.

TRUSTING GOD TO ACT

Wait for the LORD; be strong and take heart and wait for the LORD.
PSALM 27:14 NIV

There will be points in your life when you're utterly incapable of affecting the outcome of a situation you find yourself in. At times like that, you have no choice but to wait for the Lord and trust Him to act. Often, it then takes great faith to believe that God is with you, because He might seem very distant, or like He's turned away from you. This is why Isaiah said, "I will wait on the LORD, who hides His face from the house of Jacob; and I will hope in Him" (Isaiah 8:17 NKJV).

If you've sinned and disobeyed the Lord, chances are good that He actually *has* turned His face from you and isn't listening to your prayers (see Isaiah 59:1–2). But if you have sincerely repented, then there are no longer any issues between you, and you simply have to believe that God loves you and will act on your behalf.

This takes faith. You might go through a time of testing just like Job, who was convinced for several months that God was against him. During such lonely sojourns, you must trust God's Word, not your feelings, and believe that "the mercy of the LORD is from everlasting to everlasting upon them that fear him" (Psalm 103:17 KJV).

This can be a difficult time, and what will sustain you is the knowledge that God is good and that He will eventually come through for you and resolve the situation.

ALL EYES ARE UPON YOU

*"Let your light so shine before men, that they may see your
good works and glorify your Father in heaven."*
MATTHEW 5:16 NKJV

It's important that you live your Christian faith sincerely, not just put on a show when you think people are watching. However, like it or not, people *are* watching you all the time and constantly judging whether you're living what you preach. This includes fellow believers and your own children. That's why Paul said, "Be an example to all believers in what you say, in the way you live, in your love, your faith, and your purity" (1 Timothy 4:12 NLT).

Unbelievers are watching, too—both the curious who are attracted to the Gospel and the antagonistic who're looking for an excuse to criticize the faith. Peter refers to them, saying, "It is God's will that your honorable lives should silence those ignorant people who make foolish accusations against you" (1 Peter 2:15 NLT).

People are constantly watching you. It can't be avoided. In fact, it's God's *plan*—one of His chief ways of letting the world see what the Gospel can do for a person. Jesus said that believers were the light of the world, a city set on a hilltop (raised up like a stage), where everyone could see them and think about them.

And people are *especially* watching you when you go through hardships, whether they're misfortunes, illnesses, or persecution. Paul said, "God has displayed us. . .for we have been made a spectacle to the world" (1 Corinthians 4:9 NKJV). How you act when you're suffering communicates more effectively than a sermon.

UNITY IN THE SPIRIT

They were all filled with the Holy Ghost. . . And the multitude
of them that believed were of one heart and of one soul.
Acts 4:31–32 kjv

You received the Holy Spirit into your heart, the core of your being, when you put your faith in Jesus (see Galatians 4:6). Many people are very interested in what the Spirit can do for them—as well they should be, since it is He who saves them and gives them wonderful gifts! But they often overlook one of the chief purposes of the Spirit—to bring Christians into unity.

"By one Spirit we were all baptized into one body" (1 Corinthians 12:13 NKJV), so although we are each individual members, we "are all one in Christ Jesus" (Galatians 3:28 NIV). We all share in "the communion of the Holy Spirit" (2 Corinthians 13:14 NKJV).

The very same Holy Spirit who dwells in your heart also dwells in the hearts of all other believers, and He loves every one of them as much as He loves you. This is why Christians are to love one another sincerely, and why "the members should have the same care one for another" (1 Corinthians 12:25 KJV).

You may be a rugged individualist and be inclined to look out chiefly for yourself, but if you do so, you're missing out on the big picture. When God sent His Spirit into your heart, He made you to live in fellowship with other Christians. You are to look out for them just like you would a natural brother or sister.

FAITHFUL, BLESSED WORKERS

He that is faithful in that which is least is faithful also in much.
LUKE 16:10 KJV

Seventeen-year-old Joseph was taken as a slave to Egypt. He could have bemoaned his fate and sunk into despair. But Joseph's diligence, work ethic, and love for God came to the fore:

> *Potiphar. . .realized that the LORD was with Joseph, giving him success in everything he did. . .so he soon made Joseph his personal attendant. He put him in charge of his entire household and everything he owned. . . . All his household affairs ran smoothly, and his crops and livestock flourished. So Potiphar gave Joseph complete administrative responsibility over everything he owned.* (Genesis 39:3–6 NLT)

Joseph started off as a new slave learning the ropes. But he was soon promoted to be Potiphar's assistant, carrying out all his instructions. Finally, when Potiphar realized just *how* capable Joseph was, he removed himself from the picture and gave Joseph "complete administrative responsibility" over his entire estate.

Jesus told a parable about a wealthy man who rewarded two hardworking servants, setting them over his estate, and told them both, "'Well done, good and faithful servant! You have been faithful with a few things; I will put you in charge of many things'" (Matthew 25:21 NIV).

God is not the only One who rewards diligent hard work. When your boss realizes that you have a superior work attitude, and that God causes you to succeed, he'll advance you as well. If you wish to be promoted, be diligent in the details, and God will bless your work.

EXCELLING AT WORK

Do you see a man who excels in his work?
He will stand before kings; he will not stand before unknown men.
PROVERBS 22:29 NKJV

It is easy to get caught up in working for the applause of men—or simply to put food on the table—because both produce tangible results. But a man who excels in his work can do so for other reasons. For the Christian, we are called to work to the glory of God (Colossians 3:17).

A man who excels in his work is diligent. He studies the systems that are in place and tweaks them to make them even better. He knows the needs of his customers and he exceeds them. He keeps his word. He is prompt, accurate, and quick to adjust his course when he sees the need to do so.

Joseph was sold into slavery by his brothers, but he worked hard and found favor with Potiphar, the governor of Egypt, who eventually elevated Joseph to second-in-command. He literally stood before royalty, as the verse above says. But even for those of us who will never meet nobility for our strong work efforts, we will stand before the King of kings to give account someday.

If you aren't already doing so, what would it look like for you to excel at work for God's glory? Would it mean loving an unlovable boss? Would it mean allowing him or her to take the credit for one of your ideas? Would it mean going above and beyond your work description to benefit your department or company?

ACT LIKE MEN

Watch ye, stand fast in the faith, quit you like men, be strong.
1 CORINTHIANS 16:13 KJV

In his first letter to the Corinthian church, the apostle Paul tells them he plans to pass through Macedonia before visiting Corinth for the winter (1 Corinthians 16:5), if the Lord allows. Until he gets there, he has several messages for them. He wants them to take a collection for poor Christians (verses 1–4), to take good care of Timothy when he visits (verses 10–11), and to be on the lookout for a possible visit from Apollos (verse 12).

Then he adds the admonition in verse 13 that you see above. They were to stand fast in the faith and to "quit you like men." This phrase was used in the English-speaking world at the time the King James Version was translated, and it is the equivalent of our modern phrase "act like men." In other words, Paul was telling them to hold fast until learned believers could arrive to encourage them in the faith.

Here's how Bible commentator Matthew Henry describes this phrase in his *Commentary on the Whole Bible*: "Act the manly, firm, and resolved part: behave strenuously, in opposition to the bad men who would divide and corrupt you, those who would split you into factions or seduce you from the faith: be not terrified nor inveigled by them; but show yourselves men in Christ, by your steadiness, by your sound judgment and firm resolution."

Take inventory of the worldly men around you. Are they seeking to corrupt you? Stand firm against them—resolved to stay true to the faith.

STANDING IN THE GAP

*"So I sought for a man among them who would make a wall,
and stand in the gap before Me on behalf of the land,
that I should not destroy it; but I found no one."*
EZEKIEL 22:30 NKJV

When God commissions the prophet Ezekiel to chronicle a long list of sins committed by Jerusalem, Ezekiel covers all his bases: murder, idolatry, mistreatment of parents, oppression of strangers, mistreatment of the fatherless and the widows, profaning the Sabbath, acts of lewdness, bribery, and extortion, as well as her priests violating God's law. In every sense, Jerusalem had become a den of iniquity.

And yet, in the midst of such wickedness, God was looking for a man who would make a wall, and stand in the gap before Him on behalf of the land, that He would not destroy it. But sadly, He found no one. As Bible commentators point out, not every man was caught up in debauchery. But one of the few who wasn't—Jeremiah—was forbidden to pray for the city (Jeremiah 11:14). Apparently, the city had crossed the point of no return with God. The righteous had abandoned the gates, His judgment certain.

Nations fall as the righteous stop practicing righteousness. The act of falling away can be so subtle that you almost don't recognize it. A compromise here. A "small" sin there. And before you know it, you have lost your house, and then your city—not in the physical sense, generally, but in the moral sense. If God were to look for a man to stand in the gap today, would He find you there?

KEEPING THE FAITH

For we have spent enough of our past lifetime in doing the will of the Gentiles—when we walked in lewdness, lusts, drunkenness, revelries, drinking parties, and abominable idolatries.

1 PETER 4:3 NKJV

The Jews who were dispersed among Gentiles (the unconverted) had picked up many of the Gentiles' bad habits: lewdness, lust, drunkenness, revelries, drinking parties, and abominable idolatries. Peter is calling them to a different lifestyle—one the Gentiles will think is strange (verse 4), but ultimately they will have to give an account to God for their choices (verse 5).

A 2013 article on the Charisma News website cited a George Barna poll that said "61 percent of today's twenty-somethings who had been churched at one point during their teen years are now spiritually disengaged"—meaning they don't attend worship, read their Bible, or pray. But young people aren't the only ones who are disengaging. Another Charisma News article from 2015 cites a Pew Research Study, saying: "Between 2007 and 2014, the number of Americans identifying as Christians fell from 78.4 percent (178.1 million people) to 70.6 percent (172.8 million people)."

First Timothy 4:1 warns that in latter times some will depart from the faith. But it doesn't have to happen in your house, on your watch. You've spent enough of your life chasing the desires of the flesh, and you know where that leads. If you are married, teach your family the perils of chasing their own desires. If you are unmarried, gather with other believers who want to remain strong in the faith and constantly remind one another to stay on the narrow road.

GODLY PURSUITS

But you, O man of God, flee these things [the love of money and its empty pursuits] and pursue righteousness, godliness, faith, love, patience, gentleness.
1 TIMOTHY 6:11 NKJV

When the Bible tells us to flee certain sins (putting off the old man), it tells us how to do so by pursuing new practices (putting on the new man) (Ephesians 4:21–24). In the verse above, the apostle Paul has just finished warning young Timothy about the perils of loving money, and then he tells him how to fight it: pursue righteousness, godliness, faith, love, patience, and gentleness.

What exactly does that look like? Pursuing righteousness in this context isn't about our eternal standing, according to commentators, but rather it is about dealing with one another justly. In doing so, we are not seeking to unjustly profit from our relationship with them. Pursuing godliness means to do our part in the sanctification process. We can do nothing to purify ourselves of our sin, but we can put ourselves under the preaching and the reading of the Word. Pursuing faith is about taking our eyes off our circumstances and placing them above. Loving God replaces loving money. Pursuing patience means bearing with loss, injury, and persecution. And pursuing gentleness means being content with our lot.

If the love of money is strong in you, the list of pursuits above is the antidote. As you begin to pursue them, your love of money will be loosened, and you will see other spiritual victories in your life as well.

A DIVINE MEETING PLACE

And Judas, who betrayed Him, also knew the place [a garden,
over the Brook Kidron—also known as the garden of
Gethsemane]; for Jesus often met there with His disciples.
JOHN 18:2 NKJV

Even though Jesus knew that Judas was about to betray Him, He didn't vary His pattern of meeting with His disciples in the Garden of Gethsemane. In fact, He met there with His disciples just after the Last Supper. Judas would have known this pattern well, since he was one of those disciples.

The Scriptures don't say why Jesus chose to retire there on this particular occasion, but He typically did so for prayer, reflection, and lodging—away from the craziness of Jerusalem.

Western Protestants seem to minimize the need for an actual meeting place with Jesus since we can worship Him in spirit and in truth from anywhere, but there is something to be said for having a designated place in your home to meet with Him, whether it's on your front porch, on a nearby walking trail, or in a meditative garden. Much like having a dedicated office space helps us to focus better on our work than if we tried to do so from our living room, having a dedicated space to meet with Jesus clears away worldly distractions.

Do you have a place you retire to routinely to meet with Jesus? Do people in your family know that when they see you in this place, you are meeting with Him? Do even your enemies know about this place? If not, find one and begin using it today.

NO MORE PRETENSE

What this adds up to, then, is this: no more lies, no more pretense.
Tell your neighbor the truth. In Christ's body we're all connected to
each other, after all. When you lie to others, you end up lying to yourself.
EPHESIANS 4:25 MSG

Our natural inclination is to present our best, while hiding the rest. We smile, even though we are feeling down. We nod our head in agreement during a Bible study or sermon, even though we don't understand. We pray in the company of others, even when our private prayer life is nonexistent.

In the verse above, the apostle Paul is calling for an end to pretense in the Church. He isn't necessarily saying we should wear our hearts on our sleeves, or that we should shake our head in disagreement during a Bible study or sermon, or that we should not pray in the company of others if we aren't praying privately. But he is saying that pretense comes with a cost. When we lie to one another, openly or subtly, we not only harm the body but we also harm ourselves because we end up lying to ourselves.

Consider your own small group of Christian fellowship. Can you see pretense in others? How has this affected your relationships within the group? How has it affected your ability to minister to one another? If you can see pretense in them, they can probably see it in you, too. Resolve to tell them the truth, knowing it will make the ground fertile for ministry.

SUFFERING FOR CHRIST

For to you it has been granted on behalf of Christ,
not only to believe in Him, but also to suffer for His sake.
PHILIPPIANS 1:29 NKJV

Paul knew what it meant to suffer for Christ. He chronicles many of his perils in 2 Corinthians 11:24–27. They include: five lashings from the Jews, three beatings with rods, one stoning, and more. He was in constant danger, and always in need of food, shelter, and clothing.

Writing from a Roman prison, he wanted the believers in Philippi to understand that they, too, are called to suffer for Christ. The church in Philippi was known for its generosity, even sending Paul supplies when he was ministering to other churches. They may have been the only church to do so (Philippians 4:15–16). He wanted to hear only good reports about this church, even if he couldn't be with them (Philippians 1:27), so he was preparing them not to fear their adversaries. Suffering for Christ had been granted to them by God; it was a privilege.

How can we see it as any less in our own lives? The American church tends to get caught up in its rights as citizens (and biblically, there is a place for playing the citizen card), hoping to ward off suffering, often forgetting that we are called to suffer for Christ. We aren't called to seek it, but we are called to endure it when it comes. Are you preparing your family accordingly?

NO TURNING BACK

But now after you have known God, or rather are known by God, how is it that you turn again to the weak and beggarly elements, to which you desire again to be in bondage?

GALATIANS 4:9 NKJV

Most of us tend to default to the familiar. The Jews in Galatia were no exception. After hearing the Gospel and responding to it, they knew God in a far more intimate way than when they were trying to keep the ceremonial law by adhering to eating certain foods or observing certain ceremonial holy days, as the law commanded.

None of those practices had any inherent spiritual power. They were shadows of the Gospel to come. Yet Paul is writing to the Galatian church with a heavy heart, knowing they had slipped back into their old ways. "I am afraid for you, lest I have labored for you in vain," he says in verse 11. He goes on to say, "My little children, for whom I labor in birth again until Christ is formed in you, I would like to be present with you now and to change my tone; for I have doubts about you" (verses 19–20).

Today, we don't struggle with returning to the ceremonial law because most of us didn't come from that background. But we struggle with other empty rituals, such as performance-based Christianity. Formerly, we believed we could earn our way to heaven by good works. Even though we left that behind, we return to it when we believe our performance is a reflection of spiritual strength. Reject that! Return to the power of Christ in you.

BITTER AS WORMWOOD

*For the lips of an immoral woman drip honey, and her mouth
is smoother than oil; but in the end she is bitter as wormwood.*

Proverbs 5:3–4 nkjv

If we are not on continual guard against sexual immorality, we will be easily swayed away from everything we believe to be true. An immoral woman speaks directly to our carnal nature. She is persuasive and inviting, but in the end, she is as bitter as wormwood.

"Wormwood" isn't a word we normally use, but you can also find it in Revelation. When the third angel sounds his trumpet, a great star falls from heaven into a third of the rivers and springs of water (Revelation 8:10). "The name of the star is Wormwood. A third of the waters became wormwood, and many men died from the water, because it was made bitter" (verse 11). In other words, wormwood is poisonous to the point of death.

Sexual immorality is really that serious. If we do not die a physical death from disease, we certainly place ourselves on the edge of spiritual death. In his commentary, Matthew Henry said: "Uncleanness is a sin that does as much as any thing [to] blind the understanding, sear the conscience, and keep people from pondering the path of life. Proverbs 5:5 says the immoral woman's 'feet go down to death.' Proverbs 2:18 says her 'house leads down to death.'"

Are you currently in the clutches of, or being lured by, an immoral woman? Recognize that she is as bitter as wormwood. She doesn't have your best interest at heart. Turn from her and embrace life.

LOOK TO JESUS

"But love your enemies, do good, and lend, hoping for nothing in return; and your reward will be great, and you will be sons of the Most High. For He is kind to the unthankful and evil."

LUKE 6:35 NKJV

A Christian man who works in a community center in Omaha, Nebraska, was nearing the end of his shift one night when several men walked in, wanting to use the facility. The man told them they were closing and expected them to walk away. He looked away momentarily and caught a punch directly under one of his eyes, knocking him off his stool.

The man, a firm believer in the right to self-defense, said the first thing he felt for his attacker was love. The man who assaulted him was far from Christ and in desperate need of a Savior. In the truest sense of the word, the victim loved his enemy, even going so far as to begin praying for him.

Our flesh demands retaliation. The Spirit demands love, for He is kind to the unthankful and evil. We know this, first because the verse above says it, but second because we experienced it ourselves. While we were yet sinners, Christ died for us—demonstrating His love for evil, unthankful people.

As American men, we've grown up watching the likes of John Wayne, Clint Eastwood, and Sylvester Stallone portray characters who are tough, rugged men who are quick to retaliate, and this has shaped the way we view the model of manhood. Instead, we ought to be looking to Jesus.

FOR KING AND COUNTRY

Therefore I exhort first of all that supplications, prayers, intercessions, and giving of thanks be made for all men, for kings and all who are in authority, that we may lead a quiet and peaceable life in all godliness and reverence.
1 TIMOTHY 2:1–2 NKJV

Throughout history, politics have been divisive. Some Christians are deeply involved; others prefer to steer clear. No matter your natural inclination, we cannot live compartmentalized lives. Politics matter.

Our leaders determine the degree of freedom we enjoy by the laws they pass. They also send our children to war (sometimes justly, sometimes not), set tax rates, choose or confirm judges, and in some sense, they even shape the culture of the generation to follow by the legislation they pass. That's a lot of power.

What is your first reaction when political leaders, or anybody in authority, does something you disagree with? Is it vitriolic criticism? If so, that's probably a good indication that you haven't been praying for them, as Paul advises Timothy in the verses above.

Notice the three types of prayers Paul tells Timothy to pray for all people—including leaders: supplications, intercessions, and giving of thanks. Supplication is an act of asking God to help someone else—to provide for that person's wants and needs. Intercessions are asking God to intervene on somebody else's behalf. And giving thanks is an act of gratitude for that person.

Of course, tyrants and dictators ought to be opposed, and even deposed, but never without praying for them first.

FRESH INSIGHTS

Wise men and women are always learning,
always listening for fresh insights.
PROVERBS 18:15 MSG

Neil Postman, the late cultural critic who passed away in 2003, released a book in 1985 called *Amusing Ourselves to Death: Public Discourse in the Age of Show Business*. His primary concern was the way show business—television, largely—was conditioning us "to tolerate visually entertaining material measured out in spoonfuls of time, to the detriment of rational public discourse and reasoned public affairs."

In one chapter, he says that even religion "is presented, quite simply and without apology, as an entertainment." He points out that dogma, ritual, and theology are stripped away. Entertainment has replaced the sacred, in his opinion. Fast-forward thirty years and his premise seems even more pervasive.

Of course, consuming media for entertainment purposes is fine, but it will indeed shape our worldview if we aren't also consuming other media for knowledge so we can think and reason critically. Proverbs 18:15 says wise people are always learning and listening for fresh insights.

We can listen for fresh insights in more ways than simply media, though. Having coffee with a wise older man from church can be of significant spiritual benefit. You can also digest sermons or begin attending organized Christian social gatherings.

What does the balance between entertainment and the pursuit of knowledge look like in your life? What does your media diet consist of? How often do you socialize with fellow believers outside of the worship center? What are you doing to bring your life into compliance with Proverbs 18:15?

SHOW YOUR LOVE

Love. . .does not seek its own.
1 CORINTHIANS 13:4–5 NKJV

Western culture has fallen into the trap that so many decaying cultures before us fell into: We incessantly chase our own wants and desires, even in marriage, at the expense of others. But 1 Corinthians 13 tells us that love does not seek its own.

"There is, perhaps, not a more striking or important expression in the New Testament than this; or one that more beautifully sets forth the nature and power of that love which is produced by true religion," says Albert Barnes in his *Notes on the Bible*. The indwelling of the Holy Spirit changes our perspective from self to others. They are not mutually exclusive, and Paul is not saying we are forbidden to care for ourselves, but self is not the primary focus in biblical love.

You may have ordered flowers for your wife or girlfriend and had them delivered to her today. If so, that was a nice gesture. But are you in tune with her enough to know what she really wants? Do you know the desires of her heart? Her dreams? Her goals? Is she interested in working in theater? Take her to a play. Does she want to open her own boutique? Visit one with her to pick the owner's brain. Does she want to mentor young women at church? Step in and relieve her of some of her duties at home so she is free to do so.

Show her you love her, rather than simply telling her.

GIVE ME DISCERNMENT, LORD

Then God said to him: "Because you have asked this thing, and have not asked long life for yourself, nor have asked riches for yourself, nor have asked the life of your enemies, but have asked for yourself understanding to discern justice, behold, I have done according to your words."

1 KINGS 3:11–12 NKJV

If the Lord appeared to you in a dream and asked you, "What shall I give you?" how would you respond? If you are young, you might ask for a beautiful wife. If you are middle-aged, you might ask for a larger 401(k). If you are older, you might ask for a longer life.

None of those things are inherently bad, but when the Lord appeared to Solomon in a dream and asked him that very question, Solomon's answer was better:

> Now, O LORD my God, You have made Your servant king instead of my father David, but I am a little child; I do not know how to go out or come in. And Your servant is in the midst of Your people whom You have chosen, a great people, too numerous to be numbered or counted. Therefore give to Your servant an understanding heart to judge Your people, that I may discern between good and evil.
> (1 Kings 3:7–9)

Solomon wasn't really a child. He just felt like one because he lacked understanding. So he asked God for discernment, and God was pleased. God may never appear to you in a dream, but He would be just as pleased if you asked Him for discernment today.

GOD'S HERITAGE

Who is a God like You, pardoning iniquity and passing over the transgression of the remnant of His heritage? He does not retain His anger forever, because He delights in mercy.

MICAH 7:18 NKJV

The prophet Micah foresaw Judah's captivity as the nation was drawing to a close during the reigns of Jotham, Ahaz, and Hezekiah (Micah 1:1). Even still, as the prophets often did, Micah warns God's people of the impending judgment for those who had ears to hear.

While judgment and hardship were coming, so was the mercy of God for His remnant. In the verse above, Micah asks, "Who is a God like You?"—a God who delights in mercy and pardons His people's sins? Surely, no false god or idol could make such an offer.

We, as God's people, are His heritage. He was once angry with us for our sins, but He has pardoned us, having passed over our transgressions in the name of Jesus. We are His remnant—the remaining portion of humanity who longs to see God make all things new. He set redemption in progress from the beginning, knowing we would fall short.

As the head of your household, are you sure that your family knows the relevance of serving a merciful God? Do they know Him to be slow to anger? Do they understand they are part of His heritage—the latest in a long list of generations who have known God and been preserved by Him? Have you made that connection for them?

DEVOUT MEN

And devout men carried Stephen to his burial,
and made great lamentation over him.
ACTS 8:2 NKJV

As the Word of God spread in Jerusalem after Pentecost, the number of disciples began to increase, and even a "great many of the priests were obedient to the faith" (Acts 6:7 NKJV). But not all of the religious leaders in the synagogue were happy about it. When Stephen, one of the original seven deacons in the church, was questioned by the high priest, he held nothing back—calling them stiff-necked and uncircumcised in their hearts and ears, as well as resisters of the Holy Spirit (Acts 7:51).

Speaking the truth cost Stephen his life. The religious leaders stoned him to death, leading to a great persecution against the Jerusalem church, forcing many believers (except the apostles) to be scattered throughout Judea and Samaria (Acts 8:1).

The next verse says "devout men carried Stephen to his burial." Commentators vary regarding the identity of these men. At least one believes these men may have been unconverted Jews who didn't like what took place. Others believe these were members of the Jerusalem church. Either way, nobody can doubt their courage after seeing what happened to a man who crossed the authorities. But honoring the fallen at the hands of injustice meant more to them than the possible repercussions.

If persecution of believers were to spread across the country today and believers were scattered, would you be one of the devout men who took risks when the situation called for it, the way these men did?

THE DISPERSION

Peter, an apostle of Jesus Christ, to the pilgrims of the Dispersion in Pontus, Galatia, Cappadocia, Asia, and Bithynia.
1 PETER 1:1 NKJV

Known as one of the more universal epistles since it is not written to a particular church, Peter's first letter was addressed to Christians who had been dispersed across Asia Minor because of their faith. They held a special place in Peter's heart. Some believe these were descendants of the Jews who were displaced after their Babylonian captivity. And some believe that Peter, who was of the circumcised, may have played a role in their conversion.

Out of sight never means out of mind in the universal Church. When one part of the Body suffers, we all suffer. The Voice of the Martyrs shares the story about ISIS spray-painting the Arabic letter *N* on the homes and businesses of Christians in northern Iraq. This identified them as *Nasrani*—a derogatory term for Christians. They were given the choice to convert to Islam, leave, or die. More than one hundred thousand Christians fled, unwilling to renounce their faith. This has sparked a movement called "I Am N" in which fellow believers from around the world stand with them.

Does the persecuted church hold a special place in your heart? As the leader of your home, do you ever talk to your family about believers who are being persecuted around the world? Does your family pray for them? If you need some help, visit the Voice of the Martyrs website, and sign up for their e-mail news alerts and their free monthly newsletter.

LOVING THE BRETHREN

We know that we have passed from death to life, because we love the brethren. He who does not love his brother abides in death.
1 JOHN 3:14 NKJV

In the state of Nebraska, everything revolves around the Cornhusker football team in the fall—no matter how good or bad the team might be in any given season. Wedding planners check Nebraska's schedule before choosing a date, looking for a coveted off-week. Other social events like birthday parties, retirement celebrations, and anniversaries are scheduled in places with televisions so everybody can see the game.

After games, people spill into the streets to resume their normal activities, and as they meet up, they talk about the game they just watched. They are unified in their love for their team. Transplants to the region don't understand, and many even develop a strong dislike for the team and its culture because they don't feel like they are part of it. They even mock the team and its fans, but the fans are not fazed. If anything, it makes their ties to the team stronger.

In a similar fashion, the apostle John doesn't want believers to marvel or fret because the world hates us as Christians. In fact, when the world hates us, it's a good indicator that we are on the right path because they can see a difference in the way we live and also in the way we love fellow believers.

You aren't afraid to show people your passion for your favorite sports team or musical group. Don't be afraid to show them your passion for God's people as well.

SWAYED BY THE WORLD

For the wisdom of this world is foolishness with God.
1 CORINTHIANS 3:19 NKJV

Have you ever been around a new convert to a political ideology? He or she goes on and on about what one pundit or another says about their political enemies. When you interject a biblical truth that might contradict what the pundit says, the new convert becomes defensive—angry even. That emotion often drives him or her to embrace untruths. It can even happen to Christians if we aren't careful.

So it is with religion in general, and Christianity specifically. The world believes all sorts of untrue notions about the Christian faith. It falsely believes heaven can be attained through human effort; it falsely believes the Bible contains errors; and it falsely believes Christians hate people simply because we disagree with certain lifestyles. The world views Christians as overly simplistic and unenlightened.

The world's arguments are seductive, appealing to the flesh in one way or another. Little by little, they can pull us away from biblical truth we once embraced. Is this happening to you? Are you reading your Bible less frequently than you used to and listening more often to worldly pundits? Has your prayer life grown stale? Is your worship attendance more sporadic in favor of some other activity? Would you rather hang out with unbelieving friends than fellow believers?

The world rejects God and His followers. It is unwise, self-serving, carnal in nature—unwilling to accept biblical truth. If the world has begun to seep into your thinking, plug back in to Jesus and let the world's foolishness fade away.

SEETHING WITH RIGHTEOUS ANGER

"Then all these servants of yours will go to their knees, begging me to leave, 'Leave! You and all the people who follow you!' And I will most certainly leave." Moses, seething with anger, left Pharaoh.
EXODUS 11:8 MSG

In 2011, a thirty-two-year-old woman was apparently agitated over a Black Friday Walmart crowd in Los Angeles to the point that she allegedly took matters into her own hands. According to the *New York Daily News*, she was accused of dousing the crowd with pepper spray, injuring twenty, and then taking off with a discounted Xbox.

She claimed self-defense, saying shoppers were attacking her children for the Xbox. Police ruled there wasn't enough evidence to charge her, so no charges were filed. Either way, anger won the day.

Sometimes it should. In Exodus 11, Moses told Pharaoh that after every firstborn child in Egypt died because Pharaoh would not release Israel from captivity, he would be begging Moses to leave with all of God's people. He left Pharaoh's presence "seething with anger." Standing up for others in the face of tyranny is always just. It's the opposite of Black Friday anger.

As men, many of us have Black Friday anger—anger that is based on something we aren't receiving—status, attention, our just due. We might not believe such anger is a huge concern, but the Bible says otherwise: "Bridle your anger, trash your wrath, cool your pipes—it only makes things worse. Before long the crooks will be bankrupt; GOD-investors will soon own the store" (Psalm 37:8–9 MSG).

THE AROMA OF CHRIST

For we are to God the fragrance of Christ among those who are being saved and among those who are perishing. To the one we are the aroma of death leading to death, and to the other the aroma of life leading to life.

2 CORINTHIANS 2:15–16 NKJV

If you're over forty, you probably remember Drakkar Noir cologne. Maybe you even wore it in the 1980s or early '90s. It had a sweet, almost overpowering smell, so you didn't need to wear a lot of it to catch people's attention.

As far as colognes go, people had very decisive views. You were either for Drakkar Noir or against it. Some loved it, and others hated it. All these years later, you'll still hear references to the cologne in modern music and sitcoms. It has certainly left its mark.

That's what Paul is telling the Corinthian church in the verses above regarding our faith. Everywhere we go, the aroma of Christ follows us. To those who are interested in spiritual matters, we are the aroma of eternal life. To those who are not, we are the aroma of death. Notice that leaving a spiritual scent is not an option.

If someone were to ask the people in your life if you have a spiritual aroma, what would they say? Would some say you have the words of life? Would others say you are too religious? The former are grateful for you. The latter are unwilling to face their own sin. Either way, you are leaving an aroma. And that is your calling.

SPIRITUAL GARDENING

Now he who plants and he who waters are one,
and each one will receive his own reward according to his own labor.
1 CORINTHIANS 3:8 NKJV

If you've ever been around someone who can turn an ordinary conversation into a spiritual one with thought-provoking, Gospel-laced questions or observations, then you probably feel inadequate in your own evangelization efforts. For most of us, the ground we are planting in seems much dryer and less receptive to the Gospel. The next time you encounter such ground, consider the verse above.

Some of us are called to plant seeds in rough terrain, while others are called to pour a little water on those seeds to bring the Gospel to fruition. But the two aren't mutually exclusive. You can be a planter who waters on occasion or a waterer who plants on occasion. The good news is that both will receive his own reward according to his own labor. This should free us to speak Gospel truth no matter whether we are planting or watering. Both are necessary.

But the apostle Paul doesn't leave any room in this verse for not gardening in some fashion. Sitting in the pew while others garden is not an option. So that raises several questions: How are your gardening efforts going? Which role do you naturally gravitate toward? Have you played both roles at some point? Do you seek out the unconverted in your office, at the store, and everywhere else you go so you can plant or water?

WITH JESUS

*Now when they saw the boldness of Peter and John, and perceived that
they were uneducated and untrained men, they marveled.
And they realized that they had been with Jesus.*
ACTS 4:13 NKJV

When Peter and John healed the lame man outside the temple, the man did what came naturally to him—he joined Peter and John in the temple, "walking, leaping, and praising God" (Acts 3:8 NKJV). The people inside marveled, giving Peter an opportunity to point out that the man was healed in the name of Jesus—the One this very people had denied.

That landed them in the custody of the Sanhedrin, who weren't all that fond of what Peter and John were saying. As Peter testified at their trial, he accurately portrayed Jesus as the chief cornerstone in whom salvation is found (Acts 4:11–12). That's when the religious leaders began to notice that these two uneducated men who were speaking with such boldness had been in the presence of Jesus. Either they recognized them as having traveled with Jesus, or they recognized something in them that made them realize they had been with Jesus. Either way, spending time with Jesus had changed them—it had given them a boldness they never had before.

Have you been changed by spending time with Jesus? One true test is to evaluate how willing you are to proclaim His truth among people like coworkers or old drinking buddies who might not be open to hearing it. If you've come up short, spend more time with Jesus. He'll make all the difference.

A THANKSGIVING PLAN

But fornication and all uncleanness or covetousness, let it not even
be named among you, as is fitting for saints; neither filthiness,
nor foolish talking, nor coarse jesting, which are not fitting,
but rather giving of thanks.
EPHESIANS 5:3–4 NKJV

Here Paul lays out the conduct that is fitting for a Christian. The context seems to indicate that he is primarily focusing on Christians in community with one another, but it certainly applies in a broader context as well. Practically speaking, the verses above speak to one of the biggest struggles men face: the lust of the eyes, which leads to fornication.

When Paul says he doesn't want us to even name such sins among us, he is saying he doesn't want it to exist. If it does, we certainly shouldn't be stoking the fires of others by talking about it in a playful manner. In our culture, that might include comments about suggestive television commercials at Super Bowl parties or laughing at dirty jokes.

The verses above say that instead of such talk, we are to be thankful people. How might that look? If you are surrounded by guys watching a football game and one of them makes a comment about a suggestive commercial, consider having a thankful response ready.

It doesn't have to be verbal. You can pull out your cell phone and look at photos of your wife or girlfriend and thank God for her. Or you can text a Christian friend to start an edifying conversation, thanking God that your friend is available.

PROVE YOURSELF A MAN

"I go the way of all the earth; be strong,
therefore, and prove yourself a man."
1 KINGS 2:2 NKJV

At the end of David's life, he charged his son Solomon to prove himself a man. Solomon would need to be wise as he assumed the role of king. Even though he was young, he would need to act much older. David explained what that would look like: "'And keep the charge of the LORD your God: to walk in His ways, to keep His statutes, His commandments, His judgments, and His testimonies, as it is written in the Law of Moses, that you may prosper in all that you do and wherever you turn'" (1 Kings 2:3 NKJV).

Sadly, Solomon wasn't always successful. While he was indeed wise, he "loved many foreign women" (1 Kings 11:1 NKJV), and eventually "his wives turned his heart after other gods; and his heart was not loyal to the LORD his God" (verse 4). He also gathered many possessions (Ecclesiastes 2:7) and indulged in wine (Ecclesiastes 2:3) in search of fulfillment. Eventually, he laments his failures, saying: "Then I looked on all the works that my hands had done and on the labor in which I had toiled; and indeed all was vanity and grasping for the wind. There was no profit under the sun" (Ecclesiastes 2:11 NKJV).

If even the wisest of men can be turned against the Lord by his baser appetites for periods of time in his life, how much more can we? Whatever your struggles, resolve to turn to the Lord today.

LIFTING OTHERS

*Therefore let us not judge one another anymore, but rather resolve this,
not to put a stumbling block or a cause to fall in our brother's way.*
ROMANS 14:13 NKJV

It's hard not to play the comparison game with fellow believers. We look at stronger believers and wish we could pray like them, or that we had their biblical knowledge. We look at weaker believers and sympathize with them, knowing they lack basic biblical understanding. We even compare ourselves to Christians who appear to be in a similar place we are, spiritually speaking.

The latter two instances can lead to judgment. Pride says we are stronger than the weaker believer because we spend more time in the Bible than he does. And it says that the similar believer's sins might be worse than ours, so maybe we are stronger after all. Paul wanted the Roman church to stop judging one another—to stop looking at spiritual practices like certain dietary restrictions or observing one day instead of another. Instead, he wanted them to put their brothers' spiritual well-being first.

If one believer drinks wine and another doesn't, he didn't want the drinker to flaunt his freedom and perhaps cause the other to fall. The same applies to other spiritual practices. "For the kingdom of God is not eating and drinking, but righteousness and peace and joy in the Holy Spirit," Paul says in Romans 14:17 (NKJV). Rather than comparing yourself to other believers and then judging them, make their spiritual welfare of utmost importance instead. It will lead to joy in the Holy Spirit.

FOUR HUNDRED SILENT YEARS

"Behold, the days are coming," says the Lord God, "That I will send a famine on the land, not a famine of bread, nor a thirst for water, but of hearing the words of the Lord."

AMOS 8:11 NKJV

The prophet Amos records one of the saddest moments in Israel's history, when God said, "'The end has come upon My people Israel'" (Amos 8:2 NKJV). God's patience had finally reached an end, and He spoke about a dark period that was coming for His people. The pronouncement in verse 11 had to be one of the worst—they would no longer hear the words of the Lord.

After the old covenant drew to a close, God was silent for four hundred years. Protestants refer to this as the "Four Hundred Silent Years." Everything changed during that time period. Rome replaced Persia as the ruling authority. The king, Herod, was from the line of Esau rather than Jacob. And the priesthood was tainted. When God was silent, the people strayed to the point that they no longer gave God much thought.

The same could be said for a modern household that is void of God's Word. Without His instruction, we busy ourselves with other tasks and glean from other authorities. Have you stopped opening God's Word in your own home? Maybe you used to read a portion of scripture to your family at the breakfast or dinner table but have fallen away from that practice, and now you can see the difference in them. It's not too late to begin again.

REMEMBER, RECOGNIZE, RESPOND

*God put his love on the line for us by offering his Son in sacrificial
death while we were of no use whatever to him.*

ROMANS 5:8 MSG

Some will choose not to recognize Ash Wednesday for a variety of reasons. It could be that the day seems like a throwback to a time of forced rituals without an engaged heart. Others might overlook the day because it was never a part of their church experience. Then there are those who choose not to follow Jesus.

Ash Wednesday is set aside to *remember, recognize,* and *respond* to the true message of Easter. We *remember* because the ashes that mark the faithful are the burned remains of the palm branches used last year on Palm Sunday. We *recognize* that the work of Jesus on the cross led to rescue from eternal death and Him giving us a brand-new purpose for our lives. We *respond* because the One who died for us is worth living for.

For some this may be a ritual, but for others it is a meaningful way to connect to the impact brought about by a Savior who lived, died, and rose again to offer forgiveness and life.

We can remember, recognize, and respond without the ritual, but the ritual allows many to remember, recognize, and respond in a tangible way that bolsters their faith. Perhaps you have Christian friends who do celebrate Ash Wednesday. Ask your friends what things they did and thought about today, and learn something new about their Christian walk. You may be surprised at the encouragement they have to share!

WORDS LEFT UNREAD

*Such things were written in the Scriptures long ago to teach us.
And the Scriptures give us hope and encouragement as we
wait patiently for God's promises to be fulfilled.*
ROMANS 15:4 NLT

It appears you're in the mood to celebrate. Today is Read across America Day, a whole day dedicated to reading. Schools will celebrate to get the kids excited about their books, an all-day literary pep rally. Libraries may hang posters to commemorate it, and bookstores may see more customers because of it. You're reading these words, so you're celebrating, too. Surprised?

There is an even better way to celebrate. Pick up a book whose words were inspired by the God who made dirt, air, water, and language. What would it look like if we lived in a world where everyone believed that the Bible was as valuable as food, water, and oxygen? How much change would we see if we not only read the words God wrote for us, but we actually believed what was written and did what it said?

The Bible is filled with historical events, spiritual heroes, poetry, love stories, parables, and most importantly—the heart of God for all mankind. And for Christians in particular, the Bible contains vital "hope and encouragement as we wait patiently for God's promises to be fulfilled."

Words left unread have never changed anyone. Pick up your Bible today and let the change begin.

DARK NIGHT INSPIRATION

Ascribe to the LORD the glory due his name;
worship the LORD in the splendor of his holiness.
PSALM 29:2 NIV

What inspires you? For some, it's spending time with family. Others require the quiet glory of a scenic location. Still others' hearts are inspired by stories of people they may not even know, but who have done amazing things. Artists, the most famous for seeking inspiration, get excited by subjects that capture their attention, while poets and songwriters rely on experiences and feelings to share their inspiration.

Francis Scott Key, an American poet and lyricist in the 1800s, was an inspired man. However, his inspiration didn't come from something beautiful and heartwarming; it came from a firsthand perspective of war. His backstory is filled with grit and glory, pain and perseverance.

The inspiration Key felt led him to pen the lyrics to what would become America's national anthem. The words are filled with the images of war, but they are colored with hope, because when the last shot was fired, it was the ragged American flag that still waved in the early morning breeze.

Inspiration isn't always found in the beautiful and serene. Even in our darkest times we can be inspired because God walks with us. We may remember those times better than most, and in hindsight, they can become the most beautiful of all. What "dark nights" has He delivered you from? Have you given Him "the glory due his name"? You may not have Francis Scott Key's talents, but God loves to hear from you all the same.

UNPLUG AND RECONNECT

Come close to God, and God will come close to you.
JAMES 4:8 NLT

We exist in a wireless yet constantly logged-on society. Visit any mall or shopping center and you'll discover fewer people actually using their voice to communicate because they're using the texting option on their smartphones. Many will pay less attention to pedestrian traffic and more attention to the latest social media posts. Conversations in restaurants have become much different—at best, friends pause to swipe across their screens and show each other videos or pictures of family or pets, but at worst, no one looks up from their screens until it's time for the check.

Unplugging from handheld gadgets and computers is almost as rare as living off the grid. Choosing to be unconnected from modern technology seems nearly barbaric. However, those who do unplug consider the end result worth the stigma—improving their human connection with those loved ones whom they actually live with.

On this National Day of Unplugging, you can take a break from the newsfeed notifications and comments from people you barely know. In doing so, you may find you have more time to give to those who should be the most important in your life.

When you unplug, you might also discover the God who's available for real-time prayer conversation, to listen to your status updates, and to offer perfect answers to your hardest questions. He promises that when you come close to Him, He's there and will draw close to you.

TRIP-PLANNING SERVICE

*Do you see what this means—all these pioneers who blazed the way,
all these veterans cheering us on? It means we'd better get on with it.
Strip down, start running—and never quit! No extra spiritual fat,
no parasitic sins. Keep your eyes on Jesus, who both began
and finished this race we're in.*
HEBREWS 12:1–2 MSG

The practice is grueling. The conditions harsh. Yet there is excitement among the participants, and the dogs find it hard to wait. They want to find the end of their tethers and strain against the sled.

The start of the Iditarod race begins today in Alaska. Teams will brave snow and ice as they battle every conceivable obstacle to endure to the end.

Paul spoke of the Christian life as a race that must be finished and a fight that must be won. He spoke of discipline and effort, yet it is not in our own strength. We run, we fight with the knowledge that God is the One who brings us to the finish line, and He is the One who has the power and skill to win the fight.

When we're in our worst *life battles*, we can be certain that the God who brought us *to* the crisis has a plan for getting us *through* it. When it feels like He's taking you the long way on your spiritual trip, remember how He works everything together for good for those who love Him and are called according to His purpose (Romans 8:28).

INVESTING IN GOD'S GIFT

Children are a gift from the LORD;
they are a reward from him.
PSALM 127:3 NLT

The idea of an inheritance is God's idea, but His plan for an inheritance may be different than how we view the passing of values to a new generation.

If children are the inheritance we receive from God, then maybe He meant for us to take parenting as a great privilege and awesome responsibility. God doesn't want us to waste our time and opportunities with our kids, but to learn who they are so we can best teach them God's ways and perhaps, eventually, how to accept the role of seeing their children (our grandkids) as their God-given inheritance.

We're to consider our role as dads as one of the most important responsibilities we'll ever have. We can't take money, awards, or our favorite team jersey with us to heaven, but we can create an atmosphere in our homes that extends our faith and its riches to a new generation.

Jesus invited children to come to Him. As dads, we have the opportunity to show our children the way.

God described inheritance as a role of relationship, not a lump-sum cash gift. Why? Maybe our daily investments have a greater impact than an end-of-life monetary award.

Our children have always wanted more meaningful time with us. Let's give it to them.

A CONSUMING UNFORGIVENESS

Forgive one another as quickly and thoroughly
as God in Christ forgave you.
EPHESIANS 4:32 MSG

Whom do we spend the most time thinking about? Those we love? Maybe, but there's another group of people with equal or greater access to our thinking. Many will think about them every day. Who are they? Those who've hurt us.

We'll replay their misdeeds over and over again. The more we think about them, the angrier we'll get. The angrier we get, the more hurt we feel. The more hurt we feel, the more blame we place on the offender. In some cases, unforgiven offenses will consume the majority of our thoughts.

Forgiveness is something you can give even when there is no apology—even when the offender never asks—but forgiveness can feel like a one-sided gift.

On the other hand, forgiveness doesn't mean an automatic renewal of friendship or trust. You can forgive an offense, but if the offender doesn't change his behavior, he may be forgiven, but not trusted. In certain cases, it may be wise to keep your distance from some offenders who may be quick to reapply the hurt.

Humans are incapable of forgetting the hurt inflicted by others. Thankfully, God forgets every sin that we confess and removes it from us "as far as sunrise is from sunset" (Psalm 103:12 MSG). We should forgive as God forgave us so as to prevent a "bitter root" from springing up in our hearts (Hebrews 12:15 NIV), but a renewed relationship will depend on both the forgiver and the forgiven. Are you willing to let go of the offenses you've held on to?

VARIABLE RATE OFFENSE DEBT

"In prayer there is a connection between what God does and what you do. You can't get forgiveness from God, for instance, without also forgiving others. If you refuse to do your part, you cut yourself off from God's part."
MATTHEW 6:14–15 MSG

If you have a variable rate loan, then you know that your rate could go up or down. It could work in your favor, but sometimes it doesn't.

Forgiveness works in a similar way. When others hurt you, it can be easy to think of it in terms of a loan. By offending you, they have taken on a debt you want repaid.

But just like a variable rate loan, there are often changes to the terms. Revenge will increase the total repayment value. It can quickly get out of hand, and there may be no repayment that can satisfy an *offender's* debt.

While we keep track of what the offender owes, he may be unaware (or not even care) that a debt is owed. No matter how much interest you tack on to an *offender's* debt, many offenders will never meet your repayment expectations.

Offenses will happen. When we refuse to forgive, we don't gain anything—we cut ourselves off from God, who expects us to extend the same forgiveness that He's given us. When we're quick to forgive, we'll discover we save a lot of time and emotional energy. . .and we'll stay connected to God, too.

BLAME AND FORGIVENESS

Forgive anyone who offends you.
Colossians 3:13 NLT

With the disobedience of Adam and Eve, *offense* was introduced to our world. From the moment of original sin, mankind has always needed forgiveness.

If mankind can offend God through choices we make, and if God had to send His Son to make permanent forgiveness possible, isn't it conceivable that the disobedience found in all of mankind would ultimately inflict pain on others? Yeah, sin does that.

When we're offended, we often believe the experience is unique to us and no one has ever had to endure the same suffering. Maybe that's true, but offenses *will* happen to someone every minute of every day, and we don't deal with it very well.

Today is National Get Over It Day. This sounds ruthless and uncaring, as if we're magically supposed to say that the offense was no big deal and simply shrug it off as unimportant. Let this sink in—true forgiveness requires naming the sin and who is to blame. In order for God to truly forgive us, He had to pinpoint our offenses. We must do the same because forgiveness should never be trivial; it is costlier than just saying "It's no big deal."

The only way to get over an offense is to treat the issue honestly, acknowledge the hurt, and then intentionally choose to forgive specific offenses. There's more to experience in life than old hurt—it's time to get over it.

LOST AND FOUND

"We must celebrate with a feast, for this son of mine was dead
and has now returned to life. He was lost, but now he is found."
LUKE 15:23–24 NLT

He defied tradition. He ruined his father's plans. He misused resources. He lost everything. He was the day's headlines. In the muddy confines of a pigpen, it seemed like he got what he deserved.

If you're familiar with the story of the prodigal son, you know there's more to it. At first glance it would seem the father, who had been ill-used by his son, would have had every justification to disown the boy. He could have treated the wayward youth as an employee—*if* he ever considered allowing the boy to come home at all.

His name could have been repeated with disdain by all who had heard his story, but his father never allowed the negative speech to gain a foothold. The father freed the son from ridicule, humiliation, and shame. The father forgave the son before the son recognized he needed forgiving. Reconciliation began the moment a repentant son came within sight of his father.

Forgiveness offers freedom, reflects God's command to love, inspires restoration, and is the key that unlocks second chances.

AN OPTION WORTH TAKING

The only thing that counts is faith expressing itself through love.
GALATIANS 5:6 NIV

Let's take a look at forgiveness from another angle—love. The greatest commands Jesus gave were very simple: Love God and then love everyone else.

The greatest source of teaching about love comes from 1 Corinthians 13. Forgiveness is an essential part of love because love keeps no record of wrongs, is not easily angered, and is not self-seeking (1 Corinthians 13:5). When you can't or won't forgive, you will keep records of the hurts others have done to you, you will be easily provoked to anger, and you will fight for your own self-interests instead of seeking the interests of others.

Does it sound as if you can obey God's command to love while refusing to forgive others?

True love forgives. When faith is expressed through love, bitterness and resentment get an eviction notice. If love is a choice, then forgiveness is also a choice.

You can't blame the past, present, or even negative circumstances for your decisions. Forgiveness is a personal choice that doesn't excuse sin, but it can remove the burden you carry and help to heal old wounds instead of letting them fester.

And finally, forgiveness is the only chance many of us will ever get to restore broken relationships.

So when the choice to forgive presents itself as an option—take it.

THE RELENTLESS MARCH OF TIME

Teach us to number our days, that we may gain a heart of wisdom.
PSALM 90:12 NIV

Today there will be people who show symptoms similar to jet lag. They will be tired, easily frustrated, and feel out of sync. They may be late for church and blame their behavior on a politician, and they might have a point.

Statesman Benjamin Franklin introduced the idea of daylight savings time in an essay in 1784. While Ben was talking about using daylight hours for additional productivity, he wasn't suggesting changing the clock. He thought people should just get up earlier to make the best use of available sunlight. What began as a joke in the mind of Mr. Franklin became daylight savings time, which has been in place in the United States in the form we know now since the mid-1960s.

Some might compare the idea of *saving time* to cutting the bottom from a bedsheet and sewing it on the top in order to make the sheet longer—the end result just ruins your sheet. Others have found the "extra" daylight a welcome addition to their day and enjoy the change each year.

No matter how you feel about daylight savings time, it does bring up a question about how you spend your time. Each of us has a specific amount of time to use, but we can end up treating time as if it *serves* us instead of something we *spend* wisely—or foolishly. Are you using this God-given resource well?

MONDAY WITH A PURPOSE

Do your best. Work from the heart for your real Master, for God.
COLOSSIANS 3:23 MSG

Mondays are considered one of the least inspired days of the workweek. The existence of Monday may be the reason motivational posters were created.

On Mondays, you can't build on any momentum generated from the day before. You start from a standstill and remain sluggish the rest of the day. You think about all the things you could have done with an extra day off, but you can also become overwhelmed with all that needs to be done before the weekend arrives.

Monday often feels like a throwaway day. We can think of it as the day we endure so we can get to Tuesday. As much as we may loathe Mondays, God is clear that all days have meaning, all moments are important, and He has a plan for the work we do. That means that even Mondays have a purpose.

We serve a good God who gives us good gifts (Matthew 7:11). So every new day is a reason to rejoice, every Monday is a cause to celebrate, and every hour of work can be dedicated to the God who says we work for Him.

Hang in there! If Mondays are your toughest days of the week, ask God to show you some of the gifts He has in store—perseverance, cheerfulness, energy, to name a few—to help you through the day. Some of the best things could happen today—yes, even on a Monday.

NEXT QUESTION

*"Don't bargain with God. Be direct. Ask for what you need.
This isn't a cat-and-mouse, hide-and-seek game we're in."*
MATTHEW 7:7 MSG

It's easy to think that God can ask questions and we can't. However, the Bible is filled with questions, and most come from people who just wanted to understand God a little better. Questions that begin with *how long, who can be saved,* and *would You destroy* may be familiar, but scholars believe there are more than three thousand questions found between the pages of Genesis and Revelation.

Some questions had obvious answers, while others were more difficult. Some questions came from a place of great pain, while others were used to clarify. Some questions were spoken to try to trap Jesus, while He asked questions that made the hearer think.

It's natural to have questions, normal to want to learn, and nice to get an answer. God is not frustrated by the questions you might have. Knowing Jesus isn't just available for some people, but for anyone who draws close to Him (James 4:8). However, once you have your answer, be prepared for changes in how you think, respond, and live.

If prayer and Bible reading is how we talk with God, then questions should be part of the dialogue. Don't be surprised if there are times when He asks the questions. He likes answers, too.

HARVEST UNDERSTANDING

See how the farmer waits for the land to yield its valuable crop,
patiently waiting for the autumn and spring rains.
JAMES 5:7 NIV

Travel enough and you'll see farms, center pivots, and rows of corn, wheat, and beans. You'll see cattle, sheep, and horses within the confines of barbed wire. There will be trucks, tractors, and all-terrain vehicles on dirt roads and rutted trails. Even in the biggest cities you'll find farmers' markets where the products farmers grow are on display and on sale.

Because people need to eat, there will always be a need for the farming community. These are the men and women who plant, nourish, and harvest the food we take for granted, because the work behind the food is hidden when we find it on the shelf at the grocery store.

The culture of farming was very familiar to Jesus, and He used this culture to help share truth. His agricultural parables and sayings illustrated lessons from spiritual growth to bad influences, from the way we listen to where we place our trust.

Jesus knew farming was a perfect way to help people learn more about the Christian life. Beyond the impact farming has on the economy and our personal well-being, it's good to know that understanding a bit about farming can enhance our understanding of Jesus.

Spend some time in the parables (see Matthew 13), and see what farming can teach you about a lifelong walk with Jesus.

OTHERS IN FOCUS

Each of you should use whatever gift you have received to serve others,
as faithful stewards of God's grace in its various forms.
1 PETER 4:10 NIV

Social media promotes a "me first" environment, and we can all fall victim to its influence, but it doesn't have to be this way.

Our online posts routinely point to the best things that happen to *us*. They contain information that, intentionally or not, draws attention to our best qualities or achievements. There's nothing wrong with celebrating good things happening in our lives, but our celebration of ourselves, especially social media's often filtered, no-bad-days-ever depiction of us, can cause others to feel less important than us—even if that was the last thing we wanted them to think.

We take selfies and post them to show the places we've been and the people we've met, but we're *always* the center of the photo. What if we were to take some of our posts and point out the good things happening in the lives of other people? The opportunities to use social media for encouragement are greater than you may have considered before.

God always planned for us to invest in the lives of others. Beyond the likes and shares we might participate in online, we need to be intentional with all our interactions, whether they are online or not. We can't forget to invest in flesh-and-bone humanity, to reach out to our families, friends, and others whose lives may never fit into a standard shiny social media profile. Let us be faithful stewards of our gifts!

THE SHAMROCK WITNESS

"One of your altars had this inscription on it: 'To an Unknown God.'
This God, whom you worship without knowing,
is the one I'm telling you about."

ACTS 17:23 NLT

When you want to share the difference Jesus has made in your life, how do you start?

If you were Saint Patrick, you'd start by showing people a common shamrock. This man we honor today shared Jesus wherever he went—and he used each leaf of the shamrock to help people understand the idea of the Trinity—Father, Son, and Holy Spirit.

The shamrock has become symbolic of this day, but Patrick used it as a symbol of something he valued more highly than personal honor.

Patrick wasn't the first—or last—to use an object to help bring understanding. In Athens, the apostle Paul used an idol dedicated to an unknown god to help those Athenians who would listen to learn more about the one true God.

We can use things in our own culture to help people understand more about Jesus. Since God made the world and everything in it, we shouldn't be surprised when we find ways to use what He created to point all the way back to the Creator. And we ourselves and the changes Jesus has made in our lives may be the best "object lesson" that people will see.

Making Christ known is one of the best ways to show honor to the One who rescues, restores, and transforms us.

OUR SECOND GREATEST NEED

Make a clean break with all cutting, backbiting, profane talk.
Be gentle with one another, sensitive.
EPHESIANS 4:31 MSG

Moms and dads could have been all-knowing in our eyes, immune from making wrong choices—or they made mistakes that caused us to want to nominate them for World's Worst Parents. Sometimes we can only see their mistakes long after the fact, but other times even as kids we could have written a book on the subject of mistake-prone parenting because we had a front-row seat.

Every parent makes mistakes. There are no college degree programs in perfect parenting. You might wish your parents would have been more understanding, more present, or more caring. You might wish they were more of this, less of that, or just the right amount of something you can't even define.

When you become a parent yourself, you gain some firsthand knowledge of the struggles your parents went through when they were trying to make the right "perfect parent" decisions. . .and then living with their mistakes. Perhaps your own experience has created a new compassion in your heart for your parents, foibles and all.

Love is the greatest need of mankind, but forgiveness is a close second.

Nobody's perfect—that's why God *created* forgiveness. This is as true for parents as it is for children, and this would be a perfect day to think back on your relationship with your parents and try on one of God's *best* creations.

HOMECOMING

*Jesus said, "Let the little children come to me, and do not hinder them,
for the kingdom of heaven belongs to such as these."*
MATTHEW 19:14 NIV

It would seem God designed the American cliff swallow with an amazing internal GPS. Each spring, the birds leave their home in Argentina and fly six thousand miles to the American Southwest. Many swallows have chosen a structure built in the 1770s as their yearly destination.

The mission at San Juan Capistrano was not built for birds. The mission was where human visitors received comfort, guidance, and love. However, when the swallows arrived, the mission seemed suited to nesting. Nearby water and plenty of insects made the mission a welcome retreat for the weary birds.

One early worker was so irate with the birds that he smashed their mud nests to get them to leave. The leadership of the mission eventually expanded so the old stone structure could become home to the swallows when they visited America.

Jesus invites the unlikely, unwelcome, and unloved to come to Him. There are no qualifications and no exceptions. He gave up everything to make grace, forgiveness, and a home available.

We might assign the coordinates N33°30 10 W117°39 46 to the mission at San Juan Capistrano, but the swallows seem to know the church is home. Wouldn't it be nice if all the humans felt the same?

THE UNCHANGEABLE MEETS CHANGE

Jesus Christ is the same yesterday, today, and forever.
HEBREWS 13:8 NLT

Once upon a time, the first day of spring was always on the twenty-first of March. Those days are gone. Science now looks at the exact day of the vernal equinox as the official start. This year spring arrives today.

If you like warmer weather, the good news is that spring and summer have more total days than autumn and winter.

Chances are pretty good you don't particularly care how the date is set. You may be more interested in celebrating the end of winter. You might be happy that there are more warm days than cold, but it might not inspire a public happy dance.

You can fill a calendar with important dates including birthdays, anniversaries, graduations, and weddings. Other dates are coming, but you don't have any idea when they will arrive. Those dates might be when your children leave home to begin life on their own, the exact date you'll retire, or the date of an illness.

When you're unsure how to manage the next *unknown*, just remember the God who brings spring walks with you in life's rain. The God who knew you before you were born walks with you on the hardest days. He loves you, and His love and faithfulness will never change through all the seasons of your life.

A TIME TO UNITE

In Christ's family there can be no division into Jew and non-Jew,
slave and free, male and female. Among us you are all equal.
That is, we are all in a common relationship with Jesus Christ.
GALATIANS 3:28–29 MSG

Of all the people on earth, there is one group that should have the most interest in eliminating racial discrimination from their thoughts and actions, yet every generation of Christians has struggled to embrace a truth that tends to be ignored—God does not discriminate based on the color of our skin.

On this International Day of the Elimination of Racial Discrimination we can still divide ourselves from each other based on how much money we make, where we live, our skin tone, or even our ethnic heritage. We may have great intentions—like wanting people to feel comfortable by putting them in groups that match their background—but it's rarely well received.

Jesus was clear that His sacrifice was for *all* mankind. He said salvation came to the Jew and the Gentile—that's *everyone*. In His time on earth, He even preached to the Samaritans, an ethnic and religious group that the Jews called "half-breeds" and went far out of their way to avoid. As in everything, Jesus is our example of how to live and how to love.

Jesus said His love was for the world, and He didn't add a list of exceptions. Why should we? God has a family—and when we don't exclude people because of their skin color, it's larger than we thought.

THANKS FOR THE MEMORIES

Some trust in chariots, and some in horses;
but we will remember the name of the LORD our God.
PSALM 20:7 NKJV

Her name was Betty Jo, and she loved to visit nursing homes. By her own admission, she couldn't sing "worth a lick," but she always tried. Her song list was always the same.

In her own broken voice, Betty Jo seemed to perform miracles. She sang hymns, and men and women who'd withdrawn to a place of internal refuge brightened. Light came to their eyes and their lips began to move. Soon their voices could be heard, and when the singing was over, many could visit with Betty Jo. Most hadn't visited with anyone in a long time.

Did Betty Jo have some superhuman skill? No. Betty Jo just knew that when an individual is inspired to remember, her thinking clears.

Remembering is exactly the remedy God offers when we need clarity. When we're overwhelmed and suffer from a lack of inspiration, when we're tempted to trust in our strength or money or hard work (our modern "chariots" and "horses") to get by, it's remembering God's faithfulness that adjusts our perspective and allows us to return to clear thinking. Our verse today says we will remember the "name" of the Lord; Proverbs tells us, "The name of the LORD is a fortified tower; the righteous run to it and are safe" (Proverbs 18:10 NIV).

We honor God best when we remember His goodness and let that memory inspire us to follow where He leads—today, tomorrow, and into eternity.

THE WEAK GAIN STRENGTH

[God said,] My strength comes into its own in your weakness.
2 CORINTHIANS 12:9 MSG

There was a time when men gathered on Saturday afternoons at their local theater and purchased tickets to watch the latest western. Cowboys filled the screen and each roughneck was gifted with a firearm and the art of being self-sufficient. They pulled themselves up by the bootstraps, were self-made men, and while they offered help to others, they didn't seem to need any help themselves.

Moviegoers mistakenly believed that the Bible said, "God helps those who help themselves." Men didn't want to bother God and thought they were doing Him a favor by keeping their problems to themselves. Sometimes this perspective meant that men would *gut* it out and do their best to survive. Others would simply deny their struggle and hope that their luck would take a turn for the better. Neither option included asking God for help.

The Bible has never suggested we go it alone. The closest theme might be that God helps those who *ask for help*.

Why would we need a Savior if we could save ourselves? Why would we want a Savior who wasn't strong enough to handle our struggles? Let His strength make up for your weakness.

THAT'S GOOD

Then God looked over all he had made,
and he saw that it was very good!
GENESIS 1:31 NLT

Pharmaceutical companies spend millions of dollars to develop new drugs that may include unpleasant side effects. God spoke, the world came into being, and it was good.

Thomas Edison spent years looking to find the right way to make a light bulb. God said, "Let there be light." There was light, and it was good.

A factory worker blends chemicals and colors to produce a fake flower. God made His own flowers in all different colors, sizes, and scents. The Bible says they were more beautiful than the king's clothing. No wonder He scattered them over the entire earth.

Anything we have made—God has made better (or He cleans it up).

God's extravagant imagination created birds, fish, and animals of every description, mountains of every size, rivers filled with ripples, and a rich palette of humanity that inspires us.

If that's not extravagant enough, God made the stars, named them, and flung them into space. Why? So we'd have something to appreciate on the darkest night.

It shouldn't surprise us that we enjoy creating new things. After all, we were made in the image of God *and He creates*. However, it can be easy to honor God's creation or even *our own* before we honor the One who made everything we would ever need. And that's not so good.

RELATIONSHIPS BEFORE _____?

*"What kind of deal is it to get everything you want but lose yourself?
What could you ever trade your soul for?"*
MATTHEW 16:26 MSG

One of the easiest responsibilities a man can take on is the financial care of his family.

Easy?

Men are prone to become workaholics. When we're told we need to provide for our families, we tackle that responsibility by focusing our time, talent, and energy into turning our work ethic into a cash equivalent.

David, Samuel, and Eli are biblical men who struggled with their kids because work always came before being a dad.

Making money may be the easy part. Being a dad and husband is much harder because it requires an emotional investment many men struggle to make. It's easier to throw cash at a problem than to be a real and present parent. It's easier to work than listen to the struggles our family goes through. It's even easy to believe that somehow our inattention is directly related to our importance.

Because God is our Father, we can learn a few lessons from Him. He is always accessible, listens, and understands our struggles enough to offer perfect advice.

Never sacrifice your family on the altar of personal achievement. It may be possible to have wealth and a close family, but real relationships need to come before all else.

WHAT WILL YOU CELEBRATE?

This is the day the LORD has made.
We will rejoice and be glad in it.
PSALM 118:24 NLT

If you could personally create any holiday, what would you celebrate? A commemoration of dental floss, the indulgence of a caramel brownie, or the attention-grabbing completion of a perfect cannonball into calm waters?

Today is actually Make Up Your Own Holiday Day. If you wanted to celebrate your children's good grades, then this could be your day. The same is true for remembering the first time you read through the entire Bible, proposed to your wife, tried cauliflower, or overcame a bad habit.

You could use the day to celebrate something good that's happened to someone you know. Maybe you could let your kids decide what they would celebrate (you're bound to learn something). Choose both meaningful and goofy reasons to celebrate.

Maybe it would just be enough to celebrate this day because of the same reason you should celebrate every other day—God made it and that's the best reason to cheer!

It might even be meaningful to wait until the day is over and name this day for the specific ways you saw God work in the life of your family. There's no wrong way to do it, as long as you are full of gratitude and praise for what your God has done!

CATCH GOLD FEVER

The decrees of the LORD. . .are more precious than gold,
than much pure gold.
PSALM 19:9–10 NIV

It's been said that during the California Gold Rush in the 1800s the only people really making money were the business owners selling mining equipment and food. There were lots of glassy-eyed adventurers who would trade a large sum of gold for better shovels, picks, lanterns, pans, and a bag of flour or sugar.

There weren't any online shops these hearty miners could use to compare prices. They were forced to either live with what they had or pay the high store prices in the hopes of earning even more gold with their new tools. Some lost their lives in the mines, a few stopped thinking clearly, and others left their claims broken and penniless.

When gold fever hit, these miners were willing to give up everything to get the gold. They sought what they viewed as precious to the exclusion of almost every other pursuit.

If God's Word is more precious than gold, it would seem we should have a great hunger (gold fever, if you will) to follow after God and what He's said. There's good news. God always gives more than He asks, shares more than He receives, and offers more than the best rebate. We'll never regret throwing our lot in with Him.

THE TEAM

You use steel to sharpen steel, and one friend sharpens another.
PROVERBS 27:17 MSG

A lock keeps others out. A hinge opens the way. A door provides a boundary.

An engine provides motivation. A wheel facilitates transportation. Brakes end locomotion.

Everything in life has a purpose, and every purpose needs a team. For instance, if you are playing baseball, you'll need eyes to see the ball, arms to swing the bat, legs to run the bases, and muscles to do everything with precision—and that's only part of the team. We haven't even talked about head and shoulders, knees and toes.

The team Jesus had in the last three years of His life were called *disciples*. This twelve-man team worked together, ate together, and learned together. They would become the core of the first-century Church. When they didn't work together, the team suffered.

As a Christian man, you need the encouragement of other Christian men. This can come through Bible study, accountability partners, and acts of service to others.

We each have a place in the Body of Christ. We each have a job that we were created to complete. We each need to recognize the contributions of others. Like today's verse says, let's be open to sharpen those around us and to allow ourselves to be sharpened so we can be the most effective team for Christ.

WON'T BE LONG NOW

Love from the center of who you are; don't fake it. . . .
Be good friends who love deeply; practice playing second fiddle.
ROMANS 12:9–10 MSG

Ruben worked at a Christian camp in the 1980s. He always smiled, took directions well, and never voiced negative opinions.

He'd survived scarlet fever as a child and certain aspects of Ruben's thinking became limited, but he was loved by all who knew him.

He'd tell common fairy tales, but would crack himself up and laugh, forget where he was, and continue with a different story. His laughter was infectious. Soon, everyone around him would be laughing, although they weren't sure why. The more Ruben's audience laughed, the funnier his stories became.

One of Ruben's favorite jokes was, "What did the monkey say when he got his tail cut off? 'It won't be long now.'" This was always followed by a fit of laughter, demanding audience participation.

In that one simple joke, Ruben taught a lesson he might never have intended: There are times when bad things will happen. We could lament the circumstances and the end result of the incident—or we could respond by believing nothing good can come by complaining. We can turn our worst storms to God's control. A good response will always improve the story we tell.

THE PENCIL PARABLE

[Look] unto Jesus, the author and finisher of our faith.
HEBREWS 12:2 NKJV

There once was a pencil, a sharp point on one end and a soft eraser on the other. The number 2 was emblazoned on its exterior, and it was ready to be used.

The author looked at the various writing implements on his desk. First he chose a pen, but one mistake later and he had to start over. Then he tried a highlighter, but they were hard to read. He tried crayons and markers, but nothing suited the author.

He scratched his rough whiskers and grabbed the pencil. It wasn't as handsome as a fountain pen or as colorful as a marker, but it provided a satisfying and familiar scratch. When the author spelled a name wrong, the pencil erased the word and the author started again.

The pencil didn't have to be flashy to be useful. The pencil provided what the author needed. The pencil made no demands.

We can be pencils in the hands of the Author of life. God can take our unassuming lives and draft a story He's proud of. As if the number 2 on the pencil stands for "second in importance," the story being written is not authored by the pencil, but by the One who is first in importance, the Author.

WHO'S LOOKING OUT FOR ME?

I know, GOD, that mere mortals can't run their own lives,
that men and women don't have what it takes to take charge of life.
JEREMIAH 10:23 MSG

Humans are prone to wander, make mistakes, and become defeated. Earth's first couple had very simple rules to follow, but they easily became convinced to be lawbreakers.

Adam and Eve had every reason to follow a trustworthy God. However, it seemed easy to believe that God was holding all the best for Himself and that following Him wouldn't be in their best interest.

We're no different. We feel that God doesn't really understand us. We believe He wants to withhold something we want right now.

God designed us to embrace His plan and purpose, but thanks to sin, now our natural bent is to look out for ourselves. We can be convinced that things, fame, and money provide a path to the satisfaction we want, but they can't. Instead, the self-centered pursuit of these things pulls us away from God, the only One who can truly satisfy us.

We're not equipped to do life alone, so God gave us directions to follow, lessons to learn, and the Holy Spirit to lead us.

A self-focused lifestyle often leads us to misunderstanding, misapplication of what we learn, and misguided trips to places God marked KEEP OUT! In what parts of your life have you been looking out only for yourself?

OUT OF YOUR MIND

At this point Festus interrupted Paul's defense.
"You are out of your mind!"
ACTS 26:24 NIV

When they heard Paul's story, King Agrippa and the Roman proconsul, Festus, thought he was insane. From their perspective, the evidence was overwhelming. Saul of Tarsus, the brilliant Jewish rabbi and trusted member of the Sanhedrin, abandoned a promising career to join and promote the outlawed sect he once wanted to destroy. He literally went from persecutor to persecuted preacher!

Paul stood before men who held his life in their hands and babbled on about dead men coming back to life and a heavenly vision, and then he tried to persuade them to join his movement (Acts 26)! No wonder Festus thought he was crazy and Agrippa was insulted!

Others may think great adventurers are out of their minds. Adventurers want to do what others think can't be done, take journeys others think are impossible, follow a vision others can't see, and take risks others fear. But that's what makes them heroes!

Deep in the heart of every man is an adventurer, a dreamer, and a hero. Like Paul, we long to follow the wild paths of a great vision. And, like Paul, that journey—the hero's journey—begins with an encounter with the living Christ.

The journey to spiritual transformation and a radical faith in God, participating in His work in the world, and finding our place in His Kingdom is life's greatest adventure.

But we shouldn't be surprised if those around us say, "You are out of your mind!"

HOME SWEET HOME?

As long as we are at home in the body we are away from the Lord.

2 Corinthians 5:6 niv

In 2 Corinthians 5:1–10, Paul was speaking about his struggle between life and death. He realized that this physical life in some ways kept him from being "at home" with the Lord.

There is no doubt about it. We are "at home" in this physical world. Our planet is the one place in the universe where life flourishes. We were made for this place. More precisely, this world was created to be our home. Humankind, created in the image of God, was the ultimate purpose of all creation (Genesis 1:26–27).

But this world as it now exists is not our true home. We were never meant for this sin-ravaged and broken planet. We were never meant to experience the suffering and sadness of a cursed world. We were meant to enjoy intimacy with God without any barrier (Genesis 3).

Being "at home" also means being in a place where we feel comfortable, at rest, and at ease. Another way to think about Paul's insight is that the more comfortable we are, the more at home we feel in our sinful culture and society, the further away we are from being at home with Christ and enjoying our walk with Him.

We should not be "at home" with this world's values, lifestyles, and priorities. We should be restless in this world. If we aren't uncomfortable here, we will never be truly "at home" with Christ.

LEAVING HOME

When Jacob learned that there was grain in Egypt,
he said to his sons, "Why do you just keep looking at each other?"
GENESIS 42:1 NIV

It's easy to identify with Jacob's frustration. Caught in a great famine, the specter of starvation loomed over his family. But his sons denied the coming crisis and procrastinated. They sat around looking at each other as if they didn't know what to do!

Many of us are more like Jacob's boys than Jacob. We are comfortable where we are, and when faced with a long and difficult journey, we'd rather stay home. We don't move until we have to. But by then it can be too late.

This story sheds light on our spiritual lives. Like Jacob's family, we can't find what we need most where we are now. Our relationship with Christ once nourished our souls but has become as dry as a famine-plagued desert. Second, we are reluctant to move. The status quo is just easier. Third, a crisis is looming. Ultimately we will starve and die if we don't do what must be done. Our wives and families will suffer along with us. Finally, we know where to go to find what we need.

Embarking on a life-giving spiritual journey means leaving comfortable but sinful habits behind, enduring the rigors of a new and different life, overcoming barriers, and dealing with our past failures. But the riches of the Kingdom of God wait at the end of the journey.

TROUBLE LETTING GO

"Let me kiss my father and mother goodbye,"
he said, "and then I will come with you."
1 KINGS 19:20 NIV

Elisha had trouble letting go (1 Kings 19:19–21). When the prophet Elijah threw his mantle over Elisha's shoulders, he made Elisha his successor. But Elisha's first reaction was to go home and say good-bye to his parents. He had trouble letting go.

His reaction reminds us of those who made excuses for not following Christ. In His parable of the great banquet (Luke 14:15–24), Jesus recounted three kinds of things people have trouble releasing.

The first man bought land and needed to see it. He couldn't let go of his *place*.

The second man bought oxen and had to see them. He couldn't let go of his *possessions*.

The third man wanted to be with his new wife. He couldn't let go of *people*.

Both Elisha and the characters in Christ's parable had the opportunity for a new life and a tremendous adventure. But the stories end very differently.

Elisha goes back, slaughters his oxen, burns the plow, and (we assume) bids farewell to his parents. He severed the ties to his past and went after his future (1 Kings 19:21).

The characters in Christ's parable cling to their place, possessions, and people. They wouldn't let go. They lost the opportunity, missed the feast, and watched others enjoy what could have been theirs.

It's a simple truth. We need empty hands to take up our cross and follow Him (Mark 8:34–38).

HOLDING ON

Immediately Jesus reached out his hand and caught him.
MATTHEW 14:31 NIV

Following the hero's path means both letting go and holding on.

The story of Peter "walking on water" (Matthew 14:22–36) is a perfect example of this truth. Peter "let go" of the safe confines of the boat. But when he began to sink, Christ caught him, and Peter "held on" with all his strength. It reminds us of Psalm 18:16–17 (NIV):

> He reached down from on high and took hold of me; he drew me out of deep waters. He rescued me from my powerful enemy, from my foes, who were too strong for me.

Paul wrote in Philippians 3:12 that he pressed "on to take hold of that for which Christ Jesus took hold of me (NIV)."

Peter at the Temple Gate took hold of the beggar's right hand and saw God do a miracle when the lame man was healed by the power of God (Acts 3:1–10).

Like a trapeze artist, we must let go in order to reach for what can take us to new places and greater heights. Letting go and spinning through the air is an exhilarating, not a terrifying, experience. The performer knows the "catcher" will be there at the right time to catch and hold him in an iron grip and will never let him fall.

We, too, must hold on with all our strength to the love of God that holds us close. Then we can enjoy soaring free from the limits of our fears and failures.

SECOND THOUGHTS

"We can't attack those people; they are stronger than we are."
NUMBERS 13:31 NIV

Moses sent twelve spies into Canaan in preparation for the coming invasion. All of them had waited a lifetime for the fulfillment of God's promise and the conquest of the land. All of them were delivered from Egypt, crossed the Red Sea, and saw the presence of God at Mount Sinai and the miracles in the desert.

Ten had second thoughts (Numbers 13:31–33).

On the threshold of their greatest adventure, these ten took a long, hard look at the challenges and decided it wasn't worth it. They preferred the world they knew, even if it was in the wilderness, to the battles before them. It was the defining moment for all twelve spies. Ten died in the wilderness they preferred. Two reached the Promised Land and lived their most cherished dreams.

Every man faces moments when the likelihood of success seems small, the obstacles insurmountable, and the costs immeasurable. Those who turn back never fulfill their wild, wonderful dreams. Those who press on may fail, but they fail daring greatly.

On the threshold of a great spiritual adventure, of leaving behind the wilderness of this world and pursuing a great and glorious life in God, some turn back and refuse to step into that new life. They are afraid. It costs too much. Victory seems impossible.

But those who refuse to retreat press on to live an incredible adventure of faith and follow God into the promised land of a rich, full life.

No one can make that choice for us. Will we live by fear or by faith?

GOING BACK

Paul did not think it wise to take him,
because he had deserted them in Pamphylia.
ACTS 15:38 NIV

John Mark gave up. . .quit. . .ran away. So when the time came, Paul refused to let him join the second missionary journey (Acts 15:36-41).

Unfortunately, John Mark wasn't the only one who gave up on the adventure. Paul wrote that "Demas, because he loved this world, has deserted me and has gone to Thessalonica" (2 Timothy 4:10 NIV).

Faced with the opportunity to journey into new and unknown territory, some refuse to go. They are afraid. They love the life they have too much to risk losing it. They are deaf to the call and walk away from the open door.

But most of the time we just don't want to change.

We spend a great deal of time and effort creating the life we want. Once we get it, we don't really want to change. Change is hard work, stressful, uncertain, and messy. It is also absolutely essential in order to pursue the great and glorious adventure of a God-filled life.

So what is it that needs to change? There are many answers, but the sad story of Demas gives us one crystal-clear insight.

His affections did not change. He never stopped loving "this present world" with its comforts and pleasures. He loved the world more than he loved God, God's will for his life, and the great adventure of his call. What he loved drove his behavior and led him to refuse God's call and resist change in his life. So, what do you love...most?

MENTOR, PART ONE

Barnabas took Mark and sailed for Cyprus.
ACTS 15:39 NIV

John Mark was fortunate. Barnabas (Mark's cousin, see Colossians 4:10) interceded, took Mark under his wing, and kept a bad decision from becoming disastrous. His decision created a rift with Paul, but Barnabas obviously thought Mark was worth the effort.

We don't know what happened next. What we do know is that years later Paul asked Timothy to bring John Mark to him because he was "helpful to [him] in [his] ministry" (2 Timothy 4:11 NIV). Clearly, a lot had changed!

All of us need help and guidance to overcome our fears, step into a great future, and grow deep spiritual roots. Barnabas demonstrates the heart of a spiritual mentor.

First, Barnabas believed in Mark and his potential. We all need people who believe the best for us and in us.

Second, he was willing to invest. Barnabas had invested in Paul and saw that investment pay off in the apostle's life and ministry. He was willing to make that investment in Mark.

Third, Barnabas was experienced. Barnabas had been where John Mark needed to go and could show him the way. Mark was a willing follower.

Finally, Barnabas was an encourager. In fact, Barnabas, which means "son of encouragement," was actually his nickname. He was a Levite from Cyprus named Joseph (Acts 4:36).

We all need someone like Barnabas in our lives who can point us in the right direction and encourage us on the way. And we all need to do that for someone else.

Palm Sunday

FLOURISHING

The righteous will flourish like a palm tree.
PSALM 92:12 NIV

Most Christians are familiar with the events of Palm Sunday—Christ's triumphal entry into Jerusalem, the adulation of the crowds as they spread their cloaks in the streets and waved palm fronds. It was a welcome fit for a king, and rightly so! That day began the series of events that led to an upper room, a garden, a mock trial, a cross, and the empty tomb. There is no Easter without Palm Sunday.

In Psalm 92:12–15, the palm tree is a symbol of the spiritual life Christ made possible for all His children. Like the palm, we can grow, flourish, and live a fruitful life.

He made it possible for us to flourish and live joy-filled, exuberant, and meaningful lives.

He made it possible for us to sink our roots deep in the rich spiritual soil of His presence. We are planted in the house of the Lord!

He made it possible for us to have fruitful, productive lives for as long as we live, even bearing fruit in old age.

He made it possible to stay spiritually vital and healthy, to stay green and growing!

He gave us reason to shout with joy and proclaim His righteousness, power, and glory!

But we should remember that we only "flourish in the courts of our God" (Psalm 92:13 NIV). We must draw our life and strength from a deep and nourishing relationship with Him.

An "uprooted" plant doesn't flourish or produce fruit. It dies. Are you rooted in your Savior today?

MENTOR, PART TWO

Elijah and Elisha were on their way from Gilgal.
2 KINGS 2:1 NIV

Elisha's relationship to his mentor, Elijah, was essential. He could not fulfill God's call on his life without Elijah. From the scripture about the last day they were together, we discover five essential qualities of a spiritual mentor (2 King 2:1–18).

First, Elijah and Elisha were close. Elisha knew that the time had come for them to part, and he put off the final good-bye as long as he could. Three times Elijah tells Elisha to stay behind. Three times Elisha refuses.

Second, Elijah was selfless, willing to give of himself to Elisha even at the last moment. "'Tell me, what can I do for you before I am taken from you?'" (2 Kings 2:9 NIV).

Third, Elijah continued to teach his mentee, demonstrating practices that Elisha needed to complete his journey—such as parting the Jordan waters by striking them with his rolled-up mantle (1 Kings 2:8, 14).

Fourth, Elijah invested in Elisha. He spent time with Elisha and taught him after Elisha obeyed the call to be his successor (1 Kings 19:19–21).

Fifth, Elijah had what Elisha wanted, the mantle, which represented the power and presence of God. Spiritual mentors must have their own vital spiritual life; mentors cannot give another person what they don't possess. Though the mantle had no power of its own, Elijah's faith helped Elisha know, experience, and operate in the power of God until it was time for Elisha to own it for himself.

Mentors can help us. But they can't do for us what we won't do for ourselves!

THE CLEAR CHOICE

The Israelites did just what the LORD commanded.
EXODUS 12:28 NIV

The first Passover (in Exodus 12) is the story of two peoples and one choice.

After more than four hundred years in Egypt, the children of Israel were clearly influenced by its culture and religions. Getting Israel out of Egypt took a few days, but getting Egypt out of Israel took forty years.

It was a seminal moment. There was a clear choice. Israel would obey or not. Her firstborn would live or die. They would find freedom or stay in slavery. They would go to the Promised Land or choose Goshen. They chose wisely!

We all face such moments. We must decide to go on to greater heights in God or stay where we are. In that moment, life, death, our future, and the fate of those we love all hang in the balance. Sadly, not everyone chooses wisely.

The key to the story is simple. It was obedience. The way out of Egypt wasn't really the road to the Red Sea. It lay in obeying God. We do what God commands, or we don't. We leave the old life behind, or we don't. We cross the threshold of faith, or we don't. We live God's way, or we live the world's way.

They could not have crossed the Red Sea without first crossing the barrier of obedience. We will never see or experience the great things God has for us without this one simple act, doing what the Lord commands.

THE RISKS OF RETURN

Then Orpah kissed her mother-in-law goodbye.
RUTH 1:14 NIV

Orpah and Ruth faced the same clear choice—go with Naomi to a new land and life or go back to Moab and the life they knew. Orpah refused that new life.

We don't know what happened to Orpah. It seems likely she followed Naomi's advice (Ruth 1:11–13) and went home, married, raised a family, and lived the rest of her life just like everyone else in Moab. She disappeared into the mists of history.

But we do know what happened to Ruth. She lived an incredible life that far surpassed anything she could have imagined. She was David's great-grandmother, an ancestor of the Messiah, and she holds an honored place in history. But none of it could have happened without leaving Moab!

Ruth's words to Naomi (Ruth 1:16–18) set the pattern for all who cross the line from the life we have to the life of our dreams.

She committed herself to God, to God's people, and to that future without reservation. It was a long walk into a new land and a new life, but nothing could dissuade her.

Call it what you will—stubbornness, determination, grit. It comes to the same thing, the strength to follow God regardless of what comes our way. We see it in Jesus. "As the time approached for him to be taken up to heaven, Jesus resolutely set out for Jerusalem" (Luke 9:51 NIV).

Pursuing the hero's journey, the great adventure of faith, means crossing the boundary between the life we have and the life we want. It's the only way.

A "TAXING" TIME

"So give back to Caesar what is Caesar's."
MATTHEW 22:21 NIV

In a few days, taxes are due. Christians often reference these words because Christ paid taxes, too. But it raises the question: What else belongs to "Caesar"? What else do believers owe those who govern our land?

In Romans 13:1–7, Paul called on his readers to pay their taxes, but he didn't stop there. Since "governing authorities" (Romans 13:1 NIV) are an extension of God's authority, we also owe them "submission," respect, and honor (Romans 13:1, 5, 7). In 1 Timothy 2:1–2 (NIV), Paul said "that petitions, prayers, intercession and thanksgiving [should] be made for all people—for kings and all those in authority."

That's a high bar, when, as has happened so often in history, the government uses its vast power against the cause of Christ and His followers. Jesus lived under the oppression of a foreign power, and Paul wrote during a truly monstrous time of persecution when Nero ruled Rome.

Those of us who live in a democracy owe the government one more thing, our participation. We should raise our voice, vote, and exercise the great gift of citizenship in other legal, respectful, God-honoring ways.

Complaining about the government and those who govern is the "great American pastime," not baseball. Believers should not join the cacophony of angry, bitter, and disrespectful voices but participate in ways that obey scripture and bring glory to God and the Gospel.

THE ROAD TO RESURRECTION

They came to a place called Golgotha.
MATTHEW 27:33 NIV

The road to resurrection runs through Golgotha.

The road Christ walked that day was good for us. It wasn't "good" for Christ, who suffered physical, emotional, and spiritual agony few can imagine. But at the end of that road was the fulfillment of His mission, a new and resurrected life, and the immeasurable joys of glory.

It was not the road Christ wanted to follow. In Gethsemane we're told that "he fell with his face to the ground and prayed, 'My Father, if it is possible, may this cup be taken from me'" (Matthew 26:39 NIV). He would have preferred to fulfill His mission and live a new and glorious life without taking the road to Golgotha. So would we.

It just can't be done.

The trials and suffering of Good Friday were the only way to expiate the sins of the world, gain salvation for mankind, and fulfill the divine plan to redeem the world.

The challenges we face along the road to a deeper and richer life in Christ are just as necessary to break our sinful will, to teach us the lessons of godly living, and drive us to ever greater intimacy with and dependence on God. But how?

Christ shows the way: submission—"Yet not as I will, but as you will"—and trust—"'Father, into your hands I commit my spirit'" (Matthew 26:39; Luke 23:46). If we refuse to submit and trust, if we reject the way of the cross, we will never see new life, and our journey to spiritual greatness ends.

MISSING IN ACTION

Then all the disciples deserted him and fled.
MATTHEW 26:56 NIV

Where were the disciples?

John was at the cross the day Christ died (John 19:26–27). Judas, in regret-fueled despair, had killed himself (Matthew 27:3–5). But where were the others? No one knows for sure.

Their often noted and criticized desertion of Christ in Gethsemane isn't hard to identify with or understand. Running from danger is a natural response and survival is a basic instinct. We'd just like to think we'd do better.

But their abandonment in the midst of crisis illustrates two critical truths about our spiritual journey. First, we need allies and friends to travel with us. Jesus "appointed twelve that they might be with him" (Mark 3:14). For three years, they and a group of women (Luke 8:2–3) accompanied and supported Him on the journey. When His great crisis approached, He wanted them close and praying. "Then Jesus went with his disciples to a place called Gethsemane, and he said to them, 'Sit here while I go over there and pray'" (Matthew 26:36 NIV).

Second, there are places others can't or won't go with us. There are trials we must face, challenges we must overcome, and enemies we must battle alone. But that doesn't mean we are truly alone any more than Christ was alone on Golgotha. God is with us, even when we don't feel Him.

We all need a band of brothers. But we also need the strength to pursue our journey whether or not they go with us.

RACING TO THE RESURRECTION

*Both were running, but the other disciple outran
Peter and reached the tomb first.*

JOHN 20:4 NIV

It's an odd moment. Peter and John raced to the garden tomb. John got there first, but Peter entered the empty tomb first (John 20:5–8). Their reactions illustrate the response of many to Easter morning.

John stood on the outside and hesitated. We don't know why. Perhaps like so many who encounter the claims of the risen Christ, he wasn't sure. Many will stand close to the greatest joy of humankind and hesitate.

Peter took longer to get there, but he went right in. On this Easter, many are taking the long road to Jesus. Our prayer should be that they experience the majesty of the resurrection and the joys of forgiveness and new life.

Peter and John went home confused. They left the tomb with more questions than answers. Thousands will observe magnificent Easter celebrations and not truly understand its significance or know that Christ's love for them motivated His sacrifice or that they can know Him and a new life free from their past.

There was a third runner that day, Mary Magdalene (John 20:11–18). She ran to tell the apostles when she discovered the empty tomb (John 20:2), and apparently Mary ran back.

Peter and John had gone home. She stayed until she met the resurrected Christ, heard His voice, and worshipped at His feet. She alone experienced the joy and wonder of her risen Lord.

Mary won the race to the resurrection.

NO ONE SAID IT WOULD BE EASY

As for you, you were dead in your transgressions and sins.
EPHESIANS 2:1 NIV

No one said getting from where we are to where we want to be in God is easy. Anyone who says it's easy is a liar. Anyone who believes it's easy is a fool.

James said we should rejoice in trials because of what they produce in us (James 1:2–4).

Paul compared this life to the harsh discipline of an athlete in training (1 Corinthians 9:24–27).

Jesus warned us that we would have trouble in this world (John 16:33).

The Bible compares our spiritual journey to gold in the refiner's fire or clay on the potter's wheel (Proverbs 17:3; Jeremiah 18:1–5).

In his great work *Summa Theologica*, Thomas Aquinas seems to echo Ephesians 2:1–2 when he warned against "the world, the flesh and the Devil."

When we pursue Christ with all our hearts, we live a life that challenges the world around us and may prompt an angry, hostile response. They hate Him and all who follow Him.

That pursuit draws us into spiritual warfare. Our enemy uses all his power and influence to deceive us, block our way, and make sure we pay a high price for following God.

But we are our own worst and greatest enemy. We run from, resist, and resent the struggles we inevitably face. We want glory without the cross. It never, ever happens that way.

No one said it would be easy. . .just worth it!

COMMENDATIONS

"I commend to you. . ."
ROMANS 16:1 NIV

It's a stunning list.

At the end of his letter to the Romans, Paul takes time to greet, commend, and express gratitude to twenty-five individuals and, in some cases, their congregations. All of them in one way or another were of great value to his life and ministry. It's not an exaggeration to say that Paul's great accomplishments weren't possible without them.

It isn't just more difficult to make this journey alone; it's impossible. All of us need allies who will walk the road to a growing spiritual life with us. We will need help along the way.

Paul's allies were his benefactors, his coworkers, and friends. He even mentions that Rufus's mother had been a mother to him (Romans 16:13). We don't know much about most of the people on this list, but we know he valued and appreciated each of them.

Also, we know that each of them supported and encouraged him on the way. Together they provided a network of material, emotional, relational, and spiritual support. When Paul suffered, they comforted him. When Paul was discouraged, they encouraged him. When Paul wanted to quit, they challenged him. When he didn't have what it took to go on, they gave it to him. Paul accomplished great things and reached great heights standing on their shoulders.

We need to intentionally build this kind of network and work at keeping these relationships healthy and strong. We really can't "go it alone."

FUNDAMENTAL CHOICE

"Now choose life."
DEUTERONOMY 30:19 NIV

The children of Israel fled Egypt. They had crossed the Red Sea, camped at the base of Sinai, and spent forty years in the wilderness. Now they stood again at the Jordan, and Moses presented them with a stark choice—life or death.

They were approaching their greatest challenge, conquering the Promised Land. Everything this generation, which was raised in the wilderness, knew was going to be different, and they needed to be ready for the cataclysmic challenges and changes they would face on the other side of the Jordan.

All of us face moments like this on our spiritual journey. We stand at the edge of a great transformation and must choose between the future and the past, between spiritual life and death, between what was and what can be.

Moses made clear what was at stake in their decision.

Our spiritual lives are in the balance. If we balk and fail to meet the challenge, we will not experience the deep, rich, and intimate relationship with God we seek.

The future of those we love is in the balance, too. "Now choose life so that. . .your children may live" (Deuteronomy 30:19 NIV). As husbands and fathers, we must be constantly alert to the impact of our lives on those we love. They go with us or stay behind with us. We blaze the trail forward, or we settle for the status quo.

Finally, our future is in the balance. "For the LORD is your life, and he will give you many years in the land" (Deuteronomy 30:20 NIV). Whether or not we inhabit that land is up to us.

GETTING READY

*"And that you may love the LORD your God,
listen to his voice, and hold fast to him."*
DEUTERONOMY 30:20 NIV

The people approached the greatest challenge of their lives, and Moses wanted them to be ready. He knew what we should know—preparation matters.

We, too, will face great challenges, moments when it feels like life or death on our journey to spiritual growth. Success or failure in the next phase of our journey depends on preparation in this phase.

It's fascinating that his instructions had nothing to do with becoming a conquering army and everything to do with their right relationship with God. Strategies and techniques, no matter how valuable, don't matter if we are not spiritually prepared.

Moses gave four specific instructions (Deuteronomy 30:20):

First, love God. Our affections are at the core of life. We will always follow our greatest love. If He is not our one great love, we will falter when asked to sacrifice what we truly love.

Second, listen to God. God speaks to us through His Word, His Spirit, and His people. He will lead us if we listen and follow His voice.

Third, link your life to His. We must take hold of God in an ironclad grip that will not let go no matter what we face. He won't let go of us, but we must hold on to Him.

Finally, lean on His promises. God has promised greater heights in Him, no matter how difficult the journey. He will keep His promise, but we must keep faith in His promises.

A CLEAR LINE

As the time approached for him to be taken up to heaven,
Jesus resolutely set out for Jerusalem.
LUKE 9:51 NIV

Jesus knew false arrest, torture, crucifixion, and death waited for Him in Jerusalem. But He was determined. The word *sterizo* in this verse means "to make firm, to strengthen, or to confirm."

It's an amazing statement that clearly illustrates the great challenge that confronts all who pursue spiritual vitality and growth. There comes a moment when to go forward, to enjoy the life in God we hunger for, we must face a painful challenge, leave something behind, and that something in us must die.

Abraham left family behind in Haran. Moses faced murder charges in Egypt. Paul's self-righteousness died on the road to Damascus. David had his giant, Joseph had a prison, and Peter had his shame. All of them passed through their ordeal and found God waiting on the other side.

It's different for every man. Some face the painful challenge of confessing sin and making amends to those they've harmed. Some have to leave behind a career, friends, or family. Ambition, pride, selfishness, or lust must die in others. It may cost cherished relationships, pleasures we enjoy, or the future we want. It will cost. . .everything. And we know it.

But we must follow Christ, face the challenge, live through the pain, and kill what must die. Like Christ, we must be firm, strong, and resolute! If we aren't, we will fail.

But we don't have it in us. We aren't that strong. Remember. . . "I can do all this through him who gives me strength" (Philippians 4:13 NIV).

TRANSFORMERS

And we all. . .are being transformed into his image.
2 CORINTHIANS 3:18 NIV

Passing through a great challenge changes us. Peter, the coward of the courtyard, became the lion of Pentecost. Paul, the persecutor, became the great champion of the faith. David, the shepherd boy, became Israel's greatest king. Moses, who ran for his life, faced down Pharaoh and delivered his people.

Paul outlined the process of a great transformation in 2 Corinthians 3:18.

First, we encounter God with *"unveiled faces."* All pretense, self-righteousness, and hubris are stripped away. We see ourselves clearly and know who and what we are—sinners in need of a Savior, weaklings in need of great strength, and fools in need of great wisdom.

Second, we *"contemplate the Lord's glory."* Like Moses, we are transformed by confronting the glory of God. We grasp the true majesty and infinite wonder of our Savior and His love. We are humbled and overwhelmed in His presence.

Third, all this *"comes from the Lord."* We can't do any of it! No matter how hard we try, how disciplined, rule-keeping, or religious we are, we remain shameful sinners. We only wash the outside of the cup (Matthew 23:25–26). If God doesn't change us, we can't change.

Fourth, we are *"transformed into his image."* Our destiny is to be like Jesus!

Finally, we are transformed *"with ever-increasing glory."* Transformation is a process, not an event. We keep changing and will never, even in eternity, experience all the transformation or glory we long for or He intends. Hallelujah!

TAKE HOLD OF HIM WHO HAS TAKEN HOLD OF YOU

I press on to take hold of that for which
Christ Jesus took hold of me.
PHILIPPIANS 3:12 NIV

Sometimes the prize seems elusive, just out of reach. We shouldn't be surprised. No matter how much we grow in grace, there is always room to grow. And the more we grow in Christ, the more we realize how little we truly know Him.

In Philippians 3:12–14, Paul outlined his strategy for taking hold of more and more of God in his life.

First, don't expect to ever truly reach that goal. Paul didn't.

Second, the more Christ takes hold of us, the more we are captivated by His power and presence in our lives, the more we are motivated to pursue Him.

Third, forget. Let the past, with its mistakes, shortcomings, and failures, stay in the past. Don't long for what you had yesterday. Backward focus prevents forward motion.

Fourth, press on. The word translated "press on" means "to run swiftly in order to catch a person or thing." Just as athletes approaching the finish line lean into the tape, we should exert every effort and lean into God.

Finally, there is a prize! Paul defined this prize in part when he wrote: "I want to know Christ—yes, to know the power of his resurrection" (Philippians 3:10 NIV). That's not all that those who take hold of that for which Christ has taken hold of them can expect. But it is more than enough to keep us in the race!

CHOICE AND CONSEQUENCE

"From everyone who has been given much,
much will be demanded."
LUKE 12:48 NIV

The more of God we experience, the more He expects of us. It's always been that way.

Moses had the glory of the burning bush and was expected to set his people free.

Paul met Jesus on the Damascus road and was expected to bring the Gospel to the world.

Peter had the joy of three years at Jesus' side and was expected to lead the Church in the face of great persecution and in a period of incredible expansion.

There is no doubt that this is true. As a matter of fact, one of the barriers to greater spiritual life is knowing that God's call accompanies God's joy. But why? Why are we not free to just enjoy the glory of knowing God without the burden of service?

First, growing in God isn't only about us. It is also about God's glory in the world. It's not about us. It's about Him.

Second, growing in God prepares us to participate in His great work in the world. Surely our relationship with Him is precious. But God wants everyone to know that joy and He has chosen us as His emissaries.

Third, growing in God strengthens us for the inevitable challenges we face. We know Him, and we know He will strengthen, sustain, and stay with us.

Finally, it's good for us. We were created to live on purpose for a great purpose. We cannot fulfill that destiny or know that satisfaction without a great mission.

What is God expecting of you?

SETTING AN EXAMPLE

Join together in following my example.
PHILIPPIANS 3:17 NIV

Paul realized that he was leading the way and others were following him.

Every man who seeks a great adventure in God is leading the way. The question is: What kind of example are we setting? Are we living up to the life of Christ in us, or are we slipping back into old habits and patterns?

First, Paul knew his life was being watched. His example mattered. Our children, our friends, and the unbelievers who surround us every day are watching us, too. We may not think about it, but it's true. Paul took that responsibility seriously.

Second, we ought to follow the example of others who are ahead of us on the path of spiritual growth. Paul wrote, "Keep your eyes on those who live as we do" (Philippians 3:17 NIV). We set an example by following the example of others.

Third, the impact of our example has eternal consequence. In the rest of the paragraph, Paul contrasts those who follow his example and those who are enemies of the cross (Philippians 3:17–21). Setting the wrong example has disastrous consequences.

Finally, our example must have integrity. It isn't about putting our best foot forward or presenting a handsome veneer that hides the truth. How we handle our flaws and failures, how we deal with challenges and difficulties, and how we respond to temptation are part of that example.

The world has plenty of hypocrites. It's men of true integrity that are in short supply.

GLOWING IN THE DARK

All the Israelites saw Moses, his face was radiant.
EXODUS 34:30 NIV

It's one of the Bible's strangest moments. Moses returned from the presence of the Lord glowing! (Exodus 34:29–35). Others could observe the changes in his life.

In 2 Corinthians 3:7–18, Paul used this moment to illustrate the transformation believers experience in the presence of God. "And we all, who with unveiled faces contemplate the Lord's glory, are being transformed into his image with ever-increasing glory" (verse 18).

Great spiritual transformation isn't just possible—it's real! God does great work in us to transform us into Christ's image. That is our great and glorious hope!

Great spiritual transformation should be observable. Those around us should notice the difference, not because of pious posturing but because we truly are different. It isn't something we put on display. It's something we can't hide!

Great spiritual vitality can fade. Paul is clear: "Moses. . .put a veil over his face to prevent the Israelites from seeing the end of what was passing away" (2 Corinthians 3:13 NIV). Moses put the veil on because his appearance frightened people. He kept the veil on to hide the fact that the glory was fading. Our religious lives can function like that veil and hide the truth that our true spiritual vitality is waning.

Finally, great spiritual vitality can only be renewed in the presence of God. When the glory faded, Moses took off the veil and returned to the source of true transformation (Exodus 34:33–35). When he needed more of God, God was there for him. He's there for us, too.

MIDTERM EXAM

*The devil prowls around like a roaring lion
looking for someone to devour.*
1 PETER 5:8 NIV

Sometimes we think growing in grace means we've passed the test, we've overcome, we're victorious! That's true. But it doesn't mean we won't face another test. It won't be the same test, and it may be the most difficult we've ever faced. The stronger we are in God, the more threatening we are to the devil!

Peter compared this test to a roaring, hungry lion looking for prey. In 1 Peter 5:6–9, we find clear instructions on how to deal with the devil.

First, be humble (1 Peter 5:6). Pride really does come before a fall. We are most vulnerable when we think we aren't at risk. We are strongest when we depend on the mighty hand of God for our survival.

Second, don't be anxious (1 Peter 5:7). God is in control. We are secure in Him. Worry and anxiety weaken us. God cares for us, knows what we need, and is there for us.

Third, be sober-minded and watchful (1 Peter 5:8). Take the threat seriously. Be on guard against those things the devil knows he can use against you.

Resist him (1 Peter 5:9). Don't give in. Stay strong and stand firm in your faith. No matter how bad it looks, no matter how much it hurts, no matter how enticing the temptation—trust God.

Finally, remember it's a "midterm" exam, not the final. There will be another test.

AFTER. . .

After you have suffered a little while, [God] will himself restore you
and make you strong, firm and steadfast.
1 PETER 5:10 NIV

Peter reminds us that when we are tested we suffer for "a little while" (1 Peter 4:10 NIV). It doesn't feel that way. Pain stretches time. We feel like it's always been this way, and we fear it will always be this way. It won't.

But we need to understand "a little while" not in terms of this life but in terms of eternity. This life is a quickly evaporating vapor. For those who overcome, who pass the "midterm exam," joy everlasting awaits. We are "called to his eternal glory in Christ" (verse 10).

You and I can rely on God's grace to "restore [us] and make [us] strong, firm and steadfast." Tests purify us, temper us, and make us stronger. Testing won't destroy us. It solidifies those gains and prepares us for the next great step in our spiritual journey.

Perhaps the most comforting words in this passage are found in 1 Peter 5:11 (NIV): "To him be the power for ever and ever. Amen." There has never been and will never be a time when God is not sovereign. His dominion encompasses heaven and earth, spiritual and material, and includes everything that has happened to us or ever will happen!

In times of testing, life feels out of control. It may be out of our control. But it is not out of the control of God, who loved us from before time, who only seeks our good, and who has dominion over all things, including our suffering!

SO WHAT?

"Therefore go and make disciples of all nations."
MATTHEW 28:19 NIV

Heroes and adventurers come home. Those who take the journey to a greater, richer spiritual life come back to the reality of day-to-day life. But they are not the same men.

The disciples had completed an incredible journey. They saw Jesus crucified and raised from the dead, and they spent forty days with Him, twice (Matthew 28:16–20; Mark 16:14–20). Jesus called them into the future.

He answered the "so what?" question. What difference does the journey make?

Their journey and ours fundamentally changes our relationship with Christ and should result in changes in our place in the world and in us.

"When they saw him, they worshiped him" (Matthew 28:17 NIV). Our spiritual journey should change what we worship, what is of supreme value in our lives. We may enjoy the things of this world, but we no longer worship and slavishly pursue them as the source of life.

"All authority in heaven and on earth has been given to me'" (Matthew 28:18 NIV). Christ is the authority, not us. We submit to Him, obey His commands, and pursue His purposes.

"Surely I am with you always. . .'" (Matthew 28:20 NIV). But the sweetest result is our connection to Christ and His abiding presence with us. *"But some doubted. . ."* (Matthew 28:17 NIV). Seeing the resurrected Christ didn't convince all His disciples. We can expect some doubts and struggles to remain. They energize our pursuit for more of God. Doubts are not failures. They are proof of our hunger for another adventure in God!

NOW WHAT?

"Therefore go and make disciples of all nations."
MATTHEW 28:19 NIV

The "now what" depends on the "so what."

The call to go and make disciples (Matthew 28:19) and preach the Gospel (Mark 16:15) rests on the "therefore" of Matthew 28:19. Since He has all authority, since He is always with us, and since He alone is of supreme value in our lives, therefore we should. . .

Go proclaim the good news of His coming, His salvation, and the joys of life lived in His power and presence.

Go make disciples and teach others how to know Him, grow in Him, and find their greatest joy in Him. Teach them to obey His Word and live for His glory.

Go into all the world. Matthew uses the word for all "peoples," for every ethnic-linguistic group. Mark uses the word for the physical world, the cosmos. There is no place we should not go and no people we should not reach. Most of us are called to go across the street, not around the world. But all of us have the responsibility to go or to send others to the far-flung corners of the earth and the unreached people who live there.

Go because eternity is at stake. Those who don't believe are condemned (Mark 16:16).

Go in His power (Mark 16:17–18). We were never intended to accomplish this great task without His power, protection, and provision.

Our journey ends with a great call to change the world. That is our next great adventure!

GOD'S JEALOUS LOVE FOR YOU

"Do not worship any other god, for the LORD,
whose name is Jealous, is a jealous God."
EXODUS 34:14 NIV

Perhaps the thought of a jealous God calls to mind images of a person in a relationship who is pushy or overprotective. However, the full picture of God presented throughout scripture, such as in Hosea, is a heartbroken lover who has been rejected time and time again by His beloved people. This is a jealousy that isn't pushy or overbearing.

When Saint Francis of Assisi spoke of God's love, he noted that God has humbly made Himself vulnerable to the point that He allows us to break His heart. This jarring love means an all-powerful God cares deeply enough for us that He is willing to endure the pain of loss and disappointment when we turn away from Him.

God is jealous for our time and attention. When we fail to make God our top priority, He doesn't call us back with anger and obligation. He calls us back as a jealous lover who desires a relationship with us.

The costly love of God that suffered for our sake on the cross is the same jealous love of God that desires us with all of the passion tucked away in the simple message of John 3:16: "God so loved the world. . ."

Perhaps we need to believe that God loves us enough to be jealous, to allow Himself to be moved with grief when we turn away from Him. Perhaps we struggle to love and make space for God because we have yet to know and feel His jealous passion for us.

RESTORATION AFTER GOD'S REBUKE

"The LORD your God is with you, the Mighty Warrior who saves.
He will take great delight in you; in his love he will no longer
rebuke you, but will rejoice over you with singing."
ZEPHANIAH 3:17 NIV

When we fail, and we surely will all fail, we may go through a season of the Lord's discipline or rebuke. Perhaps we dread such seasons. Perhaps we even fear being cut off or losing the Lord's favor forever. Could we ever sin so grievously or repeatedly that God would ever turn us away?

Understandable as these fears may be, a season of discipline is always intended to lead us to restoration with God. In fact, if God merely let us go our own way or spared us the consequences of our disobedience, we could argue that He isn't all that concerned about us. What parent would not reach out in discipline to a beloved child with any other goal than complete restoration? Isn't God's rebuke the ultimate sign that He is truly for us, even if He isn't primarily concerned with our comfort?

And even if we pass through a season of discipline or distance from God, it is never destined to last forever. God longs to rejoice over us with singing and joy. We are His beloved people, the source of His joy and the focus of His song. How surprising it is to pass through a season of failure and discipline only to discover that God remains with us and has never let us go.

THE PROVISION TRAP

For the love of money is a root of all kinds of evil. Some people,
eager for money, have wandered from the faith
and pierced themselves with many griefs.
1 TIMOTHY 6:10 NIV

So many men feel a burden to provide for their families, and to a certain degree this is good and responsible. There are, however, lines that can be crossed when it comes to providing—when the drive to "provide" turns into a damaging love for money or a driving ambition that could undermine God's work in your life.

Paul writes about the "love of money," but perhaps we try to disguise it as something else. We justify our financial decisions and commitments, calling them wise investments, good stewardship, or planning for the future.

Isn't it wise to seek out a job that pays better, even if it means longer hours or a longer commute? Isn't it responsible to seek the best possible promotion, even if one's work is rapidly becoming an identity?

Paul hints at the way to determine whether our ambitions and investments are destructive or positive: What do we long for? Do we long for more money? More influence and power? The admiration of others? These are the very things that can undermine and essentially replace our longing for God. Money in particular supplants God's place in our lives because it can provide for our needs, provide security and comfort, and convince us that we are on the right track.

Paul reminds us that the size of the paycheck isn't necessarily the issue; it's about the object of our desires—what we pursue each day above all else.

HOW TO WAIT ON GOD

*Let all that I am wait quietly before God, for my hope is
in him. He alone is my rock and my salvation,
my fortress where I will not be shaken.*

PSALM 62:5–6 NLT

We are told repeatedly to wait on the Lord throughout the Psalms. However, this particular psalm adds a jarring addition to our waiting: wait *quietly*. The manner in which we wait is very much the test of our faith. When I wait on God, I'm tempted to make requests, to complain, to suggest solutions, and even to pray for specific outcomes, as if I know the best way for God to act in my life. Most of us can be persuaded into waiting on God, but waiting quietly is a whole other matter. Those who wait quietly have truly surrendered themselves to the direction and provision of God, for they have no other hope than the action of God.

And for the times when we stop waiting and seek our solutions or build our own safety nets and fortresses, it often takes a tragedy, crisis, or difficult situation to shake us loose. Perhaps the quiet waiting leaves us restless and fearful. However, anything that we trust more than God will not last, especially in a time of trouble that shakes our foundations.

Placing our trust completely in God does not guarantee smooth sailing. In fact, the need for God to act as a fortress suggests that we should expect conflict. Trouble is surely coming, and the question is whether we are truly waiting in expectant quiet before God.

HOW TO BLESS OTHERS

*"May the LORD bless you and protect you. May the LORD smile
on you and be gracious to you. May the LORD show
you his favor and give you his peace."*

NUMBERS 6:24–26 NLT

At an uncertain time in the history of Israel, when the people could scarcely imagine themselves as anything other than slaves and had yet to settle in a land of their own, God provided a priestly blessing for Aaron and his sons. A wandering people in search of a new land certainly needed the protection, gracious favor, and peace of God when there was so little they knew for certain.

The people of Israel rarely had smooth sailing with God. They were disobedient, rebellious, and grumbled even when God blessed them. They were rarely on their best behavior, but God mercifully encouraged them to pray for protection, peace, and the favor of God. In fact, despite their struggles, God encouraged them to imagine Him smiling upon them as He extends His unearned grace to them.

As you think about how to pray for others, consider praying that those in danger will receive God's blessing and protection. Ask God to guide them through uncertain times and to mercifully provide blessings for them. Bless them by interceding for God's favor and peace to be manifested in their lives.

When praying for others, consider asking that God will be present for them in tangible, peaceful ways. As a priesthood of believers, we have inherited the joyful role of intercession, and thankfully, God has shown us how to fill this role.

RETREAT AFTER SUCCESS

Yet the news about him spread all the more, so that crowds of
people came to hear him and to be healed of their sicknesses.
But Jesus often withdrew to lonely places and prayed.
LUKE 5:15–16 NIV

Whenever I experience success, I naturally think of ways to keep it going and build on it. Isn't that "good stewardship"? Jesus had the exact opposite response. As the crowds seeking Him increased, He immediately withdrew to be with God, lest He lose that vital connection with the Father.

This doesn't mean we must leave our work behind in order to set off for a lengthy wilderness retreat. Rather, when Jesus experienced success or His schedule started to fill up, He recognized that was the precise time to retreat. Building on success and influence isn't necessarily the best thing for our souls. We don't have to serve success, but instead we can choose to take measured steps away from our work in pursuit of spiritual renewal. Jesus' first move in the midst of "success" was to step back, and after that, He was able to step forward on firmer footing.

I have learned that whenever I have a free moment, my first move should be toward prayer, reflection on scripture, or just a reflection on my day so that I know how to pray. A full schedule is no excuse to withdraw from God or others. I can find time to pray even for two, five, or twenty minutes throughout my day by making it my first move before doing anything else. Surprisingly, I always find the time I need to get my work done.

FREED TO SERVE

"I, the Lord, have called you in righteousness; I will take hold of your hand. I will keep you and will make you to be a covenant for the people and a light for the Gentiles, to open eyes that are blind, to free captives from prison and to release from the dungeon those who sit in darkness."
ISAIAH 42:6–7 NIV

Perhaps we all know quite well that God has made us righteous and freed us from sin's power, but perhaps it's harder to consider what's next. Are we freed from sin only for our own benefit? Today's passage from Isaiah says that we have been freed in order to liberate others from bondage, both spiritual and physical. If this calling strikes you as intimidating, or if you simply don't know where to start, there's good news for you.

God holds you and shapes you. The life of God is taking hold in your life and reshaping your heart, desires, and thoughts. As God brings liberation into your life, you'll start to long to share it with others. You'll even begin to recognize the opportunities to share that light with those who are blind or to bring freedom to those who are trapped.

As God renews our minds, He also says He will take us by the hand, guiding us forward in our calling. Perhaps the thing holding most of us back is doubt that God is reaching out to us. Are you open to God's renewal and guidance? Are you too distracted? Do you need to set aside time today to allow God's renewal to begin taking hold in your life?

THE JOY OF RELYING ON GOD

But I trust in your unfailing love;
my heart rejoices in your salvation.
PSALM 13:5 NIV

We can only approach God because of His mercy, and once again it's His mercy that sustains us. I've found the greatest frustration and discouragement when I've tried to approach God based on my own merits and efforts, as if I could prove myself worthy of God's mercy and saving help.

In light of today's passage, begin by asking what you're trusting in or leaning on today. Are you joyful? Are you feeling fearful or frustrated? Our emotions and thoughts are helpful clues to what we think and practice about God. They provide the evidence of a life of faith or a life attempting to get by on its own.

While following Jesus never assures us of smooth sailing, we are assured of God's presence based on His mercy for us. If you aren't joyful today and even find yourself stuck in despair, it could be that you're trusting in yourself to earn God's mercy or simply relying on your own resources and wisdom to help yourself.

There is great joy and contentment in trusting in God's mercy and falling back on God's saving help. We don't lean on God because we've earned His help or favor. Rather, we start with His mercy, which assures us of His saving help and presence whether we are going through good times or bad.

WHO GETS THE CREDIT?

*Deliver me, my God, from the hand of the wicked, from the grasp of those
who are evil and cruel. For you have been my hope, Sovereign LORD,
my confidence since my youth. From birth I have relied on you;
you brought me forth from my mother's womb. I will ever praise you.*
PSALM 71:4–6 NIV

Today's psalm offers a surefire test for whether we are living by faith, and if
I'm honest, it's a test that I don't want to take most days. The psalmist says
that his praise shall always be of the Lord, who is his strength.

Who gets the credit in your life?

That's a question I don't want to ask myself. It's easy to get wrapped
up in my own plans, talents, and worries each day. Am I offering myself
to God and trusting God to guide my steps? Am I depending on God to
provide for my needs and to give me the strength to serve others and to
accomplish my work?

Alongside this challenging question, we have the encouraging words
that God is able to support us and to provide strength for us. We don't have
to dive into each day on our own, relying on our own discipline, willpower,
or plans to live as faithful disciples.

When trouble comes, we can cry out to God for deliverance and help.
Even if we have been distant or dependent on ourselves, we can return to
Him because of His mercy. Our God wants us to depend on Him and will
not leave us if we turn to Him.

DO YOU WANT TO BE SET FREE?

Therefore confess your sins to each other and pray for each other so that you may be healed. The prayer of a righteous person is powerful and effective.

JAMES 5:16 NIV

Jesus once asked a man if he wanted to be made well, and perhaps we should consider that question for ourselves in light of today's verse. Do you want to be set free from anger, lust, greed, or selfishness? Do you want to experience the freedom and abundant life that Jesus promised us? While we can probably tread water on our own for a while, we may never experience a true breakthrough until we humbly ask a fellow believer to pray for us as we fully confess our sins to them.

James seems to anticipate our potential objections: What if I open up my deepest, darkest secrets to someone and they can't help me? Do I want to risk exposing myself to a fellow Christian if it's not going to do any good?

James assures us that wisely choosing a righteous believer to pray for us will bring the healing we desire for our shortcomings. Whether you feel weak or stuck with a particular issue in your life, consider who you can approach for prayer this week. Your life may not turn around until you openly confess your sin and receive prayer. Do you want to be made well? Then it's time to stop hiding your secret sins and relying on yourself. We may only find true freedom when we finally confess our sins to each other.

ON FIRE IN THE WRONG WAY

When the disciples James and John saw this, they asked, "Lord, do you want us to call fire down from heaven to destroy them?" But Jesus turned and rebuked them.

LUKE 9:54–55 NIV

Zeal and passion can be tremendous assets for followers of Jesus, provided we point our zeal and passion in the right direction. When Jesus and His disciples met opposition from the Samaritans, James and John responded with zeal, asking Jesus if they should ask God to destroy them. Jesus had a different kind of zeal in mind.

Just as Jesus had responded to the Samaritan woman's controversial comments and questions with wisdom and an invitation, He had no desire to exact revenge when someone resisted Him and His message. His disciples had yet to realize that Jesus came as a doctor to heal the sick, not as a judge prepared to bring destruction. Jesus showed patience and mercy, demonstrating that God is far more concerned with changing lives than with condemnation.

We're going to meet people who are negative, insulting, and opposed to Christianity. Jesus challenges us to avoid dehumanizing them. Just as Jesus didn't come to bring judgment but to heal those who were willing, we have a similar calling to respond to criticism and opposition with patience and wisdom.

The "calling down fire" approach is too concerned with the short term. God takes a long-term, big-picture view of our world, patiently waiting for people to come to Him. In fact, God's patience isn't just for His opponents. He's also patient with His people who keep trying to call down fire from heaven.

LOVE THAT ENDURES IN TRIALS

"You loved Me before the foundation of the world."
JOHN 17:24 NKJV

I have often made the mistake of believing that God's love ensures I'll be spared trials and great suffering. If something in my life goes wrong, it's tempting to begin asking whether I've messed up in some way. The prayer of Jesus before His suffering on the cross jars us out of such notions.

Jesus was certain that God's love had remained in Him even before creation. This love had stretched for years beyond our comprehension into eternity past, and even as He faced the prospect of an extremely violent and painful death, He didn't doubt God's love for Him. His foundation was too deep and too certain for even the worst kind of death and suffering to shake Him loose.

At the start of Jesus' ministry, the Father assured Him and those present of His love for the Son. In His darkest trial, Jesus returned to this love. Even if the Father didn't spare Him from the cross and the great darkness spread before Him, Jesus clung to what He knew of God.

A preacher who had lost his eyesight shared in a sermon, "Never doubt in the darkness what God has shown you in the light." So much of spiritual perseverance depends on us remembering the ways God has acted for us in the past. Even if God seems distant in the present, we can trust that the same God who was present in the past will be there in the future.

HOW GOD TURNS FAILURE INTO DELIGHT

Who is a God like you, who pardons sin and forgives the transgression. . .
You do not stay angry forever but delight to show mercy.
MICAH 7:18 NIV

What do you imagine about God when you sin? Do you imagine an angry God, eager to turn you away or leave you alone? Do you imagine a disappointed God, incredulous that you've failed yet again?

Whether you are struggling with habitual sin or worry that your transgressions are beyond God's forgiveness, there is a promise for you: God is more merciful than we can imagine. Micah compares our Lord with the false gods of his day—deities that arose from human imagination and demanded offerings in order to be placated. He assures us that our living God is completely unlike these gods.

There is no doubt that sins and transgressions are serious and can alienate us from God, but if we confess our sins, He is all too eager to forgive and restore us. If we imagine God as angry or towering over us to strike us with judgment, the Word assures us that His anger passes quickly and that He delights in showing mercy. In fact, God takes no pleasure in judgment. God's delight is in showing mercy and restoring us. If you want to delight God, stop hiding your sin and failures. Bring them out before God in plain sight so that He can show mercy to you with His pardon and forgiveness.

TRUST FOR THE IMPOSSIBLE

"I am the Lord's servant," Mary answered. "May your word
to me be fulfilled." Then the angel left her.
LUKE 1:38 NIV

We shouldn't overlook the fact that Luke places the story of Zechariah doubting the angel of the Lord right before the story of Mary. Becoming a mother is life-changing and full of uncertainty already, but with the promise of God's Spirit coming over her and bearing the Messiah, Mary had every reason to doubt or resist the promise of God. Perhaps we can relate to Zechariah in the previous Bible story, who found the angel's promise of a child too much to take in. Mary, on the other hand, yielded herself to God, recognizing that it wasn't up to her to work out the details of God's promise. She received the promise at face value, even if the implications surely made her mind spin.

As we celebrate our mothers today, we should begin by recognizing the leap of faith they took by bringing us into the world. Bearing a child forever changes a mother's life. Nothing is ever quite the same for mothers after giving birth, and the days can be especially long for mothers as they put the needs of their children first. While flowers or brunch may be a nice start in expressing our gratitude to the mothers in our lives, we shouldn't overlook the importance of regularly lifting mothers up in prayer and seeking specific ways we can support these servants of God in their holy calling of motherhood.

THANKLESS FAITHFULNESS?

For it seems to me that God has put us apostles on display at the end
of the procession, like those condemned to die in the arena.
We have been made a spectacle to the whole universe,
to angels as well as to human beings.
1 CORINTHIANS 4:9 NIV

What is the sign of God's blessing on a Christian leader? What do we look for in the experts we trust for advice on spiritual living or Bible study? As Paul sought to correct the perceptions of the Corinthian church, he called on graphic images of prisoners being led to die in the arena at the hands of gladiators or wild animals. Paul argues that the apostles who founded the Church were not talented speakers or respectable individuals that you'd put on display. Rather, the people doing the essential work of the ministry were the ones you'd toss into the arena for sport and entertainment.

In a single sentence, Paul removes the glamour and notoriety from the work of ministry. However, there is an encouraging aspect to his message. We need not be wise teachers, experienced orators, flashy miracle workers, or skilled writers in order to share the Gospel message. In fact, Paul was criticized for being a boring speaker! Rather than trying to impress the Corinthians with his skill, Paul said that God uses plain, simple people who commit to doing the hard work of ministry day in and day out. They aren't recognized and they don't stand out. While anyone can do the essential work of ministry, there are few, if any, earthly accolades for faithfulness and effectiveness.

THE ONLY WAY TO DEFEAT SIN

So I say, let the Holy Spirit guide your lives.
Then you won't be doing what your sinful nature craves.
GALATIANS 5:16 NLT

Discipline, intentional action, and accountability are all good things that can help us overcome our sinful desires and shortcomings. We won't live as faithful disciples by accident. However, Paul shares the heart of the Gospel with us—the driving force in our lives that both unites us with God and empowers us to live in holiness. The only way we'll definitively and consistently overcome sin is to yield ourselves to the Holy Spirit. With the Holy Spirit as our guide, we'll begin to recognize the power of our own desires and, most importantly, our powerlessness in overcoming them.

The "self" will not fade away if we deny it. Our cravings are too powerful. Our senses of self-preservation and enjoyment are too appealing. We can only educate ourselves so much in the consequences of sin. At a certain point, we need a more powerful guide to show us the way forward and to redirect our desires toward the presence and power of God. Ironically, the only way to overcome sin is to stop fighting it. We won't be shaped into God's people by what we deny, but rather by whom we yield to and who guides us. By yielding our wills to God, we will find new cravings for the presence of God and will discover along the way that we have been shaped into renewed people.

HOW TO CAPTURE GOD'S ATTENTION

*But the eyes of the LORD are on those who fear him, on those whose hope
is in his unfailing love, to deliver them from death
and keep them alive in famine.*
PSALM 33:18–19 NIV

God's attention and provision don't hinge on how well we pray or how much we sacrifice. It's all too easy to turn God into a holy slot machine that demands certain practices in order to meet our needs. We run the risk of domesticating God, demanding that God meet our needs and serve our purposes. Who hasn't veered too far toward prayers heavily laden with requests and desires without honoring God's unique, all-powerful qualities?

Those who can expect provision set God apart as holy and powerful, worthy of our reverence and respect. We don't pray for God's presence and power in order to manipulate Him for our purposes. Rather, we yield to God's majestic power because we recognize our place under this awesome God, who is rightly feared.

Following quickly on this statement about the reverent fear of God, the psalmist reminds us that God's love is unfailing. We don't fear a monstrous, angry God, but we are reverent before a holy, all-powerful God who loves us deeply and will not fail us even if we have been unfaithful. As we rest in God's love for us and set Him apart as fearsome in His power, we will find the hope of His provision. Those who hope in God will find a constant, unmoving love that is deeply committed to them.

HOW TO SABOTAGE THE GOSPEL

Do everything without complaining and arguing,
so that no one can criticize you.
PHILIPPIANS 2:14–15 NLT

There is one certain way to undermine your ability to communicate the Gospel to others: engage in arguments. As we fight to be recognized, to win arguments, to justify our actions, and to make excuses for ourselves, we engage in a practice that is wholly centered upon ourselves and, even worse, has a tendency to cast blame on others. As we fight to justify ourselves, we turn others into our opponents, either blaming them for our problems or eliminating common ground with them as we argue over disagreements.

While communicating the Gospel has the potential to create peace and common ground with others, complaining and arguing will give our listeners cause to criticize us. Even if we're completely convinced that we deserve to complain or have every right to win an argument, we are reminded by Paul that there are unintended consequences that will further separate us from either our fellow Christians or those we are hoping to reach with the Gospel. As we stop fighting for our rights or to be "right," we remove a major obstacle with others and keep as many doors open as possible for the Gospel to take root and flourish in our relationships.

PEACE IS OURS TODAY

For God in all his fullness was pleased to live in Christ, and through him God reconciled everything to himself. He made peace with everything in heaven and on earth by means of Christ's blood on the cross.

COLOSSIANS 1:19–20 NLT

How would you describe your mental state right now? Are you content or discouraged? Do you feel close to God or distant from God? There are many times when I try to answer those questions and struggle with feelings of guilt and inadequacy. I wonder if I'll ever be "good enough," and I worry about where to turn next. I desperately need to read today's passage: God has already reconciled everything to Himself. The path to peace has been made wide open.

God is not distant from us. Jesus has already come to dwell among us and through the cross demonstrated once and for all that God is fully committed to making peace with us. Any barriers between ourselves and God have been finished at the cross. There is nothing we can do to improve on or supplement the cross. There is no way to make ourselves more worthy of the cross. Peace is already here. Reconciliation has been accomplished.

We also have a message with good news to share with others. God has made peace with the rebellious people of the earth. The barriers that divide us from others have been demolished with the cross. The cross is for everyone on earth. We'll only be able to share that message if we first believe that God has made peace with us.

GOD IS COMPASSIONATE TO ALL

The LORD is gracious and compassionate, slow to anger and rich in love.
The LORD is good to all; he has compassion on all he has made.
PSALM 145:8–9 NIV

I know all too well what it feels like to lose my temper and to let my anger linger. There's a good chance that you also know what it feels like to be on the receiving end of an angry outburst. Perhaps anger has gotten in the way of an important relationship or caused you to doubt someone's love for you. Today's psalm teaches us that God is most certainly capable of anger, but that anger is always slow in coming. Even when we experience God's anger, He won't dwell on it because He is so eager to love and forgive us.

This graciousness and compassion begins simply because we are God's beloved creation. God has compassion on all He has made, and the last thing He wants is to be divided from us. Although we may reject Him or go our own way for a season, He is eager to forgive and to restore us. He doesn't want us to dwell on shame or live in fear. There may be no greater tragedy than the people of God believing they could exhaust God's mercy or stray too far from His compassion. Today's psalm reveals a God who is overflowing in mercy, longing to lavish it on anyone who will turn away from their own way.

THE LIFE-CHANGING PRACTICE OF HOSPITALITY

Dear friend, you are faithful in what you are doing for the brothers
and sisters, even though they are strangers to you.
They have told the church about your love.
3 JOHN 1:5–6 NIV

Opening our homes to a missionary, minister, or fellow Christian is a simple but important way to demonstrate the love of God. John notes in his letter that Gaius, the elder he addresses in today's passage, has recognized these unknown ministers as brothers and sisters rather than treating them as strangers. It's likely that Gaius went to great lengths to host these traveling preachers in his home at a time when most people lacked significant resources. When we talk about the cost of discipleship, the ministry of hospitality may be one of the most demanding.

Inviting fellow Christians into our homes, whether for a small group meeting, a family dinner, or lodging for several days, prompts us to change our schedules, to share our resources, and to literally make space for others. More importantly, if we truly believe that we are "brothers and sisters" with fellow Christians, the proof will be in how generously we share our most sacred spaces in our homes with them. Will we invite others into our living rooms and kitchens for rest and refreshment?

Hospitality is a sacrifice, but it is a vital way to encourage and support our fellow believers. Along the way, we'll enjoy deeper relationships with our Christian family and even benefit from the blessings and prayers of those who share our homes.

FAITHFUL TO AN IMPOSSIBLE MISSION

"The people to whom I am sending you are obstinate and stubborn.
Say to them, 'This is what the Sovereign LORD says.'
And whether they listen or fail to listen—for they are a rebellious
people—they will know that a prophet has been among them."
 EZEKIEL 2:4–5 NIV

If you serve in a particular ministry or you prayerfully reach out to neighbors or colleagues, there's a trap that is all too easy to fall into when it comes time to measure your success. The Lord warns Ezekiel of this trap: measuring his success based on the responses of others. Ezekiel's calling is only to share the message that God entrusted to him. Whether or not the obstinate and stubborn people respond is well beyond his control.

Ezekiel is responsible only so far as he ensures that he has heard correctly what God has said and then communicated it. He plays the role of a prophet. If people won't listen, he may rightfully wonder if he has shared the correct message. However, in this case he has already received the bracing message from the Lord that his mission is doomed to fail.

Perhaps you aren't facing the same demanding challenges as Ezekiel today in your ministry or relationships. However, much like Ezekiel, you cannot control the thoughts, words, and actions of others. You can only prayerfully consider how God is directing you to live and speak. Sometimes your own faithfulness is the only measure of "success" that you'll have.

KNOW IT ALL NO LONGER

"This is what the LORD says, he who made the earth, the LORD who formed it and established it—the LORD is his name: 'Call to me and I will answer you and tell you great and unsearchable things you do not know.'"
JEREMIAH 33:2–3 NIV

If you aren't in a season of uncertainty, you'll soon experience one. It may reveal itself gradually or come rushing in unexpectedly. When life begins to spin out of control or you find yourself at a bend in a road that remains very uncertain, it's natural to worry about or even obsess over the future. We become attached to certain outcomes and even begin asking God for a particular future. Who hasn't struggled with doubt or at least some hard questions for God when the exact opposite thing happens!

At a time when the prophet Jeremiah confronted uncertainty and the terror of a foreign army invading, the Lord assured him that he could call out and the Lord would answer him. Of course, the Lord didn't guarantee that Jeremiah would like the answer he received. Rather, Jeremiah is assured of deeper mysteries rather than clear-cut answers and resolutions. Perhaps the answers to our prayers defy our comprehension and could take years or even a lifetime to fully unfold. Even the times when we think we understand God's ways, we'll find that there were mysteries or layers beneath our prayers that simply escaped our attention. Whether or not we want to confront these mysteries from God, the most important thing that this verse promises is the presence of God in uncertain times.

PEACE BEYOND CIRCUMSTANCES

*"But the Advocate, the Holy Spirit, whom the Father will send in my
name, will teach you all things and will remind you of everything
I have said to you. Peace I leave with you; my peace I give you.
I do not give to you as the world gives. Do not let your
hearts be troubled and do not be afraid."*

JOHN 14:26–27 NIV

Mere hours before His arrest and crucifixion, Jesus promised to send His Holy Spirit to comfort and instruct His followers. Even with the relief of Jesus' resurrection in a few days, they would have great need of the Spirit's peace and direction once Jesus ascended into heaven. Perhaps we may think they'd have all the more reason to be alarmed once Jesus ascended to heaven! However, Jesus assures us and them that it's the exact opposite: Because Jesus has sent the Spirit, they should not let fear take root in their hearts.

Jesus passes along the assurance that we can seek the direction, wisdom, and peace of the Holy Spirit. We will surely face situations where fear appears to be more than warranted. In Jesus, we can choose to turn to the Holy Spirit. This is not a guarantee that our problems will be resolved or that we'll suddenly have incredible wisdom to make the best choices. Rather, the Spirit will reassure us that we are not alone and that whatever may happen today or tomorrow, God remains with us. The Spirit guards our souls and keeps us close to Jesus, even when every other measure of peace appears to be far away.

PRAYER THAT'S WORTH THE WAIT

When your words came, I ate them; they were my joy and my heart's delight, for I bear your name, LORD God Almighty.
JEREMIAH 15:16 NIV

The act of eating is often associated with the delight of learning, meditating on, or living out the words of God. In the case of Jeremiah, he actively sought the direction of God and relied on God to speak for his prophetic ministry to Israel. Waiting on God to speak brought him joy and delight, leaving him full and content, as if he had just eaten a full meal.

Just as it can be hard to wait for a meal, it's also quite challenging to wait on God with our prayers. We may imagine someone who has waited for hours on end for an exquisite meal at a restaurant. When the steaming food arrives, it is beyond his wildest expectations, and he carefully savors each bite. Moreover, God's Word to us is abundant and life-giving for others as well. As we are nourished by God's Word, we can share what we have received with others so that they can take part in the joy and delight of God.

Waiting on God patiently takes faith and trust that God will eventually bring us the "meal" that we long for so badly. There is no other book, meal, or story that can restore us quite like the presence of God. Are we eagerly awaiting each day, leaving room on our "plates" for God to feed us? May we never settle for any lesser fare for our souls than the words of God for us.

REVEALING GOD'S HEART FOR PRODIGALS

"Say to them, 'As surely as I live, declares the Sovereign LORD, I take no pleasure in the death of the wicked, but rather that they turn from their ways and live. Turn! Turn from your evil ways! Why will you die, people of Israel?'"

EZEKIEL 33:11 NIV

While there's no mistaking the consequences that await those who turn away from God, perhaps our shame and guilt hide the true desires of God from us. If you imagine an angry God eager to judge or to catch you in your sins, let this passage change your mind. Ezekiel shows us a God who pleads with His people and begs them to change their ways. Rather than threatening His people, the Lord shows His people that there are two paths set before them and He passionately calls on them to choose the life of God found in obedience.

Each day we face choices and opportunities to move toward God or to shut ourselves off from God. If you've failed or closed yourself off from the Lord today or for as long as you can remember, the same desperate message applies to you: Turn from your evil ways! Seeing His beloved people undone by sin devastates the heart of God. The unraveling of our lives under the sway of sin is the absolute last thing He wants. God stands ready to forgive, to welcome us, and to lead us back to life. His plea for us today is simple and heartfelt: Turn back.

THE JOY OF SUFFERING

*Dear friends, do not be surprised at the fiery ordeal that has come
on you to test you, as though something strange were happening to you.
But rejoice inasmuch as you participate in the sufferings of
Christ, so that you may be overjoyed when his glory is revealed.*
1 PETER 4:12–13 NIV

Suffering and opposition for the sake of Christ isn't just a sign that we have
cast our lot with Jesus. Suffering is a way to meet with Christ on a deeper
level. As we face opposition, slander, or worse, we create a space in our
lives to more fully experience Christ. By choosing to suffer for Christ, we
are denying our own desires and our sinful natures—the very things that
come between ourselves and Him. In fact, suffering is guaranteed for us as
we take up the cause of Christ. If you are suffering for a season, God can
and will meet you and even use that suffering to bring more of His presence
and peace into your life.

Most importantly, by choosing to suffer, we are taking a step of faith to
believe that God has something better for us. We have the hope of His glory
one day as we leave our own wills behind. While our desires promise us joy
and fulfillment in the short term, these are fleeting and cannot compare
to the joy we can experience today in the presence of the Lord, let alone
when we are united with Him one day.

THE SLOW CREEP OF COMPROMISE

King Solomon, however, loved many foreign women besides Pharaoh's daughter—Moabites, Ammonites, Edomites, Sidonians and Hittites. They were from nations about which the LORD had told the Israelites, "You must not intermarry with them, because they will surely turn your hearts after their gods." Nevertheless, Solomon held fast to them in love.
1 KINGS 11:1–2 NIV

After King Solomon's wealth and wisdom are presented in striking detail, the author of 1 Kings offers a sobering note that all is not well in the king's heart: He had married many foreign women who turned him away from the Lord. It's likely that Solomon didn't think a few foreign wives could be that much of a threat to his devotion to God. After all, he lived in the epicenter of worship for Yahweh. What harm could a few foreign alliances through marriage do to his heart?

Sure enough, his heart gradually drifted further from God, and he became more tolerant of foreign gods. As he added new wives and allegiances with neighboring kingdoms, Solomon lost sight of Yahweh as he filled his time joining his wives in their idol worship. Even the wisest king was no match for the slow creep of compromise in his devotion to the true God.

As you examine your heart today, ask whether there are places or issues where you're compromising—even if it's just a little. Sin's most powerful trick is convincing us that it's not a big deal and that we can handle ourselves. It's a slow drift away from God, and we'll spare ourselves and our families pain if we recognize it sooner than later.

HONORING DISCIPLINE AND COMMITMENT

Join with me in suffering, like a good soldier of Christ Jesus.
No one serving as a soldier gets entangled in civilian affairs,
but rather tries to please his commanding officer.
2 TIMOTHY 2:3–4 NIV

As we honor those who made the ultimate sacrifice for our country, we would do well to remember that Paul looked to soldiers as an ideal of single-minded commitment and devotion to a cause. According to Paul, the model soldier prioritizes the opinion of a commanding officer and avoids the distractions of civilians. A good soldier exists for the single purpose of carrying out the orders of a commanding officer in order to win a battle. Soldiers won't leave their ranks to argue with civilians or even to address their own affairs. Their primary concern is their mission.

While Paul honors the focus and discipline of soldiers, he certainly calls Timothy to a very different kind of combat where the "soldiers of Jesus Christ" endure suffering and slander without striking back. The "soldiers" of Christ win by losing, patiently enduring suffering, and responding to our competitive culture with humility and meekness. There are many "civilian affairs" that can pull us away from the purpose of God, from entertainment to accumulating wealth to engaging in arguments that have nothing to do with sharing the good news of the Gospel. Our Commanding Officer has blessed us in order to bless others, and we'll carry out that mission most effectively when we learn from the disciplined focus of soldiers who carry out their orders under even the most demanding circumstances.

STARVING FOR GOD

*He humbled you, causing you to hunger and then feeding you
with manna, which neither you nor your ancestors had known,
to teach you that man does not live on bread alone but on
every word that comes from the mouth of the LORD.*

DEUTERONOMY 8:3 NIV

As the people of Israel journeyed through the barren wilderness strewn with rocks and sand, we can hardly blame them for worrying about what they would eat, drink, or wear while confined to such a bleak location. Gathering enough food for an entire nation in a land without set-aside fields for agriculture, irrigation, or pasture became a daily struggle for existence. How would such a large people survive forty hours, let alone forty years, in such a hostile wilderness?

While the Israelites surely considered the wilderness the last place they wanted to be, the Lord wasted no time using it for a good purpose. The wilderness was the place to learn complete dependence on God. It's almost counterintuitive for us to read this. Why in the world would God remove their reliable food supply in order to demonstrate that they needed more than bread in order to survive?

In part, the Lord used a difficult situation to teach His people complete and total dependence. They couldn't do anything clever or innovative enough to provide for themselves. Their only way out was prayer, and their only resource was God's timely help. Did God hear their prayers? Would God provide? It took a difficult journey through the wilderness to find out.

ONLY THE UNQUALIFIED NEED APPLY

*But the LORD said to Samuel, "Do not consider his appearance
or his height, for I have rejected him. The LORD does not look
at the things people look at. People look at the outward
appearance, but the LORD looks at the heart."*

1 SAMUEL 16:7 NIV

What does a king look like? If you had asked that question in the days of Saul and David, you would have heard a lot about personal appearance: height, muscular build, and even tone of voice. Of course, people longed for kings who could lead competently, but the prophet Samuel made the common mistake of confusing a kingly bearing with kingly competence. Don't we all make the same mistake of assuming that the person who looks the part is the best qualified for ministry or leadership?

The Lord turns such thinking over, declaring that He looks on the heart. The heart trumps any other measure of competence or qualification. Perhaps this means that we should change the criteria we have for our leaders, but don't overlook the possibility that this passage applies to you as well. If you sense a potential call to serve in a place or capacity that feels beyond your skill set or abilities, there's a chance that God is still calling you forward in faith. The heart that is oriented toward God can accomplish far more than accumulated wisdom and experience. If you feel woefully unqualified for God's call, you're in very good company. In fact, God takes particular delight in using the supposedly "unqualified" to bless others.

QUIET CONFIDENCE

Let someone else praise you, and not your own mouth;
an outsider, and not your own lips.
PROVERBS 27:2 NIV

National Basketball Association superstar LeBron James raised more than a few eyebrows during the 2015 NBA Finals when, after a Game 5 loss to the Golden State Warriors, he said this: "I feel confident because I'm the best player in the world. It's simple."

Most observers would agree that LeBron is the best basketball player on the planet, but many found his assertion of his own greatness a little off-putting, even arrogant. Most sports fans, after all, like a little humility in their athletes. We like these supremely talented people to "let their game do the talking."

Truth be told, most of us men like talking about ourselves. We like telling others about the things we've accomplished at work, about how great our wife and kids are, about how much we know, and about those special abilities we possess.

But God's Word warns us against not just *thinking* too highly of ourselves, but of *speaking* too highly—even when what we say is factually true. Instead, as King Solomon tells us in today's scripture, we should strive to remain humble and let others do the talking.

Confidence in one's own abilities isn't necessarily a bad thing, but we should never fall into the trap of thinking we need to give voice to our own praises. Instead, we should keep our mouths closed and let our "game" do the talking.

KEEP YOUR WORD!

Above all, my brothers and sisters, do not swear—not by heaven or by earth or by anything else. All you need to say is a simple "Yes" or "No." Otherwise you will be condemned.
JAMES 5:12 NIV

Have you ever known someone you knew you could depend on? The kind of guy who always showed up for coffee when he said he would? The kind whom you knew would keep his word when he told you he would help you with those not-too-enjoyable tasks, such as moving or painting your house?

That's the kind of friend we'd all like to have, isn't it? But, going a step further, it's the kind of friend we should strive to be.

Some Christians take the words of today's Bible verse quite literally, avoiding making any kinds of promises, taking any kinds of oaths, or entering into contracts with others. But even for someone who doesn't follow this verse by the letter (there are situations in today's world where it's impossible not to take oaths or enter into contractual agreements), there's something about James's words that strongly implies a simple but important principle: *Be a man who can be taken at his word.*

In other words, be the kind of man who is so dependable, so true to his word, that no one ever has to ask, "Do you promise?" Be the man whose "yes" can always be taken as "yes" and whose "no" can always be taken as "no."

WATCH YOUR LANGUAGE!

*But now you must also rid yourselves of all such things as these:
anger, rage, malice, slander, and filthy language from your lips.*
Colossians 3:8 niv

At a men's Bible study, a middle-aged man who had come to Jesus after decades of hard living—drinking, fighting, carousing, and cussing—shared with his brothers in Christ what God had been doing in his life.

"God has taken away the drinking, the chasing women, and the fighting," he said. "I don't want any part of those things anymore."

"Amen!"

"Praise God!"

After the impromptu moment of praise and worship had finished, the man went on: "It seems like there's one area where I just haven't changed, and that's in the way I talk sometimes. Sometimes when I get angry or frustrated, I still have a tendency to let fly with the cussing now and again, even though I know it doesn't please Him."

This sounds like he's headed in the right direction, doesn't it? Whether because of his past or perhaps a wife who constantly "reminded" him about his frequent use of profanities, he knew God isn't pleased when His people cuss and swear like longshoremen.

The apostle James wrote that "no human being can tame the tongue" (James 3:8 niv), and many of us have found that to be especially true when it comes to foul language. While it's an oversimplification to say "just stop it," we can have victory in the way we talk when we commit our speech to God and ask Him, through His Holy Spirit, to help us to speak only words that glorify and please Him.

SPEAKING JOYFULLY

He put a new song in my mouth, a hymn of praise to our God.
Many will see and fear the LORD and put their trust in him.

PSALM 40:3 NIV

Those who follow Jesus Christ have more reason than anyone to think thoughts and speak words that reflect the joy God's Word says we are to have. Jesus has promised us abundant life here on earth, as well as an eternity in paradise.

What's not to love about that?

Sadly, too many Christians play the part of Gloomy Gus (for the brothers in the faith) or Debbie Downer (for the sisters) as though they were born for it.

Have you ever known a professing believer who always seems to be complaining and grumbling about what's been going on in his life, a believer who, on the outside anyway, seems completely devoid of the joy of the Lord?

That person isn't a lot of fun to be around, is he? Which brings us to another question: Are *you* that kind of Christian?

The Bible is filled with examples of men whose life situations weren't exactly reasons in and of themselves for happy or joyful attitudes. But instead of spending their time moaning and groaning, they focused on what God was doing in and through them. The result? The joy of Lord so filled them that everyone they spoke to or wrote to could see it.

Never let it escape you that even when life throws difficulty and suffering your way, you can have the joy of the Lord so fill you that you can't help but let it affect the way you speak.

HE KNOWS WHAT WE'RE THINKING

Finally, brothers and sisters, whatever is true, whatever is noble, whatever is right, whatever is pure, whatever is lovely, whatever is admirable—if anything is excellent or praiseworthy—think about such things.

PHILIPPIANS 4:8 NIV

We've all known those married couples who know each other so well that they seem to know what the other is thinking. In truth, however, no one—not even the ones with whom we share our most intimate relationships—can possibly know everything we think.

And we should be grateful for that.

However, there is One who knows our every thought—our Father in heaven. King David knew this, which is why he wrote, "You have searched me, LORD, and you know me. . .you perceive my thoughts from afar" (Psalm 139:1–2 NIV).

God knows our thoughts—all of them. He knows the things that cross our minds that we'd never share with anyone, even our closest friends.

That's the proverbial two-edged sword, isn't it? On one hand, we're like David, who seemed to welcome his heavenly Father's loving intrusion into his thoughts when he prayed, "Search me, God, and know my heart; test me and know my anxious thoughts" (Psalm 139:23 NIV). On the other hand, we may think, *Oh no! I don't want Him to know I'm thinking about* that.

This is one of those situations when it's good to speak honestly to our heavenly Father. Since He knows our thoughts anyway, we can bring them all to Him and, like David, pray, "Search my heart and my thoughts, and help me to think on the things You want me to be thinking on."

A "HIDDEN" SIN

*"You have heard that it was said, 'You shall not commit adultery.'
But I tell you that anyone who looks at a woman lustfully
has already committed adultery with her in his heart."*
MATTHEW 5:27–28 NIV

When we read God's seventh commandment—"'You shall not commit adultery'" (Exodus 20:14 NIV)—it's easy to take comfort in knowing that we've never engaged in "the act" of sex with another man's wife.

But in today's verse, Jesus offered some tough teaching on the subject of adultery, namely that it isn't just about where we take our bodies, but (even more importantly) about the impure places our thoughts can so easily go.

Ouch!

So how do we keep those lust-inducing images from entering through our eyes and into our minds? Job, a godly man who lived thousands of years before Jesus came to earth, offers some practical advice.

Job was committed to keeping his mind from immoral, adulterous thoughts: "'I made a covenant with my eyes not to look lustfully at a young woman'" (Job 31:1 NIV).

Job was on to something, wasn't he? What we allow to enter our brains through our eyes tends to stay there—as hard as we try to make it just go away. The key, he concluded, was to be very, very careful about what we look at.

That's no easy task, especially in today's world, where seemingly every other image that comes across our field of view can be problematic. But more than anything, it's a matter of commitment. . .to your spouse, to your children, and to your Father in heaven.

PEACE AND STRENGTH THROUGH GOD'S WORD

Great peace have those who love your law,
and nothing can make them stumble.
PSALM 119:165 NIV

The writer of the epistle to the Hebrews once wrote of scripture, "For the word of God is alive and active. Sharper than any double-edged sword, it penetrates even to dividing soul and spirit, joints and marrow; it judges the thoughts and attitudes of the heart" (Hebrews 4:12 NIV).

That's a great summary of the role the Bible plays in the life of the believer. However, it doesn't mention one great benefit of spending time reading and studying the Word: It brings us peace and strength for our walk.

The writer of Psalm 119 points out that the words in the Bible (he refers to it as God's "law") have an amazing ability not just to bring us that inner peace God wants us to live in, but also to keep us from stumbling and falling into sin.

Have you been lacking peace lately? Does it seem like your life in Christ lacks power? Do you find that you're not walking with Jesus as much as you are stumbling through life? It may be a matter of putting a daily time of reading and studying the Bible higher—maybe *much* higher—on your list of priorities.

Life in the twenty-first century is busy. Once we're finished with our daily work, our family, home projects, and friends all vie for our time. But if we want the peace and strength we need to live the life God calls us to live, we can't afford to miss out on time spent with Him and His Word.

OUR SHEPHERD GOD

"As a shepherd looks after his scattered flock when he is with them, so will I look after my sheep. I will rescue them from all the places where they were scattered on a day of clouds and darkness."

EZEKIEL 34:12 NIV

In the classic hymn "Come Thou Fount," Robert Robinson, the nineteenth-century hymnist, makes this very personal confession:

Prone to wander, Lord, I feel it,
Prone to leave the God I love.

In these lyrics, Robinson, who was just twenty-two when he penned this hymn, demonstrated a keen understanding of human nature and how it is so often in conflict with the kind of relationship God desires to have with us as His most prized creation. At the time when Ezekiel recorded God's words in today's verse, people would have understood a few things about sheep that most people wouldn't today.

First of all, they would understand that domesticated sheep, not being the brightest of animals, tended to wander from their flock and from the safety of the watchful eye of the shepherd. Second, they would understand that sheep have notoriously poor eyesight and absolutely no way to defend themselves against predators looking for a quick, easy meal.

Though our human pride may tell us otherwise, God knows that we, like sheep, are prone to wandering away from the safety and security He has promised to provide us. He also knows that when we wander, we're defenseless against the temptations the world around us is sure to send our way.

There truly is no better place to be—and to stay—than under the watchful eye of our loving Shepherd Father.

RADICAL LOVE

Husbands, love your wives,
just as Christ loved the church and gave himself up for her.
EPHESIANS 5:25 NIV

Sometimes when we're trying to fully understand what God is communicating through His written Word, it's helpful to look at the context in which it was first written.

The culture at the time when the apostle Paul wrote these words was radically different from ours today. In those days, men ran everything and had total legal and social authority over their wives and children, and women had no choice but to live—submissively and probably without asking a lot of questions—under their husbands' rule.

When Paul enjoined husbands to love their wives "as Christ loved the church," he was suggesting something greatly different from the norms of the day. This was a love that served in the most sacrificial kind of way, a love that looked out for the needs and desires of someone who likely wasn't used to being treated that way by a man.

Though things have changed greatly since the days of the apostle Paul, his instructions to husbands are in many ways still a radical departure for many married men. God calls us men today to love our wives and children—and others in our circle of influence—the same way Jesus loved His people. That's a radical, self-sacrificing kind of love, a kind of love that leads first with a heart toward serving without first being served.

SEEING GOD IN HIS CREATION

"But ask the animals, and they will teach you, or the birds in the sky, and they will tell you; or speak to the earth, and it will teach you, or let the fish in the sea inform you."
JOB 12:7–8 NIV

The famous seventeenth-century English writer Izaak Walton, author of the famous fishing tome titled *The Compleat Angler: or, The Contemplative Man's Recreation*, once wrote, "Rivers and the inhabitants of the watery elements are made for wise men to contemplate and for fools to pass by without consideration."

Taking the time to get away and enjoy the outdoors is a pleasurable endeavor for just about anyone. But for a man of God, these activities offer something more, something of a truly "spiritual" nature.

One of the great things about fishing, hunting, hiking, camping, or any other activity that takes place in the context of the outdoors is just being in the places where we can enjoy those things. These are the settings where we see God's handiwork clear of man-made distractions.

No, the creation is not God Himself, but you can learn some great truths about His nature and character by looking at the wonder of what He has created.

So the next time you head out to enjoy a day—or a weekend, or a week—outdoors, don't forget to take your heavenly Father with you. It's in those settings where you can just enjoy His company, maybe even hear His voice, away from the world's noise.

THE RIGHT THING TO BRAG ON

This is what the LORD says: "Let not the wise boast of their wisdom or the strong boast of their strength or the rich boast of their riches, but let the one who boasts boast about this: that they have the understanding to know me."
JEREMIAH 9:23–24 NIV

If you've ever been around someone who spends a lot of time—not to mention his own breath—bragging about his own accomplishments, possessions, or talents, then you probably have a small clue as to why God isn't pleased with human pride and arrogance.

When we boast about our own accomplishments, about our talents and gifts, in essence we communicate a mind-set and heart attitude that what we have and what we can do are a result of our own efforts and not a result of God's blessings.

Indeed, God doesn't want His people carrying around an attitude of braggadocio. He doesn't want us expending our energy letting others know about the great things we've accomplished or about our gifts and skills.

Instead, our God wants us to make sure our words—especially those we speak in relation to our gifts, blessings, and accomplishments—point to Him as our loving Benefactor. And, as today's verse instructs us, that should begin with the fact that we know Him as our loving heavenly Father.

THE SOURCE OF OUR TEMPTATION

When tempted, no one should say, "God is tempting me."
For God cannot be tempted by evil, nor does he tempt anyone;
but each person is tempted when they are dragged away
by their own evil desire and enticed.
JAMES 1:13–14 NIV

Remember comedian Flip Wilson's famous phrase, "The devil made me do it!"? While it was part of a funny routine, it was hardly sound theology. In truth, the devil can't *make* people do anything; he can only tempt us.

The Bible teaches that temptation comes from basically three sources: from the devil (remember, Adam and Eve sinned when they gave in to the devil's temptation; also, the devil tempted Jesus Himself, though He did not sin); from the world; and from our own evil, fallen hearts (see today's verse).

Many young believers come into the faith believing that they will no longer be tempted to sin in ways they used to before they were saved. Some quickly become discouraged or disillusioned when they find that the temptation to sin doesn't just "go away."

Temptation will always be a part of our lives here on earth. It was in the beginning for humanity, and it still is today. But God can't and won't tempt us to sin. On the other hand, the Bible promises us that "God is faithful; he will not let you be tempted beyond what you can bear. But when you are tempted, he will also provide a way out so that you can endure it" (1 Corinthians 10:13 NIV).

SERVING GOD BY SERVING OTHERS

*"The King will reply, 'Truly I tell you, whatever you did for one
of the least of these brothers and sisters of mine, you did for me.'"*
MATTHEW 25:40 NIV

Today's verse—as well as some other passages like James 2:14-26—seem to
imply that serving others is a requirement for salvation. That's a real head-
scratcher for some Christians, who know that the Bible is clear that salvation
is based on faith in Christ alone and not on our good works.

When we step back and take a broader look at the entire biblical
message of salvation, however, we see that Jesus'—as well as James's—words
do not contradict or even confuse the message of salvation by faith in Christ
alone. Instead, those who by faith have received salvation and therefore
have God's Spirit living within them will be motivated to serve out of true
love for God and others.

Doing good things for others doesn't make you a Christian, and it won't
"earn" you God's eternal salvation. On the other hand, as a follower of Jesus
Christ, you'll find yourself motivated to serve others, knowing that when
you serve the "least of these," you're serving God Himself.

Do you believe God wants you to have a bigger heart for service? Have
you been wondering what kind of service He has in mind for you? Ask Him
to first give you the right motivation to serve, and then ask Him to show
you ways you can serve others.

The opportunities are all around you, and you'll find them if you just
ask and then keep your eyes open.

A SYMBOL OF FREEDOM

But for those who fear you,
you have raised a banner to be unfurled against the bow.
PSALM 60:4 NIV

On June 14, 1777, in the early years of the American War of Independence, the Continental Congress passed an act calling for the establishment of an official flag for the new nation. Originally, the flag had thirteen alternating red and white stripes and thirteen white stars set in a blue field.

The flag went through many changes in the coming decades, and today it still bears the thirteen stripes, but now it bears fifty stars, one for each state in the union. On May 30, 1916, President Woodrow Wilson signed a proclamation recognizing Flag Day on May 30, 1916. Finally, on August 3, 1949, President Harry Truman signed a bill officially designating June 14 as National Flag Day.

Some Christians have a difficult time with the idea of pledging allegiance to or saluting the American flag—or to any other physical symbol. To them, giving that kind of recognition to the flag is a form of idolatry. But when you look at the words of the Pledge of Allegiance, you see there is nothing in it that challenges our allegiance to God first.

Today, as you consider the meaning behind the American flag, it would be good to take time to thank God for the blessings of living in a country where you can speak about Him and worship Him in freedom.

FORGIVENESS OF OTHERS: GOD REQUIRES IT

*"And when you stand praying, if you hold anything against anyone,
forgive them, so that your Father in heaven may forgive you your sins."*
MARK 11:25 NIV

If you've ever been around someone who harbors anger and bitterness
toward another (for example, a man who hangs on to a wrong his wife
committed against him years earlier), you know how uncomfortable it can
be. You want to get as far away as possible, as quickly as possible.

Anger and unforgiveness are like love and faith in that they always
find outward expressions. You just can't be an angry, bitter person without
those around you seeing it in you—or hearing it from you.

God, it turns out, takes our forgiveness of others very seriously, so
seriously that Jesus instructed His followers to forgive one another from
their hearts. Otherwise, He said, God would not hear their prayers.

Have you ever been in a place with your relationship with God where
your prayers seem stale, where it seems like they aren't reaching God's ears?
There could be a lot of reasons for that—hidden sin, a particular spiritual
struggle, and even those "dry times" we all sometimes experience.

But what about unforgiveness? When you're in that place where you
don't feel like God is hearing you, take the time to examine your personal
relationships with others and ask yourself whether it's possible you're
harboring unforgiveness toward someone.

Then forgive. . .from your heart.

GOD'S PURPOSE FOR LIFE'S TRIALS

*Consider it pure joy, my brothers and sisters, whenever you face trials
of many kinds, because you know that the testing of your faith produces
perseverance. Let perseverance finish its work so that you may
be mature and complete, not lacking anything.*

JAMES 1:2–4 NIV

Albert Einstein once made an amazingly insightful observation about dealing with life's difficulties when he said, "Adversity introduces a man to himself."

When life brings difficulties our way (and it most certainly will), we see where we're really at in our walk with our heavenly Father. The old analogy holds true: When you squeeze a sponge (you being the sponge) hard enough, you're sure to see what's inside.

God never promised His people an easy ride through life. In fact, the Bible is very clear—in many passages—that trials, storms, and suffering will be part of every believer's life. If you don't believe that, just take a look at the lives of the apostles, the men Jesus chose to take His message of salvation to the world around them. We're talking imprisonment, beatings, even martyrdom for nearly all of them.

God also doesn't just automatically make you a patient person when you get saved, and He doesn't instantly make you a person of great perseverance, either. Instead, He uses a process whereby the trials and storms in your life strengthen you and make you the patient, persevering man He intends for you to be.

So when the going gets tough. . .rejoice!

JESUS, OUR ADVOCATE

My dear children, I write this to you so that you will not sin.
But if anybody does sin, we have an advocate with the
Father—Jesus Christ, the Righteous One.
1 John 2:1 NIV

It might strike some of us as a bit odd that the apostle John would use the phrase "an advocate with the Father" to describe our Savior. In the context of today's verse, the word *advocate* implies someone who pleads our case before a legal court of justice. In other words, a lawyer.

In today's legal world, a lawyer pleads his client's case—whether or not he believes that client is innocent. Our Advocate before God in heaven is different from an earthly lawyer in that He pleads the case before the Father knowing that we're guilty as charged, that we've certainly committed the offense charged against us.

This goes far beyond today's legal standard of "guilty beyond a reasonable doubt."

Jesus knows of our guilt, and so does God the Father. But when Jesus pleads our case, He, in effect, says, "Father, I know this man is a sinner. But he has come to us and confessed and repented. He has been cleansed and forgiven."

But here's the best part of this arrangement: When Jesus pleads our case, it's not before a stern judge who begrudgingly offers absolution. On the contrary, Jesus pleads our case before a loving, holy God who promises us to "purify us from all unrighteousness" when we simply confess our sins (1 John 1:9 NIV).

A FATHER'S JOY

"The LORD your God is with you, the Mighty Warrior who saves.
He will take great delight in you; in his love he will no longer
rebuke you, but will rejoice over you with singing."
ZEPHANIAH 3:17 NIV

Midway through the third quarter of the November 23, 2014, game against the Jacksonville Jaguars, Indianapolis Colts wide receiver T.Y. Hilton celebrated his seventy-three-yard touchdown reception from quarterback Andrew Luck by cradling the game ball as if it were a newborn baby.

Hilton had already practiced his celebration earlier in the day, as just hours before the game, he and his wife, Shantrell, welcomed a new daughter into their family.

Following the game, Hilton's emotions overtook him in the post-game interview with CBS. Shedding tears of unbridled joy and barely able to speak, Hilton talked about the birth of his daughter and what it meant to him to score a touchdown in her honor.

These are emotions that only a new father can understand, emotions that show themselves with tears, laughter, smiles, and even songs of joy.

The Bible tells us that our heavenly Father feels that same kind of joy when He looks at His children. In fact, today's verse tells us that His joy in us is so consuming that He breaks out in singing.

That's the kind of love and adoration only our Father in heaven can fully understand. But someday—and oh, what a day that will be!—we'll get to see it up close and personal.

LOVE GIVES. . .IT HAS TO

"Do not be afraid, little flock,
for your Father has been pleased to give you the kingdom."
LUKE 12:32 NIV

There's something about becoming a father that makes most men great givers. From the time a man first learns that he and his wife are going to be parents, he wants more than anything to give whatever he has to make sure his child has everything he or she needs—physically, emotionally, and spiritually—to grow and thrive.

In this way, earthly fathers become reflections—imperfect reflections, but reflections nonetheless—of our Father in heaven. The apostle John wrote that "God is love" (1 John 4:8 NIV), and Jesus Himself said that God loved sinful and fallen humankind so much that He gave His most precious gift: His one and only Son (John 3:16).

That's just the nature of love, isn't it? Love, by its very nature, has no choice but to give. Real love can't just be hidden away in the heart; it must find expression through gifts to its object. And the God who identifies Himself as the perfect embodiment of love doesn't just give. . .He gives *joyfully* and He gives *perfectly*.

This perfect, giving love is what the apostle James was pointing to when he wrote, "Every good and perfect gift is from above, coming down from the Father of the heavenly lights, who does not change like shifting shadows" (James 1:17 NIV).

Our God is perfect—perfect in His holiness and perfect in His giving love. He always has been, and He always will be.

SPEAKING OF OTHERS. . .

A gossip betrays a confidence, but a trustworthy person keeps a secret.
PROVERBS 11:13 NIV

Let's get real with ourselves for a moment. Most of us have a pretty good handle on avoiding the "biggies" where sin is concerned. We don't commit murder or adultery, and we'd never think of taking something that doesn't belong to us.

But many of us—dare we say *most* of us?—aren't always as careful as we need to be when it comes to how we talk about other people. Without giving it much thought, we make less-than-edifying comments about members of our families, people we work with, our spiritual leaders. . . The list goes on and on.

The Bible has plenty to say about someone who somehow finds it necessary to speak ill of other people, and none of it is good. Take a look at these descriptive biblical (King James Version) words for someone who engages in gossip: *backbiter* (Psalm 15:3), *busybody* (1 Timothy 5:13), *inventor of evil things* (Romans 1:30), *talebearer* (Proverbs 11:13), and *whisperer* (Proverbs 16:28).

God takes the things we say about others very seriously, and He tells us over and over in His written Word that gossip (even when what we say is factually true) carries with it some very serious consequences—here in this world and in the world to come.

So then, if you don't have something good to say about someone, go out of your way to find something. Otherwise, keep your negative, critical words to yourself.

LITTLE EYES WATCHING

The righteous lead blameless lives;
blessed are their children after them.
PROVERBS 20:7 NIV

Many, if not most, parents have found themselves red-faced when their little one innocently shares something embarrassing Mom or Dad did or said when they believed it hadn't been seen or heard.

Dads should never assume that their little ones aren't watching and listening. They are, and the things they see and hear go a long way toward shaping the kind of adults they will become.

Make no mistake, your kids are watching and listening to. . .

- How you talk (is it the same at home as it is in church?)
- How you treat your wife (do you lead as a servant?)
- Your consumption of various entertainment media (are you careful to watch movies and television shows that reflect a heart for godly standards?)
- Your behavior at home (are you careful not to abuse or over-use alcohol? Is your speech the same everywhere you go?)
- Your walk with the Lord (do your kids see you praying and reading your Bible?)

Whether or not they know it, fathers set the examples their children are likely to follow—in the short term and as they grow to adulthood. In other words, they are in the process of making little copies of themselves that grow to be big copies.

The greatest gift a father can give his children is to be the kind of man God has called him to be.

TIME FOR SOME HONESTY. . .

"Come now, let us settle the matter," says the Lord.
"Though your sins are like scarlet, they shall be as white as snow;
though they are red as crimson, they shall be like wool."
Isaiah 1:18 niv

The prophet Isaiah ministered in the kingdom of Judah at a time when the people had fallen into some very grievous sin. They had become both hedonistic in their behavior and complacent toward their God.

In short, they were very much like us today—lost in sin and without hope. . .at least had they been left on their own.

One of the great themes of Isaiah's prophecies—and of the entire Bible—is God's willingness to forgive and restore those who recognize their sin and turn from that sin back toward Him.

The words in today's verse are echoed hundreds of years later by the apostle John, who wrote: "If we claim to be without sin, we deceive ourselves and the truth is not in us. If we confess our sins, he is faithful and just and will forgive us our sins and purify us from all unrighteousness" (1 John 1:8–9 NIV).

We all need God's forgiveness and restoration. He has provided a way for that to happen by sending His Son, Jesus Christ, to die for our sins. Our part in that equation is to acknowledge that we are sinners and that we need to be washed "as white as snow."

AN OFFENSIVE MESSAGE

*Just as it is written, "Behold, I lay in Zion a stone of stumbling and
a rock of offense, and he who believes in Him will not be disappointed."*
ROMANS 9:33 NASB

We live in a time when many people in our culture seem to have made being
offended not just a hobby, but a pastime they pursue with passion. It's a
time when speaking the truth about the Gospel of Christ and about godly
life principles will get you labeled as "intolerant" and a "bigot."

People don't like being told that they need Jesus to save them and
change them, and they detest being confronted with their own sins. Being
told that there is only one way into the kingdom of God—through Jesus
Christ—they probably like even less.

Of course, this shouldn't shock or even surprise those who follow
Christ. It also isn't really anything new. In fact, on several occasions, Jesus
Himself warned His followers that those who faithfully live and speak for
Him would often pay a steep price for their obedience (see Matthew 5:11,
10:22; John 15:18–21).

When we share the Gospel message with others, we should be careful
to do it with wisdom, gentleness, and respect (see 1 Peter 3:15). But at the
same time, we also need to keep in mind that the truth won't always be
well received. In fact, many will find it downright offensive.

GUARDING YOUR REPUTATION

A good name is more desirable than great riches;
to be esteemed is better than silver or gold.
PROVERBS 22:1 NIV

The great Founding Father (and writer, scientist, philosopher, statesman. . . the list goes on and on) Benjamin Franklin once stated, "It takes many good deeds to build a good reputation, and only one bad one to lose it." "The First American," as Franklin is often still called, understood the value of a good name. So did the writer of today's scripture reading.

History—including some very recent history—is filled with examples of highly esteemed men who ruined their reputations (as well as their careers, their ministries, and their families) with just one misdeed. And a reputation once destroyed is exceedingly difficult, sometimes impossible, to reestablish.

You may not be a man who would make headlines with one big error in judgment, but your reputation is still important. The local or national news may not be watching, but others are—your wife, children, and the rest of your family, your coworkers, your business associates, your partners in ministry. . .those who know you follow Christ and may themselves be interested in following.

There are many things in life well worth guarding. Few if any of them are more important to protect than your personal reputation. So make sure your conduct in all areas accurately reflects who you are. . .and whose you are.

OUTWARD APPEARANCES

But the Lord said to Samuel, "Do not consider his appearance or his height, for I have rejected him. The Lord does not look at the things people look at. People look at the outward appearance, but the Lord looks at the heart."

1 Samuel 16:7 niv

Ours is a culture that puts a lot of emphasis on physical appearance. If you don't believe that, just take a look at a good percentage of the advertisements and "infomercials" that make their way onto television broadcasts on what seems like an hourly basis.

Want to lose weight? Then there's any number of new diets and exercise programs to make it happen, countless companies looking to separate you from your hard-earned cash. Looking to get rid of that wrinkled skin or gray hair? Then there are countless companies pushing creams and hair care products.

Most of us would tell others that we're more concerned with what's "inside" another person than we are with his or her physical appearance. For some, that's just a pleasantry they don't really mean when it comes right down to it. But our God says that very thing. . .and He means it.

There's nothing wrong with taking care of yourself, nothing wrong with trying to look better by staying physically fit. But where your relationship with your heavenly Father is concerned, never forget that He's far more interested in the condition of your inner man than He is with the outer man.

WHERE TO TURN WHEN YOU'RE AFRAID

When I am afraid, I put my trust in you. In God,
whose word I praise—in God I trust and am not afraid.
What can mere mortals do to me?
PSALM 56:3–4 NIV

You don't need to be an expert in child behavior to know what a small child does when he's afraid, worried, in pain, or just needs comfort. Of course, he runs straight to the arms of his loving parents (more often than not, to Mom).

It seems instinctive, doesn't it?

Life is filled with opportunities for us to be overcome by fear and anxiety. And when we enter times in our lives when we feel afraid, worried, and overwhelmed, it can be tempting just to curl up somewhere and try to wait it out alone.

Jesus once told His followers that if they wanted to enter the kingdom of heaven, they needed to do so with the heart attitude like that of a little child (see Matthew 18:2–4). Those moments of fear and worry are good examples of those many times when we need to be like little children.

When life is throwing so much at you that you feel like your fear will overcome you, do the same thing a small child does when he's afraid: Run straight to the arms of your heavenly Father, who is more than able to calm your heart. . .and calm the storm that is going on around you.

AN ACCOUNTABILITY BROTHER

Therefore confess your sins to each other and pray for each other
so that you may be healed. The prayer of a righteous
person is powerful and effective.
JAMES 5:16 NIV

The Bible tells us that we have a spiritual enemy called the devil—or Satan—who works tirelessly to tempt you, weaken you, and discourage you in your life of faith in Jesus Christ. He loves nothing more than to exploit your weaknesses and vulnerabilities and cause you to fall into sin.

And while the Word tells us that God, through His Holy Spirit, will strengthen us for our battle against the devil, it also teaches the importance of having Christian brothers who can hold us accountable, who will pray for us and give us words of encouragement in our battles against sin.

Do you have a friend like that? The kind of brother in Christ in whom you can confide? The kind of friend you are comfortable confessing your sin and your weakness to? The kind of friend who will pray for you, and even speak tough truth to you when it's needed?

That's the kind of friend you need when you're struggling with sin.

If you find yourself struggling with some particular sin and you want victory, then first ask God to give you strength to overcome. He will most certainly answer that prayer in the affirmative. Second, try making yourself accountable to a trusted Christian brother or two.

THE ONE TRUE KING

I charge you to keep this command without spot or blame until the appearing of our Lord Jesus Christ, which God will bring about in his own time—God, the blessed and only Ruler, the King of kings and Lord of lords, who alone is immortal and who lives in unapproachable light.

1 TIMOTHY 6:13–16 NIV

Nearly everybody knows of Elvis Presley as the amazingly successful musical superstar who dominated the world of entertainment in the 1950s and early 1960s. But what most people don't know is that Elvis despised the nickname that stuck with him throughout his career: the "King of Rock and Roll," or more simply, "The King."

At one concert in 1974 in South Bend, Indiana, a fan held up a sign proclaiming "Elvis is the King!" Elvis asked her to hold up the sign so he could read it, and then graciously replied, "Thank you, darling. . . The thought is beautiful, dear, and I love you for it. . . I can't accept this kingship thing, because to me, there's only one, and that's Christ."

In today's verse, the apostle Paul refers to Jesus as "the King of kings and Lord of lords," words that appear again in the book of Revelation. These words reflect perfectly the way in which God wants us to esteem our Savior—as both our Lord and our King.

Jesus is far more than a divine ruler, far more than even a benevolent heavenly monarch. He is our King, our loving King who gave everything so we could be a part of His eternal kingdom.

Who is your King today?

LOVING THE SINNER. . .

Be merciful to those who doubt; save others by snatching them from the fire; to others show mercy, mixed with fear—hating even the clothing stained by corrupted flesh.
JUDE 1:22–23 NIV

"Love the sinner, hate the sin."

This is one of those "Christian clichés" that don't appear anywhere in the Bible—at least not verbatim—but are solidly grounded in biblical truth.

Think about it: The Bible teaches that God hates sin and that we likewise are to hate sin. For example, Psalm 97:10 (NIV) tells us, "Let those who love the LORD hate evil, for he guards the lives of his faithful ones and delivers them from the hand of the wicked."

On the other hand, the Bible enjoins believers to "'love your neighbor as yourself,'" and to treat others with respect and love (Mark 12:31 NIV). Furthermore, we are called to love sinners by praying for them and by witnessing to them about the gift of salvation through Christ.

Just as it would not be loving for a doctor to refuse to tell a patient he is sick and will die unless he receives treatment, it is not loving for Christians to neglect to tell sinners that they need the Savior to save them from eternal death.

So hate sin. Hate it so much that you will go to whatever lengths are necessary to see that people are saved from its terrible consequences. At the same time, love the sinner so much that you'll pray for him and witness to him for as long as it takes.

TALKING TO YOURSELF

Why, my soul, are you downcast? Why so disturbed within me?
Put your hope in God, for I will yet praise him, my Savior and my God.
PSALM 42:5 NIV

Do you ever look at the difficulties and trials in your life and then start talking to yourself? If you don't, then you're probably in a very small minority. At some point, nearly every one of us has taken stock of our lives—or at least our current situation—and started thinking:

There's no way out of this.

Things aren't going to get better. . .at least not anytime soon.

This is just the way things are going to be for me. . . There's nothing I can do about it.

This just isn't fair!

There are all sorts of voices in our world vying for our attention, especially when life becomes difficult. Among those voices is our own.

Of course, we as believers know to be careful not to listen to the voices of the world and of the enemy of our souls, the devil. But it's also important that we don't allow our own voices to drown out that of our heavenly Father.

So when you find yourself muttering to yourself about the hopelessness or unfairness of your situation, turn your attention instead to the Lord, who is big enough and more than willing to take control of everything going on around you and in you.

As the apostle Peter put it, "Cast all your anxiety on him because he cares for you" (1 Peter 5:7 NIV).

HALFTIME

Don't waste your time on useless work. . . . Watch your step.
Use your head. Make the most of every chance you get.
These are desperate times!
Ephesians 5:11, 16 msg

Today is the first day of the second half of 2017. For most it will be just another day, but for others it will be a day of evaluation. Questions will arise. *Am I where I wanted to be at this time of the year? How can I catch up? Where did I go wrong?*

And even though you can't go back in time, it's easy to think of this day (if you knew it was the halfway point of the year) as the point of no return. After today there will be fewer hours left in the year, fewer moments to enjoy, fewer days to celebrate.

If it sounds like this is a time for melancholy, then you need to realize there's more to the story. For everything you haven't been able to do, God can do something better on your behalf. For the bad days you remember, there's a heaven God's prepared for His people to enjoy. For the moments you've missed, God has a future filled with hope available for you.

When you're not where you want to be, remember to turn back to the One who can take you where you need to be. Let His plans guide the second half of the year—"Open up before God, keep nothing back; he'll do whatever needs to be done: He'll validate your life in the clear light of day and stamp you with approval at high noon" (Psalm 37:5 msg).

CURB APPEAL

The LORD says, "I will guide you along the best pathway
for your life. I will advise you and watch over you."
PSALM 32:8 NLT

Curbs are a very useful, if not underappreciated, invention. They guide water to drains, provide a place for small boys to sit and dream on a warm summer day, provide a shape to streets, and act as a boundary for those who need to park.

Curbs are intended to keep us from going where we shouldn't go while framing the route we should take.

We need curbs. We make better decisions with curbs. We find safety because of curbs. When everyone acknowledges these boundary markers, traffic flows smoothly. Imagine the chaos if people decided it was better to drive across lawns or parks.

We have our own set of internal curbs. These are the boundaries we learned as we grew up. This might include something simple like not touching a hot stove or something more complex like not taking something that doesn't belong to you.

God has given us curbs in the Bible, His good commands that direct us how to live wisely and lovingly as His children. When we refuse to live within these curbs, we find ourselves in trouble while we ruin things that belong to other people.

Cars are perfectly equipped to ride between the curbs on the street—so are we when it comes to God's commands in scripture.

HE NEVER GIVES UP

Finish what you started in me, GOD.
Your love is eternal—don't quit on me now.
PSALM 138:8 MSG

Do you ever feel panicked, watching the days of your life stretch out before you and not knowing how to use them in the best way to become more like Christ? Or do you see the work ahead and not know if you're up to the task?

If you've ever felt anything like that, take comfort in these truths.

- God is the Author of your faith; He's writing your story (Hebrews 12:2).
- God is not a God of chaos. He's putting your life in order (1 Corinthians 14:33).
- God began a good work, and He'll complete it in you (Philippians 1:6).
- God saves through His power, grace, and love. When we believe that Jesus was the perfect sacrifice needed to make forgiveness available to all who would ask, we start a new journey that ends with us being called new creations (2 Corinthians 5:17).

You always have access to the God who is reshaping your heart, reordering your direction, and giving purpose to your tomorrow.

There's another benefit. God is faithful, and He won't give up on you. There will be moments when you're stubborn, rebellious, and unwilling to listen. He won't throw up His hands in despair. He will wait, encourage, and put detour signs in your path. You see, He knows your story and He can be trusted to do His part.

While God does the work, life transformation will require your cooperation. Go forward ready to work with Him.

THE DOG DAY OF JULY

[God] creates each of us by Christ Jesus to join him in the work he does.
EPHESIANS 2:10 MSG

This is a day that inspires patriotism, and it should. But it's also a day that often includes family, fireworks, and picnics. There's one staple for the holiday grill. If this is a typical year, Americans will eat 155 million of them. What turkeys are to Thanksgiving, *hot dogs* are to the Fourth of July.

Grilled, boiled, or eaten cooked and chilled, these meat tubes have satisfied mankind for decades. While most think of ketchup, relish, and mustard as the primary toppings, variety seems to be the thing that compliments the "dog."

Stewed potatoes, coleslaw, salsa, bacon, peanuts, and chili are just a few of the things that Americans consider when perfecting their hot dog.

Not to be outdone by a hot dog, each of us were created to be celebrated for one very important reason: God made us with inspired ingredients combined for a unique individual.

Some point to the snowflake or fingerprint to show how unique each of us are, but maybe just for Independence Day we can think of our unique personalities in terms of a hot dog. Each of us has different toppings—maybe even some that don't seem like they should go together—but we all are lovingly put together by our creative Father. With this word picture in mind, we can smile, embrace our family, appreciate freedom, and thank God for *this* day.

TWICE BORN

Jesus replied, "Very truly I tell you, no one can see the kingdom of God unless they are born again."

JOHN 3:3 NIV

We're born male or female. We're born into a certain family. We're born with a certain ethnicity and skin color.

And we're all born with a will to break God's law.

Since the very beginning, mankind has struggled to trust that God's laws were worth following. We've wondered if perhaps He is withholding good things from us.

God has things for us to do, and we ignore Him. He has things for us to stay away from, and that's what we find ourselves attracted to. God didn't *create us* to defy His law—we do that on our own.

God forgives, offers mercy, extends grace, and loves humanity because Jesus paid the price. God is holy, which means He's perfect, sinless, and set apart. Grace isn't a free pass, forgiveness isn't a green light to sin again, and mercy is a gift, not an entitlement.

We are born in sin. We are reborn to follow Jesus. The first birth is into the family of mankind. The second birth is into the family of God. Only one of those families has eternal benefits and life-changing impact. Have you been born again? And if you have, how have you been treating the grace, forgiveness, and mercy that God has extended to you?

TRUST HIM MORE

*When I get really afraid I come to you in trust. I'm proud to praise God;
fearless now, I trust in God. What can mere mortals do?*

PSALM 56:3–4 MSG

We survive in a world of broken promises. Products we buy struggle to exist beyond their warranty. Promises made by family and friends can be broken or forgotten. Something told in confidence becomes the day's gossip.

We often respond to broken promises by putting up walls, keeping things to ourselves, and never really believing anyone who says, "Trust me."

God encourages us to *trust* Him. He's never forgotten to supply the air we breathe or the sunshine we enjoy. He keeps food sources growing. In fact, He holds everything in His creation together (Colossians 1:17), even our very selves—"'For in him we live and move and have our being'" (Acts 17:28 NIV).

Some of us will still hesitate and say, "I'm not sure I can trust Him."

God is something more and different than humans. He cannot lie or sin, and He always keeps His promises (Numbers 23:19).

The more we trust God, the more trustworthy we find Him. The more we trust His ability, the less we question His authority. The more we trust His love, the less fearful we find ourselves. The more we trust in God, the less ominous life becomes.

When it's hard to trust others, it's the perfect time to trust God.

GRACE HAS A PRICE

*Should we keep on sinning so that God can show us more
and more of his wonderful grace? Of course not!*
ROMANS 6:1–2 NLT

God has freely offered grace to humanity to forgive sin and bring those who believe in Him into His family.

To demonstrate grace and forgiveness, Jesus paid a once-and-forever price—His life. He became the sacrifice for all who would accept it. Grace costs you nothing. Grace cost God the life of His Son.

While Jesus rose from the dead, the cost of forgiving grace was the most important payment in the history of mankind.

A man of integrity understands grace has a price. It isn't just a concept the mind agrees with. It changes decisions, actions, and motives.

A man of integrity brings God's command to love others into decisions, choosing to do the right thing rather than apologize after the fact. He knows he'll mess up and grace will be freely available, but he decides that sinning to *get* grace is something like abusing God's gift.

The price was high, so receiving the gift should have a life-altering impact. A man of integrity remembers what Jesus said of the sinful woman who anointed Him: that one who has been forgiven much, loves much (Luke 7:47). And this love and integrity sides with discipleship, discipline, and obedience. These are all hard things, but God's children are asked to trust Him and obey His commands. The man of integrity views this as an important, but not burdensome, directive, because he understands the immense grace that has been given him.

HE STARTED AND FINISHED WELL

Whoever walks in integrity walks securely.
PROVERBS 10:9 NIV

The Bible is filled with stories of men who started well (like King Saul) with great hopes of doing something big for God. Many of these men ended poorly. Others (like Peter) struggled at the beginning, but ended well. Still others started well—and finished well.

Daniel's story fits the last category.

He was born during an era of conflict. He existed in a time of struggling leaders and citizens who often only did what was right in their own eyes. As a teenager, he was taken from his country and taught a new culture. Somehow, in the middle of the crazy world where he found himself, Daniel wholeheartedly attached himself to the God of his people.

As a teenager, he knew God's law, including dietary requirements. He and his godly friends stood up to those who took them from their families by asking for food they knew they could eat in good conscience.

Daniel refused to compromise when he knew it was out of sync with God's will.

This man's life is an open book on what godly integrity looks like. His integrity was noticed by three kings, and Daniel was a trusted adviser for all three.

Be encouraged. No matter where you find yourself in following God, you have the opportunity to finish well.

BE STRONG: ASK FOR HELP

Oh, don't worry; we wouldn't dare say that we are as wonderful as these other men who tell you how important they are! But they are only comparing themselves with each other, using themselves as the standard of measurement. How ignorant!
2 CORINTHIANS 10:12 NLT

Guys are competitive. How do we reconcile being competitive and realizing we may not be the best? Whether it's football, video games, or trivia, there is a desire within guys to be the best.

At the end of the contest, there will be winners—and there will be losers.

Christian men can be guilty of wanting to wear a spiritual foam finger that suggests they're number one. But God calls us ignorant if we think we're somehow better than those around us.

If we're looking for a standard of measurement, we need to look at Jesus—not ourselves or those around us. Jesus was perfect in following God's commands. How about you? Jesus gave His life to rescue humanity. Have you done the same, giving your time and talents to share the Gospel? Jesus loves everyone perfectly, no matter their background or how they act. Does your love come with conditions?

We can never compare favorably to Jesus, but that's exactly why we need to stay close to Him. He ensures that any man who humbly walks with Him measures up. Ask Him for the help you need to be more like Him in every way.

MONDAY MORNING IS A GIFT

If you are a thief, quit stealing. Instead, use your hands for good hard work, and then give generously to others in need.
Ephesians 4:28 nlt

Work is God's idea. We may be anxious for the weekend, but God's *work idea* has a purpose.

While God could speak the world into existence, man would need to use his hands and skills to keep things in good shape. While God has a pretty good handle on how to manage the world, He made mankind so that they must use their minds to complete a job.

When we work, we keep ourselves from considering theft as a means of meeting our needs. When we work, we can use some of the money we earn to help those who can't work.

Work provides finances for meeting the needs of our family, offers us a sense of purpose, initiates ideas that may help others, and gives us a sense of satisfaction at the end of our day.

If we think of work as a drudgery to endure, we miss the point. Work of any kind (even volunteerism) gives us a means of helping others with something God has entrusted us with.

Your perspective of your work (and even of Monday mornings) will change when you view work as a *gift* that has the ability to bless others, honor God, and keep your mind focused.

CAUTION: THINKING AHEAD

You'll do best by filling your minds and meditating on things true, noble, reputable, authentic, compelling, gracious—the best, not the worst; the beautiful, not the ugly; things to praise, not things to curse.

PHILIPPIANS 4:8 MSG

There's a children's song that says, "Be careful, little eyes, what you see." The song continues by urging us to be careful with what our ears hear, where our feet go, what our hands do, and what our mouth says.

If we think about things that are off-limits for too long, we will see, hear, do, and say the wrong thing. When bad ideas gain a foothold, we'll go to the wrong places as well. It seems that this song for children is just as applicable to men.

We almost always become trapped when we give bad ideas too much time in our mental Crock-Pot. Bits and pieces of wrong thinking combine for a potent stew that leaves us confused and unfocused. And in those vulnerable moments, our greatest adversary, the devil, makes sure we have everything we need to tempt us to try the life that God has always warned us against.

God knows that the battles we most often lose start in the mind. Getting our thinking straight can help keep our decisions honorable.

Deciding beforehand how you'll respond to sin-influenced ideas will go a long way in helping you make the best decision when it's easier to move in the wrong direction.

A TIME TO SIMPLIFY

"If God gives such attention to the appearance of wildflowers—most of which are never even seen—don't you think he'll attend to you, take pride in you, do his best for you?. . . Steep your life in God-reality, God-initiative, God-provisions. Don't worry about missing out. You'll find all your everyday human concerns will be met."
MATTHEW 6:30, 33 MSG

Some live off the grid. Others downsize into tiny homes. Whether you call them penny-pinchers, extreme cheapskates, or Luddites, these men and women have embraced simplicity in a time when most want *more*.

While some will downsize, others will cut their own hair, make their own butter, grow their own produce, and raise their own chickens. If you think that sounds radical, you should know there are a growing number of individuals embracing a simpler lifestyle.

This isn't to suggest that you should find a tiny house and move to an uninhabited corner of the smallest county in the least populous state. Perhaps on this National Simplicity Day it's just an acknowledgment that God never asks us to complicate our lives to the point where there is no room for Him.

Having nothing to do is one problem. Having too much to do invites other dangers.

In what ways could you simplify your life? How would that impact your ability to spend time with Jesus in prayer and in His Word?

TIME TO REPRESENT

A sterling reputation is better than striking it rich;
a gracious spirit is better than money in the bank.
PROVERBS 22:1 MSG

At the end of your life, people will talk about you. When your eulogy is given, people learn something about the man you were on this earth. How do you wish to be remembered?

One pastor struggled to find something positive to say about the recently departed, but the only thing he could find out was that he was good at bingo.

Most people on their deathbeds focus on what was really important, and they often conclude they did less of the important stuff than they should have. Things like having a better relationship with God, spending time with loved ones, and loving and helping others stand out as either regrets or cherished memories at the end of their lives.

People remember us more for how we helped than how we earned our money. They care more about our acts of kindness than a mantel shelf of awards. They will respond more to a generous spirit than to our list of accomplishments.

We represent our most gracious, generous, and giving God. Men of all ethnic groups, economic backgrounds, and nationalities have discovered that being more like Him results in a *sterling reputation* and a *gracious spirit*. Becoming more like Jesus changes how people see us—because it *actually* changes us. In what ways do you want to represent your Savior better? Ask Him; He is more than willing to help you grow.

A TIME OF FAILURE

"It's time to change your ways! Turn to face God so he can wipe away your sins [and] pour out showers of blessing to refresh you."
ACTS 3:19 MSG

Men despise personal failure. We don't want to admit wrongdoing. We even hate asking for directions. Every difficulty becomes our own burden to bear.

Perhaps this is why men tend to spiral out of control when they are caught in sin. They've tried to correct things on their own, personally blamed others for their predicament, and then, when the secret is out, they decide it's no longer worth the effort, spiraling into behaviors they never dreamed possible.

Failure should bring us face to feet with Jesus. We come to Him and bow at His feet in the brokenness of a man finally willing to ask for help. There's no shame in this purifying act—it's exactly what God wants us to do. In fact, He makes a promise that He will heal us from our sin if we confess it: "If we admit our sins—make a clean breast of them—he won't let us down; he'll be true to himself. He'll forgive our sins and purge us of all wrongdoing" (1 John 1:9 MSG).

There is restoration after failure. There is hope after hurt. There is love after rebellion. It's only possible through the God who's all too aware of our failures and chooses to love us anyway.

If this describes the world you live in now, then stop wasting time. Admit your failings and ask God for the help you need.

THE BIG DIFFERENCE

"My thoughts are nothing like your thoughts," says the LORD.
"And my ways are far beyond anything you could imagine.
For just as the heavens are higher than the earth, so my ways are
higher than your ways and my thoughts higher than your thoughts."
ISAIAH 55:8–9 NLT

The biggest difference between God and man is that God is perfect—man is not.

We let people down—God can be trusted. We destroy—God makes things new. We tell lies—God speaks truth. We're selfish—God gave us everything. We want our way—God knows what's best.

These differences point to a God who's incredibly wise, but He is often thought of as foolish. For instance, His Word says we should lead by serving, find blessings by giving, and discover real life by losing what we thought was most important. In 1 Corinthians 1, the apostle Paul even states that the cross is "foolishness" to those who don't believe, but it is "the power of God" to those who are being saved (1 Corinthians 1:18 NKJV).

Sometimes we want to try to define who God is by what we experience, but God is beyond anything we can explain. He has no beginning or end. He created us and offers us restoration when we blow it. We don't have the credentials to be His children, but He welcomes us to be a part of His family through Jesus.

Thankfully, we don't have to understand everything about God to admit that He's right, trustworthy, and compassionate.

OUR GREATEST NEED

This is the kind of love we are talking about—not that we once upon a time loved God, but that he loved us and sent his Son as a sacrifice to clear away our sins and the damage they've done to our relationship with God.

1 JOHN 4:10 MSG

How do you remember your favorite days growing up? Some men remember crawling under a fixer-upper car as teenagers with big dreams, a utility light, and a wrench that could tighten bolts and remove knuckle skin in one single movement. Others remember spending time in the arcade with a fistful of quarters and an eye on the high score, lights flashing and machines beeping while other hopeful players cheered or groaned around them. Some recall their cell phones, which provided much-needed connection with friends, no less valuable though they rarely demanded skinned knuckles.

Every generation relates to our world differently and enjoys different pastimes, but one thing that never changes is the human need to love and be loved. That's why we get married and have kids. We hope that somehow the love we experience can be passed on to future generations.

God defined love. When we experience God's love, we can both love others and accept their love in a way that invites trust and inspires contentment. If we don't experience God's love, all we can reasonably expect is a less fulfilling imitation based on conditions and feelings. We will always question its legitimacy.

If you have more questions about what true love looks like, 1 Corinthians 13 can help you identify and demonstrate it in all your relationships.

TRY HARDER?

*You are not controlled by your sinful nature. You are controlled
by the Spirit if you have the Spirit of God living in you.
(And remember that those who do not have the Spirit
of Christ living in them do not belong to him at all.)*
ROMANS 8:9 NLT

When we fail—and we will—we will likely embrace the idea of trying harder. We remind ourselves that we know right from wrong, so all we need to do is police ourselves and double our efforts. After all, God gave us His laws, so shouldn't it be easier to obey them?

Who are we kidding? We tag an extra five miles per hour onto the speed limit and somehow feel law enforcement should allow a little discretion. We've become masters at riding the edge of sin and hoping we don't fall off the edge.

All the self-discipline, extra effort, and good intentions have never been 100 percent successful in keeping us away from sin, because it's never been enough.

God sent a Helper called the Holy Spirit to be both a spiritual Companion and a living Guide. We tend to ignore His influence and grow deaf to His advice. God wants to help us avoid sin, but we need to be willing to accept the help. Ask for God to open your heart to the Spirit's leading, and ask the Spirit Himself what He would show you today.

WISDOM'S SOURCE

*If any of you lacks wisdom, you should ask God, who gives generously
to all without finding fault, and it will be given to you.*
JAMES 1:5 NIV

Wisdom is often equated with the number of wrinkles on a man's face. What if wisdom comes from a place other than time alone? What if you just have to ask?

The wisdom of God comes from acknowledging Him as the Source of wisdom, accepting that wisdom as truth, and living your life according to it. Proverbs 1:7 (NIV) affirms this: "The fear of the LORD is the beginning of knowledge."

Too often we think of wisdom in terms of our personal experiences. We think we become wise by living through difficulties and learning a lesson afterward. That's a great source of common sense—and part of the reason why older folks have so much good advice to share—but true wisdom from God offers *uncommon* sense, inspired instructions from the Creator Himself on how to best live and honor Him in His world.

Maybe those young people we say are "wise beyond their years" have simply been spending time learning wisdom from its original Source.

Don't let age fool you. Wisdom is available to all, and godly wisdom surpasses the earthly wisdom of anyone you know.

The Bible contains hundreds of pages filled with what God can teach about how to be wise. Start exploring them and learn the ways God's wisdom can change your perspective.

SECURING THE INSECURE

[God said,] My grace is enough; it's all you need.
My strength comes into its own in your weakness.
2 CORINTHIANS 12:9 MSG

He was indecisive, but he wanted people to like him. He was shallow, but he had a lot to hide. He was miserable, but he wore a smile to mask the pain.

There was another man. He was demanding because it stopped any questions. He was aloof because he couldn't allow anyone to get close. He wore his pain proudly and never believed there was relief.

We've all resembled one of these men in their struggle with feelings of insignificance.

Many men believe they'll never live up to the expectations of others or are convinced they are failures.

These two men were attempting to keep others away from their secret place of pain and insecurity. Both were miserable. Both were unsure of their choices.

Only God can secure us from the outside influences and inner conflict in our lives. Our security isn't found in our own ability, but God's. We become sufficient or acceptable because of God's grace, mercy, and peace through Jesus. Though there will be hard days when our feelings sneak up on us, spending time in scripture will remind us of how Jesus loves us and came to rescue us when, in our sin, we couldn't offer Him anything in return, not even love (Romans 5:8).

Feeling insignificant is normal. Knowing we are accepted by God makes us secure, no matter what we are feeling at the moment.

HARDWIRED FOR SUCCESS?

*Earn a reputation for living well in God's eyes
and the eyes of the people.*
PROVERBS 3:4 MSG

Men seem to be hardwired to want to be considered a success. Go to most ten-year high school reunions and men will talk about how successful they are, or they may resort to reliving their high school successes.

Some men will fight for their marriages (and they should), but only to prove they're a success in marriage. They don't want to be viewed as a failure.

Men will do what they feel they have to in order to shore up the appearance of success. However, when failure comes, some men will shift direction completely. These men will embrace failure as an old friend and live as if success is no longer available. They rush to make bad choices, dismiss their wives and children because they view themselves as mistake-prone, and move from job to job because they can't find a reason to be passionate about work.

God longs for men to be authentic, transparent fighters for what's right. He longs for us to stop wearing masks and believing that if we just try hard enough we can move all outside forces to be in our favor.

Our greatest success is to be *forgiven* men of God, to be in right relationship with Him. Let's focus our efforts on knowing and pleasing Him, and then, as we put our attention on what our loving heavenly Father thinks, what others think will not matter so much to us.

HEART PROTECTION

How can a young person stay pure? By obeying your word.
I have tried hard to find you—don't let me wander
from your commands. I have hidden your word
in my heart, that I might not sin against you.
PSALM 119:9–11 NLT

Gloves protect our hands. Shoes protect our feet. Safety goggles protect our eyes. What protects our hearts?

Hearts are where spiritual decisions are made. The heart remains unprotected when we don't know which rules to follow. Accurate spiritual decisions can't be made when we have no idea what God has to say about important life issues.

When we argue that we have no time to read God's Word, we shouldn't be surprised when we break God's law. Christian men lead their families by example. Consuming God's Word is essential to demonstrating how to live a godly life.

Our decisions cannot be made simply because we feel like it's a good decision or because the majority of people we talk to have a strong opinion about it.

The integrity of the heart and the decisions it makes will always be based on the connection between consulting God's Word and a willingness to obey what we read. When we fail in either area, we resemble the heart in Jeremiah 17:9 (NLT), which reads, "'The human heart is the most deceitful of all things, and desperately wicked. Who really knows how bad it is?'"

CAUTION TAPE CHRISTIANITY

Fix your attention on God. You'll be changed from the inside out.
Readily recognize what he wants from you, and quickly respond to
it. Unlike the culture around you, always dragging you down
to its level of immaturity, God brings the best out
of you, develops well-formed maturity in you.
ROMANS 12:2 MSG

What if there was the equivalent of yellow caution tape when it comes to places, circumstances, and events that we should avoid? Would we pay attention? Would we change direction?

If you go to the theater and the movie doesn't look like it matches God's heart, imagine yellow caution tape warning you to keep out. Imagine the same to be true for individuals the Bible describes as "bad company," or maybe it's arguments you need to stay away from. This visible reminder would solve all kinds of problems, wouldn't it?

God's Holy Spirit came to be that "caution tape." We don't see visible warning signs, but if we pay attention, we'll recognize those warning signs with as much personal impact as seeing bright yellow tape blocking the way to a dangerous area.

God has always provided the warning signs—we just need to recognize them. God gave us the help we need—we just need to stop rejecting it. If we humble ourselves and fix our attention on God and the help He provides in His Spirit, we will see Him "bring[ing] out the best in [us], develop[ing] well-formed maturity in [us]."

THERE WILL BE A FUTURE

"I know the plans I have for you," says the LORD.
"They are plans for good and not for disaster,
to give you a future and a hope."
JEREMIAH 29:11 NLT

There are no problems God cannot solve, no circumstance that escapes His attention. No future that can't be adapted to His plan.

God is never surprised, never in need of education, and never in doubt. His way is perfect, precise, and practical.

In the difficult turns of our lives, we struggle, misunderstand, and then blame God. Why? We don't know the end of the story. We think what we face is unfair and that God not only doesn't make sense, but that we can consider Him malicious and untrustworthy.

What He knows—but we don't see—is that there is an ending that proves His faithfulness. We just haven't arrived at that part of the story yet.

God doesn't need to recheck His plan to see if it was correct. He doesn't need to ask someone if He should have tried a different plan. What God understands and plans for us *can* be trusted even when we struggle to make sense of it.

We're familiar with the beginning of our story. We're living the present. The future? That's the part God understands, and He promises there will be a future. Hold on. Trust your loving Creator's promise that His plan is perfect and for your good even when it doesn't seem like it.

THE ONE NAME

What marvelous love the Father has extended to us!
Just look at it—we're called children of God! That's who we really are.
1 JOHN 3:1 MSG

We are husbands, dads, employees, uncles, nephews, neighbors, plumbers, bakers, farmers, architects, writers, janitors, mechanics, truck drivers, accountants, comedians, gamers, athletes, actors, and a laundry list of other names that can define who we are and what we do.

We can also be called kind, gentle, loving, good, self-controlled, rude, rough, mean, or impulsive.

Of all the names men can be called, the one that should mean the most is *child of God*. This name defines who we are because it defines whom we follow. It indicates that God has accepted us and that we're part of a family of those accepted by Him. It suggests that we're always in a position of learning because a child never knows it all. It holds within it the promise of being coheirs with Christ, inheriting both eternal life and God's blessing and help in this earthly life: "And we know we are going to get what's coming to us—an unbelievable inheritance! We go through exactly what Christ goes through. If we go through the hard times with him, then we're certainly going to go through the good times with him!" (Romans 8:17 MSG).

Knowing who we are as a child of God helps us put all the other names we may be called into perspective. It also helps us identify with names that describe how a child of God is different from those who aren't God's children.

What's in a name? Perhaps more than you may have thought?

THE ORIGIN OF STORIES

Come here and listen, let me tell you what God did for me.
PSALM 66:16 MSG

Each song you hear has a story attached to its creation. Some of those stories are as compelling as the song itself. Horatio Spafford wrote the hymn "It Is Well with My Soul" following the loss of his four daughters in a shipwreck at sea. Matthew West wrote the song "Day One" after reading the story of a man who had made many, many poor choices and was working hard to make each day a step toward positive personal change.

You have a story, and like the psalmist, you could gather people around to hear what God has done for you, whether that's over dinner at your house, at a conference, at a prayer group, on a blog, or in a book. Finding a way to share that story is important, because your story shows evidence that the God who made you has always had a plan for you—even following your or others' poor decisions.

Depending on what you have to share, your story could provide a cautionary tale for others in their Christian lives, encouragement to the weary to continue standing strong, or an open door to welcome new stories told by those who've gained courage to speak after hearing *your* story.

At the core of your tale is the Author of your story. Whatever story you tell, give credit to God, who brings you through storms, knew your name before you were born, and prepares the way for your future.

ALL THINGS NEW

Anyone who belongs to Christ has become a new person.
The old life is gone; a new life has begun!
2 CORINTHIANS 5:17 NLT

A relationship with Jesus invites us to do things we never thought we could. Somehow impossible reactions become possible. Jesus helps us forgive when we would normally hold a grudge, love when it would be easier to hate, and share when we'd like to withhold. We become people who are generous in love, grace, and gentleness toward those who enter our path, and not because we are expecting anything in return.

God did this by making a new covenant with us. A covenant is a contract that God has bound Himself to fulfill. When we accept Jesus, there's nothing we can offer that would be considered valuable in God's sight—except ourselves.

God brings all the positive attributes, resources, forgiveness, grace, and love. It seems unfair. We get everything and He doesn't seem to get much, but this is exactly the contract (or covenant) God accepts.

Once we have access to all God offers, we find our perception, attitudes, and thoughts changed. We live life from the perspective of one who doesn't hoard time or resources, but instead extends help to others. We remember what it's like to be outside a partnership with God and want to help others discover the new covenant for themselves.

We come to Jesus just as we are, but we should never stay the way we came.

THE RIGHT CANDIDATE

Pride lands you flat on your face; humility prepares you for honors.
PROVERBS 29:23 MSG

If you spend any amount of time in God's Word, you'll notice that the men God used never seemed quite ready for the job they were asked to do. They were fearful, impulsive misfits, oddballs, and sinners, and often the least ideal candidates to do something big for God. In other words, these men were entirely average, normal, and perhaps the last to be picked for a team.

Do you ever feel average or even below average? You just might be the right candidate God can use to do something incredible.

Maybe God never wanted men who *knew* they could do something big. Maybe He likes using men who *know* they need His help.

God seems to need a little more time when He's dealing with the prideful men who know it all and don't mind sharing it. He may set aside those who seem to believe God is fortunate to have them as part of His team. God sees pride as a barrier to usefulness.

So when you feel a little inadequate, a lot out of your element, or lacking in the skills God might need, you shouldn't be surprised when God gives you something only you can do—with His help.

WHAT IS A BLESSING?

All praise to God, the Father of our Lord Jesus Christ,
who has blessed us with every spiritual blessing in the heavenly
realms because we are united with Christ.
Ephesians 1:3 nlt

Blessings are prayers at mealtimes and gifts from God. There's another blessing we'll discover over the next four days.

This blessing is a personal gift a father shares with a child. A father's blessing can give a child permission to grow up, offer freedom, and invite the child to dream big dreams and follow God's unique plan.

We *pass* the blessing when we *speak* the blessing. We cannot assume our children understand they're loved and that we want the best for them. They need to hear it from our lips and see it in our actions. A blessing can change futures, strengthen relationships, and provide a vision for their journey.

When a child receives a blessing from her father, it proves he notices her, pays attention to her heart, and knows that by giving her wings she will eventually fly.

Each child needs the blessing, but few receive it. Your children may be grown—it's never too late to bless them.

God has blessed mankind with a future and a hope. He offers a listening ear, a fully developed plan for your life, and forever companionship. He advises, He comforts, and He *blesses*.

WHAT THEY NEED THE MOST

Lord Almighty, blessed is the one who trusts in you.
PSALM 84:12 NIV

If you're married, it's possible your family has been waiting for something only you can give. They may not know how to ask. They may not even know they need this, but you have the power to build up or crush your family.

You can change futures by offering your family a *blessing*.

Abraham offered Isaac a blessing. Isaac offered Jacob a blessing. Jacob gave Joseph a blessing.

A blessing speaks life into your family. It lets your family members know you recognize their importance to you. It indicates you believe they have the ability to make good decisions. It inspires confidence and encourages hope.

Your ability to clearly tell your family members they're valued and that you believe in them can go a long way in giving them the courage to face life head-on. Too many families are waiting to be loved unconditionally by their husband or dad.

When we place conditions on our love, our families will still do everything they can to receive a blessing, but they will live with the knowledge that it probably will never happen. Give them a vision for their future that includes your backing.

You can be fifty years old and still be waiting for a father's blessing. Don't make your wife and children wait.

WHEN YOU MISSED THE BLESSING

*"God bless you and keep you, God smile on you and gift you,
God look you full in the face and make you prosper."*
NUMBERS 6:24–26 MSG

What you believed about yourself when you were a small child is likely what you believe today. We were, in many ways, children who believed what we were told by our parents, friends, or schoolhouse bullies. We each carry invisible tattoos reading *last to be picked, slow, stupid,* or *worthless.*

On bad days, you'll believe what someone said about you when you were five. It doesn't matter whether it's true or not, you'll accept it as true even when the evidence suggests otherwise.

Our future isn't defined by our five-year-old selves, but we'll act the part.

If no one's ever spoken a blessing into your life, consider this. Before you were born, God knew your name, fit you together in your mother's womb, and called you a masterpiece (Psalm 139:13–16). He wants you on His team. He created you for something only you can do. He loved you enough to send His Son, Jesus, to make it possible for you to be a part of His family.

You'll sin, but God can forgive you, and He wants to. He's never abandoned you. He's always loved you. He wants to partner with you on His plan for you.

Don't pay attention to what others called you; pay attention to His call in your life.

REVERSE BLESSING

If you honor your father and mother, "things will go well for you."
Ephesians 6:3 nlt

What if you had one or more parents who just weren't there for you? What if they didn't have what it took to show you what love looked like? What if they seemed uncaring and spoke words that couldn't be considered blessings?

Maybe one or both parents were likely never serious candidates for Parent of the Year. They didn't seem to find any joy in *you*.

You may be waiting for a blessing you've never received, validation that never came, an encouraging parent who only seemed the stuff of fairy tales, and you're in conflict. Sure, sharing the blessing with your own children is something you want to do, but giving a blessing back to a parent who never blessed you sounds like an awkward impossibility.

Some parents were likely broken by an unspoken blessing that should have come from *their* parents. Even grandparents may be waiting to be told they're loved.

As much as they may have hurt you, a rebuilt relationship may be possible when *you* give your *parents* a blessing. It may be hard, but it's entirely possible your blessing will put a noticeable crack in the walls they've built around their hearts. If this restored relationship is something you desire but you feel hesitant to try, ask God to increase your love for your parents and guide you into the right words to say and the right actions to take.

SAVED ONLY BY GRACE

Christ Jesus came into the world to save sinners, of whom I am chief.
1 TIMOTHY 1:15 NKJV

Paul wasn't just acting humble when he declared that he was the worst of sinners. He never forgot that, in his blind zeal for Jewish religious traditions, he had arrested and tortured numerous Christians and urged that they be killed. Looking back on his crimes years later, he bluntly stated that any righteousness he once thought he'd had he now realized was "rubbish" (Philippians 3:8 NKJV).

Why did God choose such a violent sinner for one of His leading apostles? Paul explained that God wanted to show by *his* example that there was no person so vile or sinful that He couldn't redeem them (1 Timothy 1:16). You might also ask why God chose Peter as a leading apostle after Peter cursed and swore that he didn't even *know* Jesus (Matthew 26:69-74). Again, the Lord wanted someone presenting His Gospel who knew that he was unworthy, who was convinced that he, and others, could only be saved by God's grace.

However, sometimes after you've been serving the Lord for a few years, have cleaned up your life, and have overcome several bad habits, you can forget what a bad state you were once in. You can begin to think that you're quite righteous and can even start to believe that you're good enough to make it on your own.

But think for a moment about the life Jesus saved you from, and remind yourself that it was by grace you were saved, not by your own goodness (Ephesians 2:8-9).

REPAYING DEBTS

Let no debt remain outstanding,
except the continuing debt to love one another.
ROMANS 13:8 NIV

Christians are to honor their debts and be faithful to pay them. When you don't have much cash, sometimes the last thing you want to think of is about repaying money you owe. You pray that they won't press you to repay immediately. In fact, truth be told, you probably wish that they'd simply forgive the debt.

Jesus said, "Love your enemies, do good, and lend, hoping for nothing in return" (Luke 6:35 NKJV), so you might think, *If they were a true Christian, they wouldn't expect me to repay them. They'd forgive my debt*. But that's missing Jesus' point. He was saying that if you lend money to an *unsaved enemy* because he needs it, do so with the full knowledge that he likely won't repay you. He *is* an unbeliever and an enemy, after all.

It's wonderful when someone is in a position to forgive a debt, but they may be unable to, or may not feel that they should, so it's your responsibility to repay them—even if you have to do so little by little over an extended period of time. It will teach you discipline and faithfulness.

You can pray that God will supply the money to repay them. And yes, you *can* pray that, if they're in a position to do so, they'll have mercy and forgive the debt. But don't attempt to impose this desire upon them.

The only debt you should never finish paying off is your obligation to love others.

NOT KNOWING WHERE YOU'RE GOING

*By an act of faith, Abraham said yes to God's call to travel
to an unknown place that would become his home.
When he left he had no idea where he was going.*
HEBREWS 11:8 MSG

Exactly 525 years ago, on August 3, 1492, Christopher Columbus set sail from Spain with three ships. Unlike Abraham, Columbus knew—or so he thought—where he was going: He intended to sail across the Atlantic Ocean and arrive at Japan by a westerly route. However, he ended up someplace completely different—the Americas.

As for Abraham, God said, "'Leave your native country. . .and go to the land that I will show you.'. . . So Abram departed as the LORD had instructed. . . When they arrived in Canaan. . .the LORD appeared to Abram and said, 'I will give this land to your descendants'" (Genesis 12:1, 4–5, 7 NLT). He didn't know till he got there that this was the place.

The Lord might also call you to uproot from a safe, familiar location and set sail for the unknown. You may have sensed God calling you, you may have been offered a better job elsewhere, or circumstances may have conspired to make the move obvious, so like it or not, you launch out. God has wonderful plans for you, but often in order for them to come to pass, you have to step out in faith.

Don't be afraid. God has promised, "I send an Angel before thee, to keep thee in the way, and to bring thee into the place which I have prepared" (Exodus 23:20 KJV).

OVERCOMING DESPAIR

He lifted me out of the pit of despair, out of the mud and the mire.
He set my feet on solid ground and steadied me as I walked along.

Psalm 40:2 nlt

The prophet Samuel had anointed David to be the future king of Israel. This was the clear will of God, so obviously God planned to keep David alive so this could happen. At first, David didn't doubt it. But after living like a fugitive in the wilderness for several years, constantly looking over his shoulder, his faith became worn down. "David kept thinking to himself, 'Someday Saul is going to get me. The best thing I can do is escape to the Philistines. Then Saul will stop hunting for me. . .and I will finally be safe'" (1 Samuel 27:1 nlt).

There's no indication that David prayed about this decision. He fled to the land of the Philistines due to his own discouraged reasoning, and this move ended up causing him serious problems.

Perhaps you're in a similar situation. You were convinced that something was God's will for your life, so you stood strong for quite some time, despite severe tests. But perhaps recently you've begun to grow weary and frayed around the edges.

God knows this is a human tendency, so He encourages you in the words of Paul, which say, "Let us not grow weary while doing good, for in due season we shall reap if we do not lose heart" (Galatians 6:9 nkjv). The Word also says, "Fight the good fight of faith" (1 Timothy 6:12 kjv), so keep fighting and believing.

KIND TO THE UNGRATEFUL

Love ye your enemies. . .and your reward shall be great,
and ye shall be the children of the Highest: for he is kind
unto the unthankful and to the evil.

LUKE 6:35 KJV

One thing that disturbs many Christians is Jesus' command to love their enemies. It just seems so far beyond what they're capable of or willing to do that they write it off as some unrealistic ideal that only the most super-spiritual, mature saints can ever attain to. But Jesus said that loving your enemies was sure proof that you were a child of the Highest God.

Why is this? Because God is loving and patient by nature. He loves the unthankful and is kind even to evil people. And as His child, you're to emulate your Father and show this same love and kindness.

You may have difficulty even showing kindness to those who don't express due thankfulness, let alone showing love and kindness to people who are evil and show no sign of repenting or changing. Yet Jesus, after explaining God's loving nature in Luke 6:35 above, added, "Be ye therefore merciful, as your Father also is merciful" (verse 36).

He doesn't expect you to be naive about where they're at or deny that they're evil, but He asks you to "overcome evil with good" (Romans 12:21 KJV). And yes, He knows that this is a difficult thing to ask. That's why He promises that "your reward shall be *great*" for obeying Him.

INTERNATIONAL FRIENDSHIP DAY

A man who has friends must himself be friendly,
but there is a friend who sticks closer than a brother.
PROVERBS 18:24 NKJV

Friendship Day is celebrated in many countries today, particularly in South America and parts of Asia. In a note of humor, in 1998, Winnie the Pooh was named the world's ambassador of friendship at the United Nations. You'd think that the outgoing Tigger would have been a more logical choice, particularly for Asia, but they must've had a reason. . .

When you need a friend, however, a stuffed toy simply won't do. There's nothing like a heart-to-heart talk with a real person. Solomon said, "A friend is always loyal, and a brother is born to help in time of need" (Proverbs 17:17 NLT). Whether you always get along with family members or not, they're still likely to help you when you're down. But today's verse says that "there is a friend who sticks closer than a brother." What does that kind of friend look like?

Proverbs 18:24 (NKJV) says, "A man who has friends must himself be friendly." That means more than simply smiling at people passing by. It means being loyal to friends when they're no longer popular and helping them in their time of need. Being loyal also means giving tough love sometimes. Scripture says, "Faithful are the wounds of a friend" (Proverbs 27:6 NKJV). As a true friend, you will tell others when they're off the mark, faithfully correcting them. Clearly, these verses are a call to a deep, enduring relationship, not simply a reminder to greet someone on Friendship Day. Be that kind of friend.

AVOID ARGUMENTS

Refuse to get involved in inane discussions; they always end up in fights.
God's servant must not be argumentative, but a gentle listener.
2 TIMOTHY 2:23–24 MSG

If you're often tempted to get drawn into arguments, you might not see it as a fault. You may simply think that you're being honest and "telling it like it is," or setting other people straight. But the fact is, most quarrels generate far more heat than light, and end up creating hard feelings. Plus, they often descend into emotional exchanges rather than reasoned discussions. This is especially true of political and religious arguments—although it could also describe many marital disagreements.

Ask yourself what you spend the most time doing during a typical argument. Are you patiently listening to the other person, trying to understand his or her point of view, or does "listening" mean impatiently waiting for your turn to speak? The Bible says that God's servant must be a "gentle listener." Does this describe you?

Granted, there *are* times, especially when someone is teaching dangerous false doctrine, when you must "contend earnestly for the faith" (Jude 1:3 NKJV). But you must contend with facts and solid reasons, not with a raised voice and intimidating emotions and body postures.

Solomon said, "Starting a quarrel is like opening a floodgate, so stop before a dispute breaks out" (Proverbs 17:14 NLT). Know what's actually worth disputing and what's not. Whether you feel you're right or not, often the wisest thing that you can do is to simply avoid getting drawn into an argument in the first place.

PROTECTED IN GOD'S SHADOW

He who dwells in the secret place of the Most High
shall abide under the shadow of the Almighty.
PSALM 91:1 NKJV

How do you find rest and calm when there's trouble and rumors all around you—when enemies seek your ruin and the winds of adversity are howling? You must stay close to God. You must dwell (consistently live) in the shelter of the Most High and abide (remain) under His mighty shadow. But what does it mean to remain under God's shadow?

Much of the Negev in southern Israel is one vast, barren, unforgiving desert baking under the heat of the sun and frequently blasted by high winds. Travelers took shelter behind great rocks during windstorms and rested in their shadow during the hottest part of the day. God is just like that to His people. He is a "shelter from the wind and a refuge from the storm. . .and the shadow of a great rock in a thirsty land" (Isaiah 32:2 NIV).

Because you're a Christian, Jesus lives in your heart. The Spirit of God's Son dwells in you. But there is more to the picture. He said, "'Abide in Me, and I in you'" (John 15:4 NKJV). Jesus lives in you, but you must also live continually in Him. This means seeking Him in prayer and staying close to Him by obeying Him.

God is a Great Rock in a hostile landscape, and He is more than able to protect you. So stay close to Him, in His shadow.

THE INDWELLING WORD

Let the word of Christ dwell in you richly.
COLOSSIANS 3:16 NKJV

Jeremiah said, "'When I discovered your words, I devoured them. They are my joy and my heart's delight'" (Jeremiah 15:16 NLT). But what does this mean? How can you *eat* God's Word? You do this by taking His words into your mind and heart, meditating upon them and absorbing them, and allowing them to inspire you and give you life. Just as you must chew, swallow, and digest natural food, so you must take God's Word into your very being.

Paul wrote that you are to be "nourished in the words of faith and of the good doctrine which you have carefully followed" (1 Timothy 4:6 NKJV). You allow the Word of Christ to nourish you and dwell in you richly when you make time every day to read it and learn from it. This can be difficult to do in today's busy world, especially if you have a high-demand job that taxes you mentally, physically, and emotionally every day. You may have so much to do that you feel you don't have time to take in God's Word.

But failing to read the Bible is like failing to eat regular meals: You may get away with it for a little while, but eventually this habit will catch up with you. You'll feel weak. And if you do without spiritual nourishment, you won't know right from wrong. So take in a meal of scripture today. "Your word I have hidden in my heart, that I might not sin against You" (Psalm 119:11 NKJV).

LAUGHTER AND WELLNESS

A cheerful heart is good medicine,
but a crushed spirit dries up the bones.
PROVERBS 17:22 NIV

Many modern doctors affirm the truth of this scripture by embracing laughter therapy, which teaches that people who cut loose and laugh will begin to enjoy improved health.

Doctors know that laughter is a natural medicine. It benefits people's physical and emotional beings. It can aid in preventing heart disease by increasing blood flow and improving the way blood vessels work. Laughter has the ability to relax a person's entire body and relieve stress. It can also strengthen the body's immune system and release endorphins to alleviate pain.

Life is often serious business, but it's possible to be sober and serious to the detriment of your health. And definitely if you have a crushed spirit—a discouraged, depressed state of mind—your health is going to suffer. There are quite a number of psychosomatic illnesses caused by little more than negative mental attitudes.

It will do you a world of good to rent a comedy movie and spend a couple of hours laughing. You can't live a life of unrelieved seriousness, stress, and worry without suffering for it. And besides the benefits to your physical and emotional health, laughter lightens your mood and causes you to have a more hopeful attitude. A happy, positive attitude will help you face life and rise above difficulties.

"For the happy heart, life is a continual feast" (Proverbs 15:15 NLT). So enjoy laughter as much as you can.

A LIVING SACRIFICE

I plead with you to give your bodies to God because of all he has done for you. Let them be a living and holy sacrifice...
This is truly the way to worship him.
ROMANS 12:1 NLT

You might sometimes think that being a disciple of Jesus is nothing but privation and suffering, since several verses talk about dying to self and killing your desires. Romans 12:1 describes laying yourself on God's altar as a "living sacrifice," and that might worry you since another verse says, "Those who are Christ's have crucified the flesh with its passions and desires" (Galatians 5:24 NKJV). You might begin to think that *truly* following Jesus is a life void of pleasure and fun.

Certainly you'll be called upon to make personal sacrifices out of love for God and others, and certainly you must not give in to the *sinful* passions and desires of your flesh—such as hatred, murder, adultery, and greed—but you will have many desires that are perfectly in line with the will of God. That's why He promises, "Delight yourself also in the LORD, and He shall give you the desires of your heart" (Psalm 37:4 NKJV).

So don't be afraid to yield your body as a "living sacrifice." Let His Holy Spirit have His way in your heart. Listen to Him when He tells you to say no to a selfish desire, or urges you to crucify hatred, jealousy, and covetousness. He wants what's best for you, and though you'll die to sinful passions and desires, you'll be truly coming alive.

LETTING IT PASS

Overlook an offense and bond a friendship;
fasten on to a slight and—good-bye, friend!
PROVERBS 17:9 MSG

Everyone makes mistakes, but some men are definitely more prone to speak without thinking and cause offense. Other men are always scarfing up the last donut—their third one—without asking whether you'd had one yet. Or they borrow a valuable tool and lose it. . .then inform you that they can't afford to replace it at this time. And you need it for work on Monday. Then the ball is in your court. How do you respond?

Hopefully, you'll be able to let the donut go without too many problems. It is, after all, a rather minor offense. But it may be more difficult to forgive hurtful words or larger losses, especially if this isn't the first time they've happened. But think carefully before you react. Is this really worth losing a friend over? Probably not.

You can still express your disappointment and let him know how this makes you feel, calmly. And you probably should express your emotions. It's not wise to hold a grudge. Leviticus 19:18 (MSG) says, "'Don't. . .carry a grudge against any of your people.'" It then goes on to say, "'Love your neighbor as yourself,'" which is the whole reason why you shouldn't nurse grudges.

God's commandments about love and forgiveness have practical applications in your everyday life and in the workplace. They may not be easy to implement, but they're guaranteed to work.

INTERNATIONAL LEFTHANDERS DAY

*When the children of Israel cried out to the LORD, the LORD
raised up a deliverer for them: Ehud the son of Gera,
the Benjamite, a left–handed man.*
JUDGES 3:15 NKJV

In past generations, if a child was born left-handed, this trait was viewed as abnormal and unacceptable. Some higher-ups got the idea into their heads that when left-handed children went to school, they should be forced to learn to write with their right hand. Eventually, they realized that they were going to a lot of trouble over nothing and causing perfectly normal children to feel rejected.

International Lefthanders Day promotes awareness of the challenges of being left-handed in a right-handed world. For example, left-handed workmen must adapt in order to use tools designed for right-handed workers.

But there are also advantages: Left-handed people often have above-average levels of creativity and imagination. For example, the southpaw hero Ehud came up with an inspired method to stop the Moabite king who was oppressing his people. In ancient Israel, men always wore weapons on their left thigh. But Ehud concealed a dagger on his *right* thigh, where the guards didn't think to look. Then, when he was alone with the dictator, he whipped it out and slew him.

We all have talents, abilities, and quirks that set us apart from other people—and which others sometimes think odd. But Paul challenges believers, asking, "Why do you judge your brother? Or why do you show contempt for your brother?" (Romans 14:10 NKJV).

Some people are just different from others, and you must learn to accept them.

DON'T LOSE YOUR CROWN

Hold on to what you have,
so that no one will take away your crown.
REVELATION 3:11 NLT

James said, "Blessed is the man who endures temptation; for. . .he will receive the crown of life which the Lord has promised to those who love Him" (James 1:12 NKJV). This crown symbolizes your salvation and is a gift—free and undeserved—to those who believe in and love Jesus.

Elsewhere, Peter speaks of another crown: "When the Chief Shepherd appears, you will receive the crown of glory that will never fade away" (1 Peter 5:4 NIV). Many Bible scholars believe that when Peter speaks about the "crown of glory," it's *separate* from the crown of life. Can someone have more than one crown in heaven? Jesus does. "On his head were many crowns" (Revelation 19:12 KJV).

When promising "the crown of glory," Peter was talking to older, mature Christians who watched over the church and set an example for other believers. The crown of life is given to *all* believers, and cannot be taken from you by any man, but the crown of glory is an award for exceptional service.

Unlike the crown of life, however, it appears that people *can* lose this crown by not fulfilling what God has called them to do, as Revelation 3:11 warns. If God has given you a task to do and you neglect it, He will have to find someone else to do it. . .and they will receive the reward originally intended for you. So be faithful to obey God and fulfill your calling.

AVOID DRIFTING AWAY

We must pay the most careful attention. . .
to what we have heard, so that we do not drift away.
HEBREWS 2:1 NIV

Most people who leave their faith in God behind don't make a sudden, deliberate decision to do so. Rather, they slowly drift away, little by little, day by day. They gradually become colder to the Lord, lose interest in prayer, reading the Word, and fellowshipping with other Christians, and, over time, value their relationship with God less and less.

Hebrews 2:3 (NIV) asks, "How shall we escape if we ignore so great a salvation?" But that's what many people do. They don't dramatically revolt against God. They simply ignore Him for prolonged periods of time. Eventually such people become "nearsighted and blind, forgetting that they have been cleansed from their past sins" (2 Peter 1:9 NIV). First, they become nearsighted, their eyes out of focus. Eventually they completely lose all spiritual sight.

They often still go through the outward motions of being a Christian, but their heart has departed. They question the basic beliefs of the faith and believe it's irrelevant to their life in this modern world.

What is the solution? How can you avoid this happening to you? You must pay careful attention to what you have heard from the Bible. When you hear the Word, ponder it and allow it to change you. "'Today, if you hear his voice, do not harden your hearts'" (Hebrews 3:7–8 NIV). Pray and ask God to renew your relationship with Him. And determine to truly *live* your faith.

MEDITATE ON GOD

Be still, and know that I am God.
PSALM 46:10 KJV

There's a time to earnestly pray for what you need, and there's a time to praise God for providing all your needs. But there is *also* a time to meditate, to simply think deeply on who God is for an extended period. At times like that, focus entirely on Him and keep your mind from wandering. God will reward you with a deeper knowledge of His nature and His love.

Some Christians shy away from meditation, thinking that Eastern religions have a monopoly on it, but the Bible talked about meditation thousands of years ago, long before any modern fads. God commanded, "Be still, and know that I am God" (Psalm 46:10 KJV). You are to still your heart and focus on knowing Him—that He is almighty God, exalted above all else, supreme, holy, beautiful, and glorious in every way.

You should also meditate on the wonderful things God has done in your life and in the lives of others. Think of His miracles, both great and small. "I meditate on all Your works; I muse on the work of Your hands" (Psalm 143:5 NKJV).

Also, when you read the Bible, don't simply hurry through it. Pause at a verse and meditate deeply on its meaning. "Oh, how I love Your law! It is my meditation all the day" (Psalm 119:97 NKJV). Paul said, "Meditate on these things; give yourself entirely to them" (1 Timothy 4:15 NKJV). Meditate on God and the things of God today.

LOVE DRIVES OUT FEAR

There is no fear in love; but perfect love casts out fear,
because fear involves torment. But he who fears
has not been made perfect in love.
1 JOHN 4:18 NKJV

This is a beautiful scripture, but what exactly does it mean? Well, in the verses leading up to this, John wrote: "We have known and *believed* the love that God has for us. God is love, and he who abides in love abides in God, and God in him. Love has been perfected among us in this: that we may have *boldness* in the day of *judgment*" (1 John 4:16–17 NKJV, emphasis added).

Elsewhere, Paul wrote: "I am convinced that neither death nor life. . .nor anything else in all creation, will be able to separate us from the love of God that is in Christ Jesus our Lord" (Romans 8:38–39 NIV). If you've believed this amazing love God has for you, and are convinced that *nothing* can separate you from it, then you know you have nothing to fear from God in the day of judgment.

These are basic Christian truths, but it's good to be reminded of them. Sometimes you may worry that you're not *good* enough to be saved. That's true, by the way. None of us are good enough to deserve salvation. We are all utterly dependent on the mercy of God. That's how you were saved in the first place, and nothing has changed there.

When you know that God loves you more than words can express, and that nothing can separate you from His love, this drives out all worry and fear.

DON'T BE COVETOUS

Don't set your heart on anything that is your neighbor's.
EXODUS 20:17 MSG

In the New King James Version, Exodus 20:17 says, "'You shall not covet. . . anything that is your neighbor's.'" But *covet* is a bit of an archaic word, not in common use today. You might have a vague idea that to be *covetous* means to be greedy or selfish, but what exactly does it mean? *The Message* translates *covet* well: "Don't set your heart on anything that is your neighbor's."

The dictionary defines it this way: "To desire wrongfully, inordinately, or without due regard for the rights of others." Thus, if you covet your neighbor's wife, you'll eventually seek to commit adultery with her—not caring about the pain this causes her, her husband, and their children.

If you covet your neighbor's wealth, you'll seek ways to get it from him—or coveting will cause you to be bitter that you don't have what he has. The Bible advises, "Keep your lives free from the love of money and be content with what you have" (Hebrews 13:5 NIV). In fact, you do well if you keep your life free from covetousness of *all* kinds. You spare yourself a lot of trouble if you're just content.

One good way to be content with what you have is to remind yourself of the tremendous rewards that you'll one day have in heaven. God will abundantly compensate you for your lack in the here and now. That's why Jesus said, "'Blessed are you who are poor, for yours is the kingdom of God'" (Luke 6:20 NIV).

BETTER DAYS AHEAD

"You will surely forget your trouble,
recalling it only as waters gone by."
JOB 11:16 NIV

Sometimes you're made to pass through a valley of suffering, and more often than not, it has to do with family issues, financial crises, or health problems. At the time, you may not even be certain that you'll survive. It looks like you'll crash. Perhaps you disobeyed God, or you acted rashly or inconsiderately to others, and now the consequences of your actions are rising like floodwaters around you. Or perhaps problems have come upon you for no fault of your own.

Yet, difficult as your circumstances may be, and difficult as it might be to believe it, soon enough you'll be laughing again and will forget your troubles. They'll be as waters that have evaporated away. David said of God, "For his anger lasts only a moment, but his favor lasts a lifetime; weeping may stay for the night, but rejoicing comes in the morning" (Psalm 30:5 NIV). It's vital to remember when passing through tests that God's favor lasts your entire lifetime; His discipline, by contrast, is usually brief.

God doesn't get any pleasure out of causing His children to suffer, yet some Christians have been led to believe that God is primarily focused on holiness, indignation, and punishment. He does allow suffering, true, but it usually only lasts long enough to bring about good in your life. "The LORD comforts his people and will have compassion on his afflicted ones" (Isaiah 49:13 NIV).

KEEP HIS COMMANDMENTS

"If you love Me, keep My commandments."
JOHN 14:15 NKJV

Jesus made it very clear what it meant to be His follower. It goes without saying that you have to believe in Him, and as a Christian you do that, but do you wonder at times whether your faith is genuine, if you truly *know* God? Many Christians ask themselves this from time to time. The Bible even advises, "Examine yourselves as to whether you are in the faith. Test yourselves" (2 Corinthians 13:5 NKJV).

And *how* do you test yourself? The apostle John gave a very simple litmus test. He wrote, "By this we know that we know Him, if we keep His commandments" (1 John 2:3 NKJV). It doesn't get much simpler than that.

But which commandments are most important? According to Matthew 22:36–39, the two greatest commands—the ones you must make *certain* to obey—are "to love God with all your heart" and to love others as you love yourself. John also gave a very simple answer, saying, "This is His commandment: that we should believe on the name of His Son Jesus Christ and love one another" (1 John 3:23 NKJV).

There are a number of other doctrines that you must believe to be sound in the faith, but it's absolutely foundational to love and believe in God and His Son, and to genuinely love your neighbor. If you have this foundation in place, you cannot only be assured that your faith is genuine, but you'll be certain to *grow* as a Christian.

ENTERING INTO GOD'S PRESENCE

Let us come before his presence with thanksgiving.
PSALM 95:2 KJV

The book of Psalms commands God's people to come before His presence with thankful hearts, and even to "come before his presence with singing" (Psalm 100:2 KJV). In Old Testament times, the temple in Jerusalem was the place where God sometimes manifested Himself as the Shekinah glory in the innermost chamber, the holy of holies. Thus, when people entered the temple, they went with an attitude of reverence and awe, offering thanks to God for His goodness and singing songs of praise.

Likewise today, when you worship God, it brings you into His presence. As a Christian, you must remember that you're not praying to a distant deity who may or may not be listening, but you are entering into the very throne room of God. "Let us therefore come boldly unto the throne of grace, that we may obtain mercy, and find grace to help in time of need" (Hebrews 4:16 KJV). You have an audience with your Father, and He's attentive to what you're saying.

But have you ever prayed and, while you were praying, realized that although you were speaking words, you didn't really have faith that you were actually talking to God? You weren't quite sure that He was listening? The problem may have been that you failed to enter His presence *before* you began praying.

Before you begin asking God for things, make sure that you've entered into His presence. And one of the best ways to do that is with a thankful heart and praise.

GETTING DISTRACTED

"While your servant was busy here and there,
the man disappeared."
1 Kings 20:40 niv

One day a prophet of God called out to King Ahab after a critical campaign and said, "Your servant went into the thick of the battle, and someone came to me with a captive and said, 'Guard this man. If he is missing, it will be your life for his life. . .' While your servant was busy here and there, the man disappeared'" (1 Kings 20:39–40 niv).

This was a parable to show Ahab that he, king of Israel, was guilty for letting the wicked king of Aram go free after he had defeated him. However, let's focus here on *this* important thought:

Many men have, at times, become so busy with a little here and there that they failed to focus on what was truly important. They allowed themselves to get sidetracked in nonessentials and before they knew it, they'd fiddled away their time. Either they get continually distracted from a task, or else they simply keep procrastinating.

The Bible tells you that you must cultivate the virtue of self-control (2 Peter 1:6 niv). Paul said that men of God must be "self-controlled. . .and disciplined" (Titus 1:8 niv). Even if you're bored with a task, such as a project at work, you must put forth the effort to focus on it and finish it. Or even if you shy away from a responsibility because it's difficult or unpleasant, such as disciplining a child, roll up your sleeves and do it. You'll be glad you did.

CONTROLLING YOUR EYES

*"I made a covenant with my eyes not
to look with lust at a young woman."*
JOB 31:1 NLT

Job lived during an era when polygamy was acceptable, yet he had only one wife. And wealthy men who didn't want the complication of extra marriages could simply take concubines. Job was the richest man in the East, yet he was satisfied with *one* woman. It helped that she was—judging by the beauty their daughters inherited (Job 42:15)—exceptionally lovely. But *most* men's eyes still would've wandered. Why didn't Job's?

Job realized that unless he determined ahead of time not to look lustfully at beautiful women, that his eyes naturally *would* wander—and one thing would lead to another. So he made a covenant (a commitment, a promise) *not* to allow his eyes to linger. Then, when faced with temptation, he refused to lust.

In modern times, men are constantly being bombarded with sexually provocative sights, both in the media and in real life. Even if you don't go looking for it, it can ambush you. If you haven't given thought to the matter ahead of time and determined your reaction, you almost can't help but gawk. But it can be very habit-forming and addictive.

The secret to victory is to gain control of your thoughts *beforehand* and determine not to look in lust, even if a woman deliberately tempts you. "Do not lust in your heart after her beauty or let her captivate you with her eyes" (Proverbs 6:25 NIV). Look away, if necessary. Ask God to help you. And don't give up.

CONFIDENT IN CHRIST

*In him and through faith in him we may
approach God with freedom and confidence.*
EPHESIANS 3:12 NIV

So often when men pray to God for a pressing need, a sense of sinfulness rises up to discourage them. The thoughts frequently come in waves: *You're unworthy. God won't answer your prayers. You might as well stop praying.* This is the voice of the enemy. His name, Satan, means "accuser" in Hebrew, and he doesn't just accuse *you* of sin. The Bible calls him "the accuser of our brethren" (Revelation 12:10 NKJV). He accuses *all* believers.

If you've given your heart to Christ, God has forgiven you and made you an heir of His eternal kingdom. If there's current sin that you haven't repented of, however, it will hinder God from blessing you in this life (Isaiah 59:1–2). That's why His Holy Spirit convicts you to repent (John 16:7–8).

But know this also: God *will* forgive you as you confess your failings to Him (1 John 1:9). The devil may try to accuse and condemn you, telling you that God won't forgive you—but don't listen to that lie! God *does* forgive. "Let us therefore come boldly to the throne of grace, that we may obtain mercy and find grace to help in time of need" (Hebrews 4:16 NKJV).

Are you in a time of need? Are you desperate for mercy? Christ's death on the cross, His shed blood, has made the way to His Father's throne open. Your sins are forgiven in Christ. You can come to God's throne with your prayer requests, boldly and with confidence.

GOD CARES ENOUGH TO ACT

Anyone who wants to approach God must believe both that he exists and that he cares enough to respond to those who seek him.

HEBREWS 11:6 MSG

You can believe in God, yet lack faith that He cares enough to respond to your heartfelt prayers. Many men believe that God exists and sent His Son to die for their sins; they even concede that He answered prayers in Bible times, but they have little faith that He *still* does. They've been disappointed when past prayers weren't answered, and this has led them to believe that God doesn't involve Himself with people today except in truly unusual circumstances.

They basically believe that God has already done about as much as He is ever *going* to do, and that from here on, it's up to people to work hard, seize opportunities, and take care of themselves. Small wonder that they don't bother to spend much time in prayer! No surprise that they end up thinking that they can pretty much manage life without God's help. They believe that they *have* to.

It's true that God expects you to work hard to provide for yourself and your family, and that He expects you to think hard to solve many of your problems, but God is still very active in the world. He still helps the helpless. And He still helps ordinary people who find themselves in unexpected difficulties.

Yes, He cares. And yes, He responds to those who earnestly seek Him. But you have to continually seek Him and not give up easily.

FEELING LIKE A FAILURE

God is not unjust; he will not forget your work and the love
you have shown him as you have helped his people.
HEBREWS 6:10 NIV

Sometimes you may feel like a failure, as if your whole life of attempting to serve God has amounted to nothing. . .or to precious little. What do you have to show for years of faithfulness? You haven't even managed to lead your neighbor to the Lord. And then there's that rebellious child who, despite your admonitions and prayers, seems determined to go his or her own willful way.

Isaiah expressed his frustration this way: "I said, 'I have labored in vain; I have spent my strength for nothing at all. Yet what is due me is in the LORD's hand, and my reward is with my God'" (Isaiah 49:4 NIV). Even though he was despondent, he still couldn't help but believe that God saw his heart and would reward him accordingly.

Hebrews 6:10 (NIV) says, "God is not unjust; he will not forget your work and the love you have shown him as you have helped his people." He sees everything you do, and because He's *not* unjust, He will surely reward you. After all, by helping His people you were showing love for God Himself. The same principle is at play in the following verse: "Whoever is kind to the poor lends to the LORD, and he will reward them for what they have done" (Proverbs 19:17 NIV).

It's worth it to serve the Lord. You may feel like you've failed, but God sees your faithfulness.

PRACTICING HOSPITALITY

When God's people are in need, be ready to help them.
Always be eager to practice hospitality.
ROMANS 12:13 NLT

The ancient Hebrews were urged to show kindness to strangers, to show hospitality by taking them into their homes for the night (Job 31:32). They were expected to feed them, and were responsible to protect guests under their roof. Examples of this are Lot taking in two strangers (who turned out to be angels) in Sodom, and the old man in Gibeah taking in the man from Ephraim and his concubine (Genesis 19:1–3; Judges 19:14–21).

These days, such hospitality is rare. With so much crime and users eager to take advantage of soft-hearted people, it's considered dangerous and unadvisable. Granted, you should use wisdom when inviting strangers into your home for the night.

But the Bible still says, "*Always* be *eager* to practice hospitality" (Romans 12:13 NLT, emphasis added). So let's look at other important ways of showing hospitality. What about when a new family comes to your church, doesn't know anyone, and needs friends? Are you eager to practice hospitality? Do you talk with your wife about inviting them over for lunch? Do you help them get settled into your town?

And what about when poor families in your church are struggling without basic needs—without warm clothes, food, or other necessities? Do you simply smile, wave, and say, "Depart in peace, be ye warmed and filled" (James 2:15–16 KJV), or do you reach out in practical ways to help them?

Keep your eyes open. There are many ways to be "a lover of hospitality" today (Titus 1:8 KJV).

AVOID PRIDE OF ACCOMPLISHMENT

By the grace of God I am what I am, and His grace toward me
was not in vain; but I labored more abundantly than they all,
yet not I, but the grace of God which was with me.
1 CORINTHIANS 15:10 NKJV

After Jesus departed, His apostles began to proclaim the Gospel. Jesus had told them, "'You shall be witnesses to Me in Jerusalem, and in all Judea and Samaria, and to the end of the earth'" (Acts 1:8 NKJV), and He had commanded, "'Go into all the world and preach the gospel'" (Mark 16:15 NKJV). However, for the next twenty years, all twelve apostles remained in Jerusalem, content to preach mostly in nearby Judea and Samaria.

Paul, meanwhile, was going "into all the world," to far-flung cities of the Roman Empire. So he wasn't exaggerating when he said, "I labored more abundantly than they all." But those accomplishments didn't make Paul think that he was better than others. He had just finished stating, "I am the least of the apostles. . .not worthy to be called an apostle" (1 Corinthians 15:9 NKJV).

Paul was aware that God was using him to accomplish great things, but he also knew that it was the power of God doing the healing miracles, anointing him to speak, and changing lives—not him. And he was also painfully aware of his own unworthiness.

When you accomplish something great, don't put on false humility and say it's nothing. If it was praiseworthy, acknowledge the fact. Admit that God used you. But be sure to give Him the praise for using you.

CAST YOUR CARES ON GOD

Cast your cares on the LORD and he will sustain you;
he will never let the righteous be shaken.
PSALM 55:22 NIV

This passage of scripture has been a source of great comfort to millions of believers, yet some people protest, "I wish it *were* that simple! When huge problems come, you simply calmly hand them to God and He takes care of everything?" This is a valid question, so let's look at this verse in context.

Earlier in the psalm, David spoke of serious threats, of conspiracies, of battles raging against him, and of the stinging betrayal of friends. (This likely happened during the civil war when Absalom revolted.) David confessed his fear, saying, "My heart is in anguish within me; the terrors of death have fallen on me. Fear and trembling have beset me" (verses 4–5).

David was eventually able to cast his cares on God and experience peace, but it wasn't a quick or easy process. He also had to plan, strategize, and lead his forces against his enemies' attacks. And he had to pray desperately day after day, several times a day. He said, "Evening, morning and noon I cry out in distress" (verse 17). David *continually* cast his cares and fears upon God, until he finally received assurance that God had heard him and would answer.

Yes, you *can* simply calmly hand small problems over to God, but when huge problems assail you, you may have to desperately and repeatedly cast your cares on Him. And He will answer.

RECOVERING THE LOST

If you know people who have wandered off from God's truth, don't write them off. Go after them. Get them back and you will have rescued precious lives from destruction.

JAMES 5:20 MSG

It's easy to write off people who have backslidden from the faith. You tell yourself that it's a free country, and it's their decision, after all. And these things are true. Plus, you tell yourself, they knew full well what they were doing when they went back to their worldly ways. And that, too, is true. But the question is: are you *concerned* about them? Do you pray for them and reach out to them?

Jesus said:

> *"What man of you, having a hundred sheep, if he loses one of them, does not leave the ninety-nine in the wilderness, and go after the one which is lost until he finds it? And when he has found it, he lays it on his shoulders, rejoicing. And when he comes home, he calls together his friends and neighbors, saying to them, 'Rejoice with me, for I have found my sheep which was lost!'"*

(Luke 15:4–6 NKJV)

Jesus took it for granted that *every* person listening would be motivated to scour the desert for a lost sheep, asking, "What man does *not* go after it until he finds it?" And how much more valuable is a person than a sheep?

In the end, the person must make up his own mind whether he'll return to the Lord or not, but you can be a big part of helping restore him.

THE NATURE OF LOVE

If I have a faith that can move mountains, but do not have love,
I am nothing. If I give all I possess to the poor. . .that I may
boast, but do not have love, I gain nothing.
1 CORINTHIANS 13:2–3 NIV

You may wonder, "How could I give all that I possess to alleviate the suffering of the poor, and *not* have love? Isn't such giving a clear proof of love?" Besides, Jesus told the rich young ruler, "Sell your possessions and give to the poor, and you will have treasure in heaven" (Matthew 19:21 NIV). But Paul clarifies that even if you give all that you have to the poor, but have selfish motives for doing so ("that I may boast"), you'll gain nothing and receive no reward.

Paul goes on in verses 4-7 to give the definition of love. Love is *not* boastful or easily angered; love is patient, kind, humble, honors others, seeks others' benefit, and keeps no record of wrongs. So even if you go through an outward show of charity, but are boastful, easily angered, impatient, envious, proud, self-seeking, or unforgiving, you aren't motivated by God's love.

Jesus also promised that if you have great faith you can say to a mountain, "'Be removed and be cast into the sea,'" and it will be done (Matthew 21:21 NKJV), but as Paul pointed out, "If I have a faith that can move mountains, but do not have love, I am nothing." So *love*—love God and others—first and foremost, and you'll be greatly rewarded in all you do.

INTO THE WIND

Then [Jesus] said to his disciples, "Let us go back to Judea."
"But Rabbi," they said, "a short while ago the Jews there
tried to stone you, and yet you are going back?"
JOHN 11:7–8 NIV

We humans love to move with the wind.

When I sail with friends, we long for that wind thirty degrees astern. When I'm riding my bike, I love it when I get a tailwind on the way home!

But then I noticed something when I walked our collie, Symba, on windy days: If it was breezy, he put that sensitive snout into the air, savored all the aromas that were coming to him, and insisted on walking *into* the wind. It was the same whether the wind carried pleasant odors to him or odors that seemed to bring him a challenge, such as other dogs that might be a threat or people he didn't know.

And then I thought of all the characters in the Bible who walked—with God—*into* the wind:

Moses to face down Pharaoh, to free God's people from horrible bondage; Daniel to face down Nebuchadnezzar and his advisers trying to destroy the Jewish people. Paul to Rome, to take the Gospel to the single most dangerous place he could go.

Jesus, to face the authorities whom He knew would stop at nothing to kill Him.

Me, to walk joyfully and graciously with Jesus, among people at work who love their immorality.

Into the wind.

I hope I've learned a little from my collie.

INNER ROOMS

*"But when you pray, go into your room, close the door
and pray to your Father, who is unseen. Then your Father,
who sees what is done in secret, will reward you."*
MATTHEW 6:6 NIV

When you really want to pray, any place can be a secret place.

Jesus told us not to pray outwardly, in ways that draw attention to ourselves. He told us to go into an inner room, where nobody can see us, and trust the One who hears us in that secret place.

But an inner room doesn't have to be an inner room. I've got a hundred inner rooms that I use to hide the fact that I'm praying.

Nobody really believes that you're praying if you're also chewing gum. Chewing gum makes a good prayer room.

Nobody really believes that you're praying if you've got headphones coming from your phone or iPod. This is especially true when you're doing that little rock-and-roll head bob. They don't know that you're emphasizing your prayers, not rocking to the music. Headphones make a good prayer room.

Nobody really believes that you're praying if you've got your nose in a book. . .like this one.

Nobody believes you're praying if you're floating on a lake or the ocean in a water hammock with a baseball cap shielding your face from the sun.

Nobody believes you're praying if you're writing or typing intently on your laptop. . .only you're typing your prayers.

A hundred prayer rooms. Ways to pray "without ceasing" (1 Thessalonians 5:17 NKJV), in secret, to the God who sees in secret.

THE POOR CYNIC

But I give [a] judgment as one who by the
Lord's mercy is trustworthy.
1 CORINTHIANS 7:25 NIV

One of my coworkers, a lady about my age, had a parent who died, leaving her as administrator of her parents' estate, as I had been of mine a few years before. We were talking in the break room. I told her how my experience was wonderful, in a way, in the midst of the difficulties: There was not a single person in my family whom I could not trust. In fact, some even volunteered information that would reduce their share of the inheritance and increase everybody else's. It made the experience a lot more gratifying. Most of them are Christians, and they're all very sincere people.

My friend was having exactly the opposite experience. She couldn't trust anybody in her family; she was having to fight everybody. My poor friend was surrounded by grasping, lying people.

So now she trusts nobody. She assumes that everyone is lying to her. She fends for herself alone. . .even when she doesn't have to!

And I can show her that she doesn't have to, that there is a God whom she can trust, just as—in me—she has a friend she can trust. Now I try doubly hard to be reliable for my poor friend in the break room, so that she doesn't become a complete cynic.

Have pity on the poor cynic. Give him, or her, someone to trust: first yourself, then your Trustworthy Savior. . .

OXYMORON

"The one who is unwilling to work shall not eat."
2 Thessalonians 3:10 niv

"Oxymoron": a contradiction in terms. "Jumbo Shrimp"; "Army Intelligence"; "*Labor Day Holiday.*"

It just seems odd to me, celebrating my "labor" by taking a day off.

As though we can celebrate our labor while not actually wanting to work.

For a while I was on the management team responsible for hiring and firing at work in the central supply/surgical instrument department of a large city hospital. I developed a philosophy that I still hold: Don't look for someone who *needs the job*; look for someone who *wants the work*. (Actually, the ideal is someone who exemplifies both.) But someone who doesn't want the work will do us no good. There's *lots* of work.

I also learned that most jobs are not so much a matter of skill, but of will: if someone is willing to do the work, he or she can usually be taught the job.

But I keep coming back to that key: *want the work*. It's the key for me, too. Notice that the verse does not say, "If one doesn't have a job. . ." but, "If one is unwilling to work."

One thing I've always hated about work is getting there and then spinning my wheels on piddly stuff.

And I think that should be our attitude as Christians: "Give me the job, and then let me get to it!"

We should need no supervision.

Bulldogs. At work, Christians should be known as exactly that.

Bulldogs.

Show us the work, and watch us shine.

NERVOUS, NERVOUS, NERVOUS

For what I received I passed on to you as of first importance:
that Christ died for our sins according to the Scriptures, that he was
buried, that he was raised on the third day according to the
Scriptures. . . . But by the grace of God I am what I am.
1 CORINTHIANS 15:3–4, 10 NIV

We are God's ambassadors. This means that people will hold God to whatever we say about Him. On top of that, if what we tell people about God is wrong, He isn't going to back it up.

Yet He will hold us accountable for it.

Quite a spot to be on. We'd better explain Him correctly, or God will hold us accountable. As will the world.

We catch it coming, and we catch it going. Who on earth can handle that kind of responsibility? The answer is. . .nobody can. I can't. You can't.

That's why the stories He asks us to tell are so breathtakingly simple. Whether it's the story of Jesus or our own story that we tell the world, they're both almost impossible to get wrong!

Plus we have the Holy Spirit to back us up, to give our words power, and to prod us if we go off on some tangent.

And He has left us His Word, which tells the life of Jesus, and what He did to save us, four times—in black and white, unmistakable. And surely we know our own testimony! This isn't metaphysics. It isn't some convoluted quest for enlightenment. There is little to be nervous about.

FAT 'N' HAPPY

Nehemiah said, "Go and enjoy choice food and sweet drinks, and send some to those who have nothing prepared. This day is holy to our Lord. Do not grieve, for the joy of the LORD is your strength."
NEHEMIAH 8:10 NIV

My place is near a chain of fishing lakes that are famous throughout the area. I have a close friend who is way more of a fisherman than I am, so I invited him to go out with me. He had a tough time catching anything, but when he did, he marveled at the size.

After a while he told me why he thought it was so hard to catch fish here. He usually fished reservoirs and other places with tons of fish but little food. The fish jump at anything even resembling a lure or a worm because they're so hungry. "Your fish are too fat 'n' happy," he said. "These lakes are too rich. They don't need the food, so we have to work harder to entice them."

I think it's that way with us and the devil. If we're fat 'n' happy on grace, fat 'n' happy on praise and thanks, fat 'n' happy on prayer and that great feeling of serving someone else, fat 'n' happy on obeying our Lord, fat 'n' happy on God's Word, then the devil's lures just don't have much attraction.

Yes, I know I just compared my friend and me to the devil. But we're both fat 'n' happy on most of that stuff I just listed, so that's a temptation we can handle!

SIN?

*Dear friends, if our hearts do not condemn us, we have confidence
before God and receive from him anything we ask,
because we keep his commands and do what pleases him.*
1 John 3:21–22 niv

Overcoming sin: it's the challenge of every Christian's life. We struggle, we strain, we "put things before the Lord" that we don't like in our lives, we attack one area at a time, and we do a lot of good. We trust God, we ask for the Holy Spirit to help us in practical ways, and He does it. This is all great, but there is a side of this that gets little notice. Most of us overcome sin daily in ways we don't even recognize, ways we can easily build on.

Church. Worshiping God. That's not sin. Shut-in visitation, prison visitation, prayer or devotions with the family, devotional books. No sin there. Relaxation. Recreation. Exercise. Working on the "honey-do" list. Yes, I know it can be overdone. But when I ride my bike, am I sinning? Not likely. I'm staying healthy; I can maybe live and serve the Lord longer. No sin there.

Family barbecues? Sitting on the porch with my wife? Any sin there? No!

When we spend our energy for God's kingdom, when we spend our energy on the good, we don't leave energy or time for sin. That is, indeed, overcoming sin; and we barely even realize it. Then, when we look at all the sins that don't happen in our lives, it gives us momentum to build on, to keep sin out of our lives.

MYSTERY

Now we see only a reflection as in a mirror; then we shall see face to face.
Now I know in part; then I shall know fully, even as I am fully known.
1 CORINTHIANS 13:12 NIV

Mystery.

It's a shame it's such a dirty word to so many people.

But if we can't live with some mystery—and some mysteries—we're likely to be uncomfortable in the kingdom of God.

Partly, it's a personality trait. Some of us are just left-brained, mathematically and mechanically inclined, who like to figure out everything to the point of perfection. My dad was like that: an accountant, an amazing mathematician, a bit of a perfectionist. Though we looked very much alike, our minds worked in exactly opposite ways. He was the epitome of a left-brained, mathematical, systematic thinker; I'm the epitome of a right-brained, poetic, emotional thinker. So what surprised me was the degree to which he expressed the wonder, the awe, the mystery of his faith—the degree to which this precise man was willing to admit what he didn't know, what no one can know. . .yet. I think it strongly affected how I came to accept the faith.

It's a principle that's true throughout life: Be confident of what you do know; readily admit what you don't know; don't shy away from what you can't know.

I have always been impressed that these are Paul's words—*Paul's* words, the words of the theological genius who wrote *Romans*: "We see but a poor reflection in a mirror. . ."

GOD'S WILL

Do not withhold good from those to whom it is due, when it is in your power to act. Do not say to your neighbor, "Come back tomorrow and I'll give it to you"—when you already have it with you.

PROVERBS 3:27–28 NIV

Some obvious things just plain escape me for a long, long time.

There are a couple of obvious ideas about God's will that I didn't combine for years. Idea One: "Nobody's here by accident." God knows where we're going to go, therefore He must have prepared things for us. Idea Two: We all need to find out what God wants us to do, and we shouldn't wait any longer than we have to before we find out.

Here's the combination that escaped me for the longest time. I am where I am; and if I come into contact with something that needs to be done for God, and I can do it, I should do it. So I think I've "found God's will." It always seemed such an elusive concept.

But in most cases, God's will isn't elusive, slippery, or unclear at all. The problem for me is that my combination almost makes it too clear. I'd rather be way more "spiritual" about things, more analytical. But Galatians 6:10 (NIV) brings me back to earth: "Therefore, as we have opportunity, let us do good to all people, especially to those who belong to the family of believers."

We are where we are by God's will. The needs we are presented with, we should meet if we can. To me, that's 90 percent of God's will, plain and simple.

GOD'S HONESTY

In those days Hezekiah became ill and was at the point of death.
The prophet Isaiah son of Amoz went to him and said, "This is what
the LORD says: Put your house in order, because you are going to die."
ISAIAH 38:1 NIV

It was the only time I ever laughed in my wife's face. I had just graduated with a degree in English and journalism. But no job. She said I should get my teaching certificate, that I'd be a great high school teacher. I was way too sophisticated for that. I almost took it as an insult. But I also have this wacky sense of humor. . .

Fourteen years of teaching high school later, I was glad for her honesty.

If we can't handle God's honesty, we will never be able to handle His truth.

Earlier, my wife had made a point that she *didn't* need to make: When I communicated with people, I was either way above their heads, or way too blunt: tactless. God had already been showing me this as people who I thought were friends would begin shying away as they got to know me.

So later, after teaching, I worked as a hospital chaplain for seven years. If you can't be tactful, you can't be a chaplain.

God's truth is easy; His honesty—truth in the particulars—is hard.

Hezekiah reacted to God's honesty, repented of his attitudes, and lived. He didn't need God's truth; he needed God's honesty.

As do we.

Our lives depend on it.

HOW LONG?

*"As in the days when you came out of Egypt,
I will show them my wonders."*
MICAH 7:15 NIV

The women have to avert their eyes, cover them, or the pain snaps through their eyes straight into the front of their heads. They know it's the right tomb. It has the same stone, though it's been moved. And that's the cloth that Jesus' body was rolled in, blood and all.

But suddenly two men are there in lightning-bright garments. Such brilliance replacing such gloom throws them to the ground. They're stunned and amazed. Something unimaginable is happening. But the instruction is simple: "Get up, and go tell his disciples."

Later, they follow Jesus north to Galilee. Jesus is speaking, and a low cloud rolls down the slope—they'd seen it happen on these mountains a thousand times—but then this cloud is blowing back up to the sky with Jesus on it, hands outstretched.

Then, suddenly that headache again: The same two men (*men?*) blazingly dressed, and they barely hear what these men say because of the wonder of how they look and their amazement at what just happened. They can't stop staring. But then the two men say, "What are you doing standing here? He told you what to do!"

How long has it been since God's wonders have left us speechless? Have we seen grace in the trust of a child, grandeur in a sunset, a forest, or a tall ship? How long has it been since an angel has had to bring us back down to earth while we were standing open mouthed with wonder?

STRIPES AND PLAIDS

However, each one of you also must love his wife as he loves himself.
Ephesians 5:33 NIV

Dad was the typical retiree. He had his old clothes, and he wore them. Striped and plaid, gray and khaki, he wore them. When he went out with Mom, he always looked great. But at home, or just to a store? Striped and plaid. Mismatched everything. The typical retiree.

So I finally concluded something about how I dress. It's important how I look when I'm out with my wife. But something else occurred to me. It's just as important how I look *for* her. When I'm painting or working on the car or the boat or the lawn mower, I get out my junk clothes. But when she has to look at me, I've determined to dress to please her. Nothing fancy; just take a little care.

It isn't any harder to dress in stuff she likes than to dress carelessly. And this attitude bleeds over into other areas, too.

This isn't just for wives, but for friends, family, the girlfriend, the fiancée. It's an extension of the attitude the Lord wants me to have in every part of my life: I need to do things for others a little better than I have to.

Especially for my wife. More especially: when I don't *have* to.

HEARTS IN REVERSE

"Others, like seed sown on rocky places, hear the word and at once receive it with joy. But since they have no root, they last only a short time."
MARK 4:16–17 NIV

I was in a discussion with a group of other Christians. A question came up about a friend who seemed to be losing her faith. The question was, "How can somebody do that?"

The discussion went back and forth until a thought hit me. So I said it. "We talk about people who have a mental belief in Christ, but it never finds its way down to their hearts. It sounds like the opposite happened to your friend. Maybe she had a heartfelt belief in the Lord, but it never made it from her *heart* up to her *head*."

I had to repeat it twice. . .because they had heard the opposite so many times.

I've known people who had a highly emotional experience with the Lord that seemed quite deep. And then they turned away from their faith. It never got from their heart to their head.

And what happens, then, when the emotion fades—what happens when your heart fails you and the emotional situation that inspired you to call on the Lord fades—and you can't fall back on what you know because you don't know very much?

We need to grow in our emotions and our understanding at the same time. Until our hearts and our minds complement each other, we will never mature as Christians.

RAISED FOR OUR FORGIVENESS

He was delivered over to death for our sins
and was raised to life for our justification.
ROMANS 4:25 NIV

Peter and John stayed close to Jesus after He was arrested, and John—being "known to the high priest"—was allowed into the high priest's confines, where Jesus was first interrogated. John went back to bring Peter in (John 18:15–16). It was shortly after this that Peter denied, with curses, that he even knew Jesus.

It is a measure of Peter's later honesty and humility that he let the account of his denial be put into writing. But I think I know why. It would explain his extraordinary relief at seeing his Lord alive again.

Peter was the first disciple to enter Jesus' tomb. And in Luke 24:34, reference is made to Jesus appearing to Simon Peter alone, before the famous "closed doors" appearances to the eleven disciples. Why this concentration on Peter?

The denial.

Here's Luke again: When Peter disowned Jesus for the third time, "the Lord turned and looked straight at Peter. . .and [Peter] went outside and wept bitterly" (Luke 22:61–62 NIV).

What an incredible moment. I'm almost surprised it was Judas who committed suicide. Peter had heaped on Jesus His own personal crucifixion. So when Peter met Jesus alive again and found that He would absolve him from his guilt in person *because He had risen*, the relief—mixed with shame at having denied his Lord—must have hit Peter like a tidal wave.

Crucified to forgive our sins, risen to deliver that forgiveness. What a delivery that was for Peter!

And for us.

NOTHING

For we know that our old self was crucified with him so that
the body ruled by sin might be done away with. . .
because anyone who has died has been set free from sin.
ROMANS 6:6–7 NIV

It is the inescapable paradox of Christianity: to be made everything, I must become nothing.

In this area, it seems to be "two steps forward, one step back" for me most of the time. But it helps me to remember Screwtape.

Screwtape?

In C. S. Lewis's book *The Screwtape Letters*, Screwtape is a trainer of beginning "tempters." He gives instructions to his student, Wormwood, about his early mistakes in tempting his target. Wormwood tried to tempt his young Christian subject with the big things: lying, theft, adultery, giving up his faith. But Screwtape criticized him: Don't try to get him to deny his faith; just get him to spend a little too much attention on himself. A little frivolity, a little wasted time or money, and then let it snowball. Make him think he's just a *little bit* of something when he knows—before the Lord—he's nothing.

That works on me. Maybe not putting myself *first*, but putting myself *somewhere* instead of nowhere, concentrating on myself. Get me concentrating on myself—on how good *or* how horrible I can be—instead of concentrating on the Lord, who is all in all.

"For we know that our old self was crucified with him so that the body ruled by sin might be. . ."

Might be "cleansed"? "Changed"? "Helped"?

No: "done away with."

To be free is to sink my nothing into His everything.

TOMORROW, AND TOMORROW, AND TOMORROW

Now listen, you who say, "Today or tomorrow we will go to this or that city,
spend a year there, carry on business and make money." Why, you do not
even know what will happen tomorrow. What is your life? You are a mist
that appears for a little while and then vanishes. Instead, you ought to say,
"If it is the Lord's will, we will live and do this or that." As it is,
you boast in your arrogant schemes. All such boasting is evil.
JAMES 4:13–16 NIV

I have this terrible feeling about what God thinks of all our plans. We express ourselves with a confidence in the future that God calls pride. The fact that we are accustomed to doing it makes it no less an offense. It doesn't matter how culturally ingrained our offenses are; they're still offenses.

I know many, many Christians, including myself when I'm not careful, who exude confidence in the future and in our plans for it. "Next year we will implement such and such a program; these investments will come in at X percent; after five years our membership will increase to X." This scripture calls such statements arrogance. That it is culturally ingrained arrogance doesn't help.

It is born of rank self-sufficiency. It's not the healthy self-sufficiency of doing our best and taking our responsibilities seriously; it's the self-sufficiency of claiming authority over an area that is exclusively God's domain: the *future*.

So God says make your plans, but don't trust your plans. Make your plans with a very light hand, and. . .

Trust Me.

SPIRITUAL DEPENDENCY

Recalling your tears, I long to see you, so that I may be filled with joy.
I am reminded of your sincere faith, which first lived
in your grandmother Lois and in your mother Eunice and,
I am persuaded, now lives in you also.
2 TIMOTHY 1:4–5 NIV

It's one of the saddest situations I encounter: spiritual dependency.

Too often Christians let others become their compass, and when the compass is gone, the dependent Christian has no pole to point to. So he or she just spins.

Paul wrote to Timothy, the son of his soul, what Paul probably knew would be his last letter. In it, he gave the key to avoiding spiritual dependency, quoted above.

There are those who feed off others' spiritual dependence on them: some pastors, parents, or just people with dominating personalities. And there are those who make themselves dependent, who might simply be followers or might admire another's supposed spirituality. But here's the key: they can somehow never bring themselves to actually make that spirituality a part of themselves.

Such was not the case with Timothy. The spiritual tradition and maturity that lived in his mother and grandmother, and in Paul himself, now lived in him. It's the opposite of spiritual dependency. Spiritual dependents are empty of faith—and of almost everything else. They depend on someone else's faith.

I simply ask them: Are you walking in your mentor's footsteps, or is he taking all the steps for you?

They need encouragement from those whose walk is steady. . .to start taking their own steps, before it's too late.

GUS

Remember those in prison as if you were together with them in prison,
and those who are mistreated as if you yourselves were suffering.
HEBREWS 13:3 NIV

Tenth grade. I had just started at Howe Military School. I needed a friend, and I found one.

Agustin Benitez. I don't remember if we were assigned a room together in the Company B barracks, or whether we requested one. I did know that no one wanted to room with little Gus because he ground his teeth when he slept. Didn't bother me. I had grown up in a house less than a hundred yards from the Grand Trunk Western railroad tracks, with only a few trees between. Nothing kept me awake!

We normally switched roommates every three weeks. But Gus and I stayed together through at least three switches. Gus fascinated me, and his life angered me.

Gus's family were refugees from the Castro regime. (His brother was in Company A.) And Gus was intense. They had fled Cuba when Gus was eight. Gus remembered—vividly remembered. Gus's life had a focus, an intense, purposeful, meaningful focus. . .that my life lacked.

Free Cuba. Free Cuba.

And his focus helped form my focus: Christians persecuted and murdered by communist regimes. And a free Cuba.

I've lost contact with Gus, but I haven't lost contact with persecuted Christians. Gus's bulldog tenacity for a free Cuba became the battery powering my prayers and efforts in behalf of Christians—and non-Christians—being persecuted by communists and Muslims.

They need our daily prayers.

So does Gus, and everyone else who works to free them.

A LITTLE PLATO

"Because you have rejected the word of the LORD,
he has rejected you as king."
1 SAMUEL 15:23 NIV

Even God had a hard time finding a decent politician.

The ancient Greek philosopher Plato said many wise things. His "Allegory of the Cave" describes a world where people basically waste their lives on shadows of the real things. It still describes life on this planet quite well.

He gave another allegory, the "Allegory of the Ship." It's simple: There is a struggle over who is going to be captain of a ship. Plato asks the question: Who is likely to win? Someone who is good at running a ship, or someone who is good at gaining power?

You know the answer.

We in the United States live in an elective republic. The same question applies: Who is more likely to win an election? Someone who is adept at administering my township/city/county/state/country, or someone who is adept at getting my vote? The two skill sets are often mutually exclusive. Plato's point is excellently made. How often do we elect people who have no clue how to represent us? It's because the people who want power the most are generally the ones who get power. These are not generally good public *servants*.

We have to be very discerning with our vote and our support. The first person to want power is the last person we should give power to. I look for candidates—especially believers—who have a history of effective administration and *service* in their backgrounds, and support them.

If I can find any.

DELIGHTFUL PRAYER

Take delight in the LORD,
and he will give you the desires of your heart.
PSALM 37:4 NIV

The last part of that verse is so nice; the first part is so hard!

In this psalm, many prayers are answered, yet the word *prayer* is never mentioned. We are told to "commit," to "wait," to "delight in" the Lord, and then He will give us "the desires of our heart," He will "make your righteous reward shine" (Psalm 37:6 NIV). But the word *pray* is nowhere to be found.

I ask myself how few things there are that I actually "delight in"—not just "like," not "enjoy," but "delight in." There aren't many. And how many other things must I avoid "delighting in" if I am truly to "delight in" the Lord?

All of them. Here's the mystery: Psalm 37 treats this process of shedding all delights other than Yahweh Himself as the process of *prayer*. How do I know? Because it's answered! It's the commitment to the Lord, the delighting in, the waiting for, that is answered.

Prayer is the growing process of the child of the living God, no more and no less. It is the devotion to Jesus that multiplies, differentiates, and strengthens the cells of our reborn spirits. Prayer is the expression of desire for our spirit's Father to work His will in ways His child cannot. But the child does not think of himself: His eyes are on his Father. He loves what his Father loves, delights in what his Father delights in. That process is . . .

Prayer.

And it will be answered.

WHEN LIFE HURTS

But we have this treasure in jars of clay to show that this all-surpassing power is from God and not from us. We are hard pressed on every side, but not crushed.

2 Corinthians 4:7–8 niv

I waded the rocky stream with my sandals on. Unlike the surrounding country, the stream was shaded by trees. Soon my whole body felt cooler, even though the wind in my face still felt like someone had opened the door of an oven.

Before long, I realized that the scenery wasn't going to change. The stream wound endlessly through low rock-strewn hills. I slowed down, feeling among the rocks in the streambed, just to pass the time. One rock felt strange. It felt smooth and sharp-edged at the same time. I kept the toe of my sandal gently against it, feeling down with my hand to uncover it.

It was a pottery perfume bottle, but it felt extremely brittle, as though it had shattered but not yet fallen apart. I cupped it in my hands like crystal. It was stronger than it seemed, though. The stopper still fit perfectly, still sealed the tiny bottle, but came out easily. (*That's strange. And why doesn't it just float away?*) In the bottom were a few drops of ointment. It had a strong fragrance, like black licorice.

It was a miracle that it hadn't come open in that stream over the years. It was another miracle that it hadn't fallen to pieces in my hand. How it had survived the battering and the pressure was beyond me. . .

First Day of Autumn

A WORLD WITHOUT CLOCKS?

One of those days Jesus went out to a mountainside to pray,
and spent the night praying to God. When morning came,
he called his disciples to him and chose twelve.
LUKE 6:12–13 NIV

At my job, I have to be very aware of time, for the sake of the surgeons and their patients. As Christians, we often have to be aware of the clock. When we need to be somewhere or do something on time, we should be known for being prompt.

On vacation, however, I heard about something called "Island Time." It's when you forget the clocks and burn the schedule. (I'd been doing this for years; now I had a term for it.) Sometimes we need to live on Island Time. Can I tell my three-year-old grandson, "Yes, let's go for a walk. You've got eight minutes"? Can I say to my aging mother-in-law, "Yeah, I'll work on your leaky toilet seal, but I'm stopping after forty-five minutes"?

And just as there is no substitute for Island Time spent with loved ones, so there is no substitute for Island Time spent with God. Time spent in prayer, Bible study, reading, thinking about how we can help friends or loved ones, or just plain rest often needs to be open ended.

Conscientious about our scheduled obligations—free with time for those we love. One gets the grace of us remembering the watch; the other gets the grace of us ignoring it.

Time on my watch—or Island Time. I know which is better; but in this world, we need to be good at both.

JOSEPH AND POTIPHAR

When [Joseph's] master [Potiphar] heard the story his wife told him, saying, "This is how your slave treated me," he burned with anger. Joseph's master took him and put him in prison, the place where the king's prisoners were confined.

GENESIS 39:19–20 NIV

Potiphar's wife accused Joseph of trying to seduce her, when it was actually the other way around. "She caught him by his cloak and said, 'Come to bed with me!' But he left his cloak in her hand and ran" (Genesis 39:12 NIV). When I've heard it referred to that Potiphar "burned with anger," it's always been assumed that he was angry at Joseph. I looked again; that's not *what it says*. It just says Potiphar was furious. If he was furious at Joseph—a slave from parts unknown—his option was clear: kill him.

But he doesn't. I think he knows full well that his wife is lying (certainly not for the first time!), and that he'll have to take over the responsibilities that Joseph was handling. But he can't side with the slave against his wife. So he treats Joseph about as well as he can, sending him to a prison for the privileged, though that's still no picnic.

Joseph is forgotten for two years, then begins his rise from the ashes to vice president of Egypt.

And all because God saw Joseph doing one thing, the one thing that He longs for from all His people.

He saw Joseph refusing to sin. We should take a hint.

Refuse to sin. It's where everything else begins.

GOD'S LITTLE HELPERS

*Now Sarai, Abram's wife, had borne him no children. But she had
an Egyptian slave named Hagar; so she said to Abram, "The LORD has
kept me from having children. Go, sleep with my slave;
perhaps I can build a family through her."*
GENESIS 16:1–2 NIV

God promises Abram (Abraham) a son, who will be the beginning of a great nation. This promise of descendants is repeated and repeated. Eventually Sarai (Sarah), who is old and barren, gets the bright idea of giving her servant, Hagar, to Abraham to bear this child of promise. This is not an unusual arrangement for that time. They would of course prefer to have children together, but Sarai thinks she is too old.

So Sarai, God's little helper, decides to give Yahweh's promise a little boost with her own little plan. The first result of this plan is hatred between the mothers and their children. The end result of this plan is the deathly, scorpions-in-a-bottle hatred between Arabs/Muslims and Jews that continues unabated to this day. This hatred continues because, while only the Jews' claim is legitimate, both are true.

Why doesn't God reveal to us the whole timeline of His plans for our lives? Why does He force us to live with day-to-day, one-step-at-a-time trust in His long-range plans?

He remembers Sarai and Abram, and the cost of humans playing God's little helper.

Let's let God be God. Let's do what's at hand with all our heart (Colossians 3:23–24) while we listen for God's leading; then let's trust the God who knows the end from the beginning.

THE OTHER SIDE OF THE CALENDAR

Be not forgetful to entertain strangers:
for thereby some have entertained angels unawares.
HEBREWS 13:2 KJV

Do the spiritual beings become aware of time as they travel between worlds?

When an angel came to visit Daniel to reveal some of the events of the last days, he said, "The prince of the Persian kingdom resisted me twenty-one days. Then Michael, one of the chief princes, came to help me" (Daniel 10:13 NIV).

Clearly the angel talked about "twenty-one days" because it was a time reference that would make sense to Daniel, and because he is talking about earthly kingdoms. How do angels measure time normally? Surely not in days.

This passage hints at one way they measure time: completed tasks. This angel fought the "prince of Persia" until the fight was won, but described it in earth days. Then it was on to the next job: visit Daniel. He's been praying.

This might give us a hint about the intensity of what's happening on the angelic side of our calendars, the back side of each date that we don't see, where we get helped unknowingly by the best and strongest angels, where their tasks are measured not by time, but by success.

Do we think of how, and when, and where these successes break through to our side of the calendar? When we write on our calendars, do we think about the angels' side of that calendar?

Have we prayed?

THE BEST THINGS

"His master replied, 'Well done, good and faithful servant!
You have been faithful with a few things; I will put you in charge
of many things. Come and share your master's happiness!'"
MATTHEW 25:21 NIV

I once had a very wise Bible college professor who said something that has stuck with me. (He also had a name I can't forget: Halton D. Starr. It's the only time I ever encountered the first name "Halton.") There are some things I'll spend a lifetime applying, and this is one of them:

> *You don't get the best things*
> *by going after the best things.*
> *You get the best things*
> *by going after the important things.*

I know what he meant by "best things," because he explained it. "Best things" meant loving relationships, good marriages, good children, spiritual truths and gifts, effective ministry, peace of mind, happiness, even financial security; all the stuff that makes life meaningful. He meant that you don't wind up with all that good stuff by going after it directly.

You get that big stuff by minding the little stuff along the way. Take "happiness," for example. We don't get "happiness" by saying to ourselves, "I'm going to make myself 'happy' today!" Happiness comes almost unconsciously when we get other things right: our relationships, our obedience to God, our daily walk with Him.

Same thing with love. It doesn't come today because I sweat and strain after love. It comes because—and while—I'm doing the little things right with folks, like kindness and concern.

Get the little things right—the *essential* little things—and the big things tend to follow.

See You at the Pole

REBELLION

But Peter and John replied, "Which is right in God's eyes: to listen to you, or to him? You be the judges! As for us, we cannot help speaking about what we have seen and heard."

Acts 4:19 niv

I wrote a saying. I want to print it on a T-shirt for my next trip to Cedar Point. On the front, where the pocket would be, I'm going to print *Rebel for Jesus* and on the back *Rebel against the Culture: Do What's Right*.

When I was a teacher, I was cosponsor of an exchange program between some students at my Christian high school and students from a partner school in Moscow. This was about six years after communism fell in Russia. When the Russian students came here, they split their time between my school and a public high school. Many things surprised them; one thing freaked them out. They were shocked to find that in our "free" country, the Bible couldn't be taught in our public schools. It was the first thing that changed in their schools after communism fell. Bible classes started popping up immediately.

They thought that we Christians were rather cowardly for not rebelling against such limitations. They were probably right. But sometimes we rebel in the ways we can.

Sometimes we rebel for righteousness at a pole.

And then we spread that rebellion with all the power, wit, tact, energy, creativity, and wisdom we can.

Not angry rebels—joyous rebels. Smiling rebels. Rebels for the faith.

Walk tall and straight, rebels, like the pole you meet at. And let your smile wave like the flag that tops it.

DARKNESS ON THE OFFENSE

"If then the light within you is darkness, how great is that darkness!"
MATTHEW 6:23 NIV

I've investigated this for years. It is an investigation that has often brought me to tears, not the least for myself. I have spent my life investigating darkness.

It's a pity, really. People have been looking for the middle ground between darkness and light for generations. They call it "agnosticism" or "humanism" or any number of other names. They live as though some middle ground is there. But then. . .it's lost again. No place to hide, from either light or darkness. For anybody.

For I have found—and here is the danger—that Jesus was right when He said that darkness is not the *absence* of something. It is an offensive, spreading, radiating force.

The sad thing that I have seen is that there is no neutral act. There are only radiations of darkness or radiations of light. Jesus spoke here of the "light" that is in us being "darkness." That is, darkness *radiates* from us just as light would: a self-centered woman who has "faith" in miracles—for herself; young men whose dullness of heart and lack of care about their own souls are the tread marks of the tanks of Satan; people thinking they're just "passing time."

Neutrality? Humbug! We're all on the offensive with *something*.

THE MIRACLE OF PSALM TWENTY-TWO

"My God, my God, why have you forsaken me?"
MARK 15:34 NIV

With these words, Jesus quoted the opening phrase of Psalm 22.

Yes, He was expressing His despair. The presence of sin will do that. But when a Jew of that time heard a portion of a psalm quoted, he would remember the whole psalm. Psalms were sung every Sabbath at the synagogue, so it's like any song you've heard since you were a kid: you remember the whole thing.

Psalm 22 was a psalm of shame for those who were crucifying Jesus. It predicted exactly what they were doing ("They hurl insults. . . 'Let the LORD rescue him.'" Psalm 22:7–8 NIV). After they heard Jesus say this, and were thus reminded of the whole psalm, they were gone!

It also predicts the result of this martyrdom: "All the families of the nations will bow down before him" (verse 27).

Not only did Jesus' Jewish hearers remember the whole psalm, but when Jesus quoted the first line, He remembered it, too. So when He expresses the first lines, He also expresses the beautiful hope of the whole psalm: "He has. . .listened to his cry for help" (verse 24).

This is not just despair; this is not just torture predicted; it is despair leading to faith in a glorious future. Jesus was in such control that He could use this psalm to declare all of this to those around Him. . .

And to Himself.

God, help us to do the same in our times of despair.

THE ESSENCE OF JOY

And then the lawless one will be revealed, whom the Lord Jesus
will overthrow with the breath of his mouth and destroy
by the splendor of his coming.
2 THESSALONIANS 2:8 NIV

There are two sides of joy.

The Red Wings hadn't won the Stanley Cup since 1955. I was way too young to remember that, but what I do remember (barely) is them losing the Cup to pretty much everyone through the sixties. They lost again in the '95 Cup finals. So when they won in '97 with Stevie Yzerman, Vladimir Konstantinov, and the gang, we were dancing in the Miller household.

Was that joy? It was very close. It certainly was happiness! Was it the "essence" of joy? Certainly not.

But I can't help it. I love winning!

I loved it when I played tennis; I loved it when my son was an all-state goalkeeper.

It's why Jesus rose from the dead: the joy of winning!

So whenever I think of Jesus and His return, those goose bumps come back. And it turns into real joy.

In a perfect world, an idea like "winning" would be inconceivable, irrelevant. There would be nothing and no one to defeat. But this isn't a perfect world, especially within ourselves. So for us to win, in this life we have to lose. . .ourselves.

Because that's the only way to attain the second side of joy: the personal presence of the ultimate Winner, who writes His autograph all over our souls:

Jesus.

COURAGE FOR THE FIGHT

"Have I not commanded you? Be strong and courageous.
Do not be afraid; do not be discouraged, for the LORD
your God will be with you wherever you go."
JOSHUA 1:9 NIV

During this month of October, we will be examining the encouragement of God as found in the Bible. Nowhere is this illustrated more clearly than in Joshua 1:9, as Joshua's faithfulness is rewarded by his being allowed to enter the Promised Land.

Joshua and Caleb were two of twelve spies sent to reconnoiter the new land that God had promised to give to the people of Israel after the exodus from Egypt. As ten of the twelve spies tried to convince Israel that the enemy was too strong, Joshua and Caleb pleaded with the people instead:

> *"The land we passed through and explored is exceedingly*
> *good. If the LORD is pleased with us, he will lead us into that*
> *land, a land flowing with milk and honey, and will give it to*
> *us. Only do not rebel against the LORD. And do not be afraid*
> *of the people of the land, because we will devour them.*
> *Their protection is gone, but the LORD is with us. Do not be*
> *afraid of them."*
> (Numbers 14:7–9 NIV)

Now, standing on the precipice of the Promised Land, God gives Joshua a convincing promise of His presence. Hear this word of God to you today: What is God calling you to do for Him? How would you approach it if you heard these words as clearly as Joshua did?

FAITH WHEN IT REALLY COUNTS

"Do not rebel against the LORD. And do not be afraid of the people of the land, because we will devour them. Their protection is gone, but the LORD is with us. Do not be afraid of them."

NUMBERS 14:9 NIV

Joshua and Caleb were the only two men over forty years old who were allowed to enter the Promised Land. After forty years of wandering in the wilderness, these two men carried God's promise to their people as they faced the monumental task of taking the land that God had promised to them. Their courage is exemplified in today's passage as they urge their people to believe in God's presence, blessing, and encouragement.

Their faith in God was a gritty, all-encompassing, as-if-their-lives-depended-on-it kind of faith. Why? Because their lives actually *did* depend on God's promises. If Joshua was to lead Israel into God's promise, he would have to feel God's presence on a second-by-second basis and step out in faith, trusting that God would come through and stand true to His promises.

Understand this: Joshua's job as the leader of Israel was to encourage the people to attack fortified cities in the face of overwhelming odds. Through forty years, his confidence in God's strong arm had not wavered. And God rewarded Joshua's determined faith as He called him to bravery in the face of imminent battle.

Joshua's story of determined, consistent faith is strong encouragement for us today as well.

FORTITUDE IN THE FACE OF BAD NEWS

The LORD gave this command to Joshua son of Nun:
"Be strong and courageous, for you will bring the Israelites into
the land I promised them on oath, and I myself will be with you."
DEUTERONOMY 31:23 NIV

In Deuteronomy 31, Moses and Joshua have been called to the tent of meeting to hear from God. God tells Moses that the time for Moses' death is near. God Himself predicts the failures of the people of Israel to follow Him once they take possession of the Promised Land:

> *"These people will soon prostitute themselves to the foreign*
> *gods of the land they are entering. They will forsake me and*
> *break the covenant I made with them. And in that day I will*
> *become angry with them and forsake them; I will hide my*
> *face from them, and they will be destroyed."*
> (Deuteronomy 31:16–17 NIV)

Imagine being Joshua in this situation: called to move ahead into battle, knowing that the people he will lead will eventually "be destroyed" because of their unfaithfulness. At that moment, many men might simply ask, "Well then, what's the point?" But there's no sign that Joshua was deterred.

So often in life we find that we can only control how we react in the face of opposition or bad news; there's not much we can do to control the reactions or responses of others to adversity. And we find, as did Joshua, that God rewards our personal faith in Him when the going gets tough.

WE ALL NEED CONTINUED ENCOURAGEMENT

"Be strong and courageous, because you will lead these people
to inherit the land I swore to their ancestors to give them."

JOSHUA 1:6 NIV

Today's call to Joshua mirrors almost exactly the one we read in the previous day's devotion. If Joshua had stood at the tent of meeting, seen the Lord's physical presence in the pillar of cloud, and heard His audible voice of encouragement, why did God feel it necessary to give Joshua this additional reminder?

That's a great question. Think for a moment about how you might answer that for yourself. In these post-New Testament days, we don't often hear of people being able to see and hear God's presence. Shouldn't this have been enough to encourage Joshua for the rest of his life?

Yet God knew Joshua would need to hear these words again. So often we, like the disciple Peter, move forward in faith and "step out of the boat," out of our comfort zone. But soon the waves of adversity rise around us, and our courage wavers (Matthew 14:22–33). God knew that Joshua would be leading a fearful people into a difficult situation, and that he would need God's continued reassurance.

How often do we find ourselves looking in fear at our surrounding circumstances rather than looking to God and trusting in His strength? Yet we can find that same reassurance by daily searching the scriptures for that guidance, and by asking for God's encouragement through the Holy Spirit in our prayers.

PROSPERITY AND SUCCESS—
GOD'S DEFINITION, NOT OURS

"Be strong and very courageous. Be careful to obey all the law my servant Moses gave you; do not turn from it to the right or to the left, that you may be successful wherever you go. Keep this Book of the Law always on your lips; meditate on it day and night, so that you may be careful to do everything written in it. Then you will be prosperous and successful."

JOSHUA 1:7–8 NIV

Every man longs to be prosperous and successful in life. We all want to be able to have a meaningful occupation, to provide for our families, and to lead the next generation to God. We want to live a faithful life in front of God and at the end hear the emphatic words, "'Well done, good and faithful servant!'" (Matthew 25:21 NIV).

Joshua's desire to be prosperous and successful was no different from ours. And the stakes were desperately high. In addition to leading a family, he was also leading a nation into hostile territory. And God gave him the surefire formula for success: an unwavering focus on God's revealed Word, leading to a resolute trust in God's promises.

Do not miss this word to you, *you personally,* today: The *only* sure way to prosperity and success, as God defines it, is by faithfully reading and following God's revealed Word. God has provided the path, with His promise of success, in His Word to you. Follow that template, and rest assured.

LOOKING BACK AT GOD'S FAITHFULNESS

"Do not be afraid. Stand firm and you will see the deliverance the LORD
will bring you today. The Egyptians you see today you will never see
again. The LORD will fight for you; you need only to be still."
EXODUS 14:13–14 NIV

As we watch Joshua prepare to lead the people of Israel into the Promised Land, let's look back for a moment at God's work in Joshua's past.

Moses and the Israelites, including Joshua, stood at the edge of the Red Sea. God had delivered them from slavery in Egypt, but Pharaoh, true to form, had changed his mind—he wanted his free slave labor back. So the Egyptian army pursued the nation of Israel as they left Egypt.

Panicked, the nation of Israel despaired at their impending slaughter. But God's reassurance to Moses was, in a word, astounding: "Moses, you don't have to lift a finger. I've got this."

Those of us who know the story know what happened:

> But the Israelites went through the sea on dry ground, with
> a wall of water on their right and on their left. That day the
> LORD saved Israel from the hands of the Egyptians, and
> Israel saw the Egyptians lying dead on the shore. And when
> the Israelites saw the mighty hand of the LORD displayed
> against the Egyptians, the people feared the LORD and put
> their trust in him and in Moses his servant.
> (Exodus 14:29-31 NIV)

Keep this story in mind today as you face your own adversity.

WORSHIP, NOT WARFARE

Joshua commanded the army, "Shout! For the LORD has given you the city!". . . . When the trumpets sounded, the army shouted, and at the sound of the trumpet, when the men gave a loud shout, the wall collapsed; so everyone charged straight in, and they took the city.

JOSHUA 6:16, 20 NIV

Armed with the memory of the defeated Egyptians lying dead on the shore of the Red Sea, Joshua moved to take Jericho in faith, following perhaps the most bizarre battle plan ever executed. God wanted to demonstrate His superiority in the face of Israel's fortified opposition, so He commanded Joshua's army to commit to a ritual of *worship* rather than warfare.

For seven days, Israel's army walked around the locked-tight walled city of Jericho. Instead of army commanders leading the procession, priests were in the front. Instead of troops brandishing their weapons and symbols of strength, the ark of the covenant was the most visible symbol. And instead of scaling the walls and engaging in hand-to-hand combat, the people needed only to wait for God to act and to open the way.

Have you been praying in the face of a seemingly insurmountable circumstance? Have you tried to act to resolve the situation, and perhaps experienced failure and frustration? Redouble your trust in God to work on your behalf. He understands the details of your dilemma much more completely than you do, and He knows what's most needed. Remember God's faithful activity in the past. Trust, and then obey.

HAMSTRUNG BY OUR OWN SIN

Joshua said, "Alas, Sovereign LORD, why did you ever bring this people across the Jordan to deliver us into the hands of the Amorites to destroy us? . . . . Pardon your servant, Lord. What can I say, now that Israel has been routed by its enemies?"

JOSHUA 7:7–8 NIV

This scene, following so closely on the heels of God's resounding success at Jericho, stands as a strong lesson for us today.

Joshua's efforts to take the small outpost of Ai were hampered by one man's personal sin. At Jericho, a man named Achan had taken some of the plunder for himself against God's specific commands. He had hidden it under his tent.

In the face of being routed by the few troops at Ai, Joshua despaired and looked for answers. God led him to Achan and revealed his sin, and after Joshua carried out God's punishment, Israel was able to move forward in their campaign to take the Promised Land.

How often does our own personal sin hamper God's work in our lives? As men, we often keep secrets from our wives, from our families—even from ourselves. Unconfessed sin in our lives is a scourge, a cancer that saps our strength and leads to defeat and despair. Even men who lead high-profile, highly effective ministries are not immune as greed, pride, sexual sin, and other evils sometimes hamstring their effectiveness.

Think today about how this may be true for you, and pray about what God wants from you in the face of this reality.

GOD: OUR DIVINE CHEERLEADER

Then the LORD said to Joshua, "Do not be afraid; do not be discouraged. Take the whole army with you, and go up and attack Ai. For I have delivered into your hands the king of Ai, his people, his city and his land."
JOSHUA 8:1 NIV

Yesterday we looked at how the unconfessed sin of one man stopped the army of Israel in its tracks, and how our own unconfessed sin might do the same in our lives.

Yet God's words today show us how God stands eager for us to get past our sin. God's plan for Joshua was to move forward, not stand still. Rather than hampering God's plan, God wanted to see the sin removed so that He could continue His work in the lives of the people of Israel. His promises were not taken back because of Israel's sin.

How true this is in our own lives! God has a relentlessly positive inclination toward us. He's cheering for us to move forward in His power; we are encouraged and emboldened by the Holy Spirit He has given to those who believe in Him. Sin is a desperately disastrous reality in our lives, to be sure; however, God desires that we confess that sin and move on in His power and in His strength, for "if we confess our sins, he is faithful and just and will forgive us our sins and purify us from all unrighteousness" (1 John 1:9 NIV).

How will this faithful promise encourage you today?

ENCOURAGING OTHERS IN YOUR CIRCLE

*When they had brought these kings to Joshua, he. . .said to the army
commanders who had come with him. . . . "Do not be afraid;
do not be discouraged. Be strong and courageous. This is what
the LORD will do to all the enemies you are going to fight."*

JOSHUA 10:24–25 NIV

As we leave the story of Joshua today, we see him encouraging his
commanding officers. Five Amorite kings had formed an alliance to fight
against Israel, and God moved in power to defeat them. Ever eager to follow
God's call and continue Israel's campaign, Joshua continued to encourage
his commanders as God had consistently encouraged him.

How have you seen God's faithfulness demonstrated in your own life?
Perhaps you've seen answers to prayer in the face of disease, marital strife,
or financial distress. Perhaps you've felt God's peace and comfort when the
answers to your difficult circumstances were long in coming.

If you've felt God's encouragement, how can you mirror Joshua's words
today? Can you encourage your coworkers, your spouse, your friends in
the face of their own difficult circumstances?

If God has shown Himself faithful to you, commit today to communicate
that faithfulness to at least one other person who is experiencing a tough
life situation. Your words of empathy may be the ones that reveal God's
power in that person's own life.

Nervous about doing this? "Do not be afraid. . . Be strong and courageous"
(verse 25). God can—and will—empower you to encourage others.

ITCHING FOR A FIGHT

From Hebron Caleb drove out the three Anakites—
Sheshai, Ahiman and Talmai, the sons of Anak.
JOSHUA 15:14 NIV

Let's not leave the book of Joshua without looking at the life of Caleb.

In Joshua 14, we learn Caleb followed God "wholeheartedly" (verses 8, 9, 14). In this, Caleb followed the formula for prosperity and success that we read about in Joshua 1:8. (Sound familiar? See October 5's reading.)

Joshua 14 tells us of Caleb's desire to take his inheritance (promised to him by Moses) in Hebron, even at eighty-five years old. This octogenarian was still itching for a fight—the same fight he was eager to engage in as a forty-year-old, the first time he encountered these giants. At that time, his confidence in God's power overflowed: "'We should go up and take possession of the land, for we can certainly do it'" (Numbers 13:30 NIV).

What was Caleb's secret? He still relied—again, wholeheartedly—on God's strength, not his own. Even after forty-five years, Caleb believed that God's promises would be fulfilled. He knew his role in this mission, and he was eager to advance against his enemies and prove God's power once again.

This message is for us, whether we're eighty-five, forty, or twenty. Patience, trust, and wholehearted devotion make us ready to take on life's most difficult challenges and pursue God's mission. When we follow God as Caleb did, we're ready to move forward in faith, no matter when God calls us to action.

GOD-INSPIRED OPTIMISM

"On that day Moses swore to me, 'The land. . .will be your
inheritance. . .forever, because you have followed the LORD
my God wholeheartedly.'. . . . The LORD helping me,
I will drive them out just as he said."

JOSHUA 14: 9, 12 NIV

A negative spirit is always a mark of self-reliance. To follow God whole-heartedly, as Caleb did, includes an unwavering trust in God's encouragement and empowerment. Along with that comes a confident optimism in God's presence and His power in our lives—an eagerness to engage with God in His mission.

Caleb, forty-five years earlier, exuded this confident optimism. And now, at eighty-five years old, he welcomed the challenge to engage in battle against the Anakites.

"Been there, done that" never entered Caleb's lexicon. He refused to leave the battle for the young men of his clan. Seeing the finish line of the race he started decades earlier, he redoubled his effort and charged into the hill country, confident in God's ability, not his own. Imagine the Anakites, shaking in their size 25 boots as Caleb approached, weapons drawn. They never stood a chance in the face of Caleb's divinely empowered onslaught.

Are there challenges you've been waiting years to accomplish? Are you ready to reengage, confident that you're accomplishing what God has called you to do?

Caleb's story was still being told years later (Judges 1:20). This is the very definition of "prosperous and successful" that we've been talking about this month (Joshua 1:8). Follow Caleb's example of faith, and leave a legacy worthy of God's warriors.

GIDEON: GOD'S STRENGTH, OUR WEAKNESS

The angel of the LORD came and sat down. . .where. . .
Gideon was threshing wheat in a winepress to keep it from the
Midianites. When the angel of the LORD appeared to Gideon,
he said, "The LORD is with you, mighty warrior."
JUDGES 6:11–12 NIV

As we continue to look for God's encouragement during this month of October, let's focus on Gideon. God's people were oppressed by the Midianites; God's prediction about the people of Israel had come true (see October 3's reading).

But as we've learned so far this month, God is always looking for ways to advance His purposes despite our sin. So God sent His angel to Gideon, who was working in secret so that his grain wouldn't be stolen by the regular raids of the Midianite troops.

Does it seem strange to you that the angel would call Gideon a "mighty warrior"? As far as we know, Gideon hadn't done anything to demonstrate courage. So here's the principle for today: Deep down, *we truly are who God says we are.*

Perhaps you've been discouraged by a poor performance review at work. Perhaps you've recently gone through a divorce that you didn't want. Perhaps you're facing your retirement years, convinced that your most productive years are behind you.

Be encouraged today! Gideon had no idea that God would use him powerfully to deliver His people, yet God's plan for his life prevailed. Remember, *you are who God says you are.* Pray to be used as Gideon was, no matter what your life circumstances are today.

QUESTIONING GOD'S PROMISES

"Pardon me, my lord," Gideon replied, "but if the LORD is with us,
why has all this happened to us? . . . . The LORD has abandoned us and
given us into the hand of Midian." The LORD. . .said, "Go in the strength
you have and save Israel out of Midian's hand. Am I not sending you?"
"Pardon me, my lord," Gideon replied, "but how can I save Israel?
My clan is the weakest in Manasseh, and I am the least in my family."
The LORD answered, "I will be with you, and you will strike
down all the Midianites, leaving none alive."
JUDGES 6:13–16 NIV

The reading for today demonstrates one thing: God works out of our weakness, not out of our strength.

Gideon's questions are real. He hasn't seen the promised blessing of the Lord in his own life. His family has been harassed; the food has literally been stolen out of his hands under this Midianite oppression.

When the Lord tells him to defeat the invading army "in his own strength," he objects again. He's the runt of the litter in the smallest family of his Israelite clan.

How like God it is to use our weaknesses to demonstrate His own power. This is why Paul taught, "For Christ's sake, I delight in weaknesses, in insults, in hardships, in persecutions, in difficulties. For when I am weak, then I am strong" (2 Corinthians 12:10 NIV).

When we admit our utter reliance on God, that's when He moves in to do His divinely ordained work.

TESTING GOD'S PROMISES

Then Gideon said to God, "Do not be angry with me. Let me make just one more request. Allow me one more test with the fleece, but this time make the fleece dry and let the ground be covered with dew." That night God did so. Only the fleece was dry; all the ground was covered with dew.

JUDGES 6:39–40 NIV

Gideon's weakness shows through in the face of God's call on his life. Not once, but twice, he asks God for a visible sign that he will have success in defeating the Midianite army.

Please take a few minutes to read the entire chapter in Judges 6. You'll find God reassured Gideon time and time again that He would do as He had said and work through Gideon to save His people Israel. Yet He also allows Gideon's questions, and answers them without showing anger or frustration.

When we're called to move into an unfamiliar or uncomfortable situation where the outcome is in doubt, God allows our questioning. He provides wise counsel from others when we ask; He leads us in answer to our prayers.

Let's look at Gideon not as a doubter, but as a man convinced of his own inability to do what God has asked him to do—utterly reliant on God to be true to His word and act on His promises. Sometimes God allows us to come to the end of our own strength so that He can prove Himself stronger.

GOD-INDUCED PANIC

The three companies blew the trumpets and smashed the jars. Grasping the torches in their left hands and holding in their right hands the trumpets they were to blow, they shouted, "A sword for the LORD and for Gideon!" While each man held his position around the camp, all the Midianites ran, crying out as they fled.
JUDGES 7:20–21 NIV

Judges 7 details how God worked through weak Gideon and his winnowed-down troops to utterly confuse and defeat the marauding Midianite army. It's well worth the read, so please find a Bible and read the story in Judges chapter 7.

Once again, we see God relentlessly encouraging Gideon, urging him to move forward in power and in faith. God's positivity in urging Gideon encourages us today as well, as He essentially says, "Gideon, with Me running the show you can't possibly lose. I am faithful; I will do what I have promised." And the rout ensues: the Midianite army is decimated in the confusion.

God's promises to us in Jesus Christ stand in the same power. When we confess our sins, when we follow His Word, when we faithfully pray for the leading of the Holy Spirit, then we will be "prosperous and successful"—as He defines prosperity and success in accordance with His will (Joshua 1:8 NIV).

Using Gideon as an example, surrender your life over to God's strength and guidance. Watch Him work powerfully on your behalf to make you the man He wants you to be—at work, in your family, and in your community.

SAMSON'S LAST BATTLE

Then Samson prayed to the LORD, "Sovereign LORD, remember me.
Please, God, strengthen me just once more, and let me with one
blow get revenge on the Philistines for my two eyes."
JUDGES 16:28 NIV

Samson was a judge over Israel for twenty years. During the time of his reign, he demonstrated his great strength time and time again, routing the Philistines many times and in multiple ways.

Today's passage leads us to Samson's final stand. As with Joshua and Gideon, Samson's prayer of reliance on God comes at a critical time—a time during which Samson has the opportunity to demonstrate God's power and strength and strike a major blow against God's enemies and their false religion. God, through Samson, destroys their temple and kills thousands.

Judges chapters 13 through 16 detail the life of Samson, known throughout history as both a hero and a deeply flawed man. Yet we read one recurring thing about Samson in these chapters. First, the "Spirit of the LORD began to stir him" (Judges 13:25 NIV) when he was a young man. Then, three other times in Judges (14:6, 14:19, 15:14) that same Spirit is in evidence right before he marks another great act of strength.

Samson's strength came from the same Spirit (note the capital S) that empowers us today. Strength, courage, honor, and the ability to demonstrate God's power within our circles of influence—all of this comes from the Holy Spirit living within us as believers in Christ. How will you move out in faith today?

FINISHING WELL

Then Samuel left for Ramah, but Saul went up to his home in Gibeah of Saul. Until the day Samuel died, he did not go to see Saul again, though Samuel mourned for him. And the LORD regretted that he had made Saul king over Israel.

1 SAMUEL 15:34–35 NIV

The prophet Samuel, leader of Israel after the time of the judges, also presided over the anointing of Saul, the first king over Israel. He anointed Saul at God's command, and King Saul ruled over Israel for forty-two years.

By all accounts, God chose and empowered Saul during his reign. Why then do we read about God's regret at the end of Saul's reign?

Late in his reign, Saul's disobedience dogged him. He relied on himself against God's specific commands. In Saul's life, we come to understand a powerful truth—that finishing well is critical to the legacy we leave in this life.

Pastor James MacDonald writes, "You could decide to destroy your life by 5:00 tonight. And would God forgive you? Yes. But would you bear the consequences of that decision for the rest of your life? Yes, you would! Don't ever mix up God's forgiveness and [real-life] consequences."

Samuel, who'd invested decades of his life into Saul, mourns Saul's failure. God even regrets His choice of Saul, despite the king's multiple decades of faithful leadership. And Saul, frustrated at his own failures, ends his own life ignobly (1 Samuel 31).

Make no mistake: finishing well matters.

WAITING FOR GOD'S PROMISES

*So Samuel took the horn of oil and anointed him in the presence
of his brothers, and from that day on the Spirit of the
LORD came powerfully upon David.*

1 SAMUEL 16:13 NIV

In the story of Samuel anointing David to be king, we hear an echo of our earlier readings: As with Samson, God's Spirit moved powerfully in this young man; as with Gideon, David was the youngest and the smallest of his family. Yet God told Samuel to anoint Jesse's youngest son, following God's direct command (1 Samuel 16:1, 12).

Notice one important truth at the outset of his story: David had to wait. And wait. God's promise was slow in coming, even though David had been anointed by God's own prophet.

God's timeline is often far from what ours would optimally be. King Saul lived and reigned for a significant amount of time—and David even spent time in his service—before David was eventually crowned king.

Are you waiting for God's promise to you to be fulfilled? Then you stand in a long line of heroes in the Bible: Noah, who built a boat over multiple decades before he ever saw a drop of rain; Abraham, who waited decades for his son Isaac to be born (when he was one hundred years old!); and now David, who waited patiently and faithfully for God's story to develop before he was crowned king over Israel.

Make no mistake: God's timelines are intentional. Faithfulness and patience in the meantime will be rewarded.

WHAT'S YOUR SLING?

"The LORD who rescued me from the paw of the lion and the paw of the bear will rescue me from the hand of this Philistine."
1 SAMUEL 17:37 NIV

When we read of David's anointing, sometimes we wonder what the older brothers were thinking: *This scrawny kid, God's anointed?* Yet we have no indication that David inspired the hatred that an earlier upstart, Joseph, provoked in his older brothers (Genesis 37:5, 12–32).

David's father sent him to the front lines of Israel's battle with the Philistines to resupply his older brothers. There, David heard about Goliath's arrogance in the face of God's people. Evidently his brothers were only too happy to have him engage this giant, and even King Saul saw the fire in David's eyes and gave him his blessing (1 Samuel 17:37).

As this boy approached Goliath in battle, God's Spirit encouraged David's own spirit. As we've seen with other men in this month's readings, David was eager to prove God powerful in the face of God's enemies. He relied wholeheartedly on God to fight for him, trusting in God to engage—and to win.

This kind of practical faith is the hallmark of the man of God. David approached Goliath with what he had, using his God-given talent with the sling to fell the giant. How has God equipped you to face your own circumstances? What's the sling in your hand, and what are the stones in your pouch? God will use what He's given you to accomplish His purposes.

WHEN OPPOSITION PROVES OUR MISSION

From that day Saul kept David with him and did not let him
return home to his family. . . . Whatever mission Saul sent him on,
David was so successful that Saul gave him a high rank in the army.
This pleased all the troops, and Saul's officers as well. . . .
And from that time on Saul kept a close eye on David.

1 SAMUEL 18:2, 5, 9 NIV

Sometimes the opposition we experience is the surest sign that we're doing what God wants us to do.

You've heard the line from the 1974 film *The Godfather, Part II*: "Keep your friends close, but your enemies closer." Saul, seeing David's obvious success, brings this young warrior into his household. Even Saul's son, Jonathan, who would be next in line for the throne, sees David as God's chosen and forms a close alliance with him.

As Saul sees his influence waning, his frustration grows. And as David continues his faithful service, we watch Saul allow his fear and paranoia to consume him.

If you've experienced opposition to your efforts to be God's man at work, at home, or in another circle of influence, take heart from David's story. Continue to be faithful in your prayerful pursuit of God's purposes. You may find that your godly example angers others who are jealous of your quiet confidence in God's presence in your life. Remain faithful and wait for God to bless your efforts.

Pay less attention to the Sauls and more attention to the Jonathans in your life.

GOD'S SOMETIMES-OBVIOUS BLESSINGS

When David had fled. . . he went to Samuel at Ramah and told him
all that Saul had done to him. Then he and Samuel went to Naioth
and stayed there. . . [Saul] sent men to capture him. But when they saw
a group of prophets prophesying, with Samuel standing there as their
leader, the Spirit of God came on Saul's men, and they also prophesied.
Saul was told about it, and he sent more men, and they prophesied too.
1 SAMUEL 19:18, 20–21 NIV

Sometimes, as we learn from this amazing passage, God chooses to deliver His favor and encouragement through very visible signs.

David was on the run from King Saul, who had tried to kill him not once, but twice. Samuel had taken David in and the two of them hid from Saul together. David must have known that Saul would send men to come and apprehend him.

How must David have felt when he saw Saul's messengers overcome by God's Spirit?

How must Saul have felt when he heard about it—not once, but twice?

God's favor, His idea of being "prosperous and successful" (Joshua 1:8 NIV), manifests itself in different ways for different men. Some men enjoy material prosperity as they follow God's plan for their lives. Do you know any such men? Are you one of them?

David enjoyed God's visible favor even though he was on the run—a very different kind of success. Let this story help you begin to redefine what prosperity and success mean in your own life.

ALLOWING GOD TO WRITE THE STORY

[David] said to Saul. . . "This day you have seen with your own eyes
how the LORD delivered you into my hands in the cave. Some urged me
to kill you, but I spared you; I said, 'I will not lay my hand on
my lord, because he is the LORD's anointed.' See, my father. . .
I cut off the corner of your robe but did not kill you."
1 SAMUEL 24:9–11 NIV

Despite having to constantly run from Saul, David's faith remained strong. His commitment to God's will and God's timing was absolute. Finding himself in the back of a cave while Saul sat tantalizingly within his grasp, David exercised almost unbelievable self-control. Even David's troops encouraged him to kill Saul, yet David resisted. He was content to let God be the one writing his story, refusing to take matters into his own hands.

How many men would have acted differently in this situation? How many men act in haste and trust in their own wits and instincts, hastily moving forward into business or personal situations that are fraught with potential consequences?

David wasn't going to usurp the throne of Israel. God had anointed him, and he trusted in God to make him the leader of His people whenever God wanted.

Are you facing a big decision? A major life change? Commit yourself to a time of prayer, of seeking God's face. Search the scriptures for God's leading, and discuss your situation with trusted and godly advisors. Time spent this way is never wasted.

FACING THE BLOODY BATTLES WITH FAITH

*Then David and all the men with him took hold of their clothes
and tore them. They mourned and wept and fasted till
evening for Saul and his son Jonathan.*
2 SAMUEL 1:11–12 NIV

David was Israel's anointed king. But after hearing of Saul and Jonathan's death, he didn't celebrate; instead, he and all of his men mourned. This is further evidence of a man filled with God's encouragement and empowerment—one who trusted God to write his life story.

David was soon crowned king over the tribe of Judah (2 Samuel 2:4), but he knew that a bitter battle was about to begin, one that would end with him being crowned king over all of Israel. David had been encouraged by God's signs throughout this difficult journey, but he also knew he had more bloody work to do.

Second Samuel chapters 1 through 5 read like a blockbuster thriller movie plot, filled with intrigue, battle, bloodshed, and eventual victory. And David, at the age of thirty, eventually begins a legendary forty-year reign.

After taking Jerusalem, we read this of David: "Then David knew that the LORD had established him as king over Israel and had exalted his kingdom for the sake of his people Israel" (2 Samuel 5:12). Honoring God's work in the past, David now begins the next phase of his life most appropriately: by giving God all of the credit for everything that had happened in the past.

We're wise to share a perspective similar to David's when we look back on our own lives.

A PROMISE OF LEGACY

"'Your house and your kingdom will endure forever before me;
your throne will be established forever.'"

2 SAMUEL 7:16 NIV

In our quest to find God's encouragement in the Bible this month, we'll find no declaration more encouraging than this one, spoken to David through God's prophet, Nathan.

This promise echoes God's lavish promises to other men in the Old Testament—to Adam: "Be fruitful and increase in number; fill the earth and subdue it. Rule over. . .every living creature that moves on the ground" (Genesis 1:28 NIV); to Noah: "I establish my covenant with you: Never again will all life be destroyed by the waters of a flood" (Genesis 9:11 NIV); to Abram: "As for me, this is my covenant with you: You will be the father of many nations" (Genesis 17:4 NIV). These global promises were given by a generous God to His faithful followers.

In the New Testament, Paul makes this critical observation about King David:

> "After removing Saul, [God] made David their king. God
> testified concerning him: 'I have found David son of Jesse, a
> man after my own heart; he will do everything I want him to
> do.' From this man's descendants God has brought to Israel
> the Savior Jesus, as he promised."
> (Acts 13:22–23 NIV)

You and I also stand in this line of promise along with Adam, Noah, Abram, and David. We have the promise of Jesus, the fulfillment of all of the other promises God made in the Bible combined.

Eternal promises given by a grace-filled God to His unworthy followers. Amazing!

GOD MAKES BEAUTY OUT OF BROKEN THINGS

[David, to Bathsheba] "I will surely carry out this very day what I swore to you by the LORD, the God of Israel: Solomon your son shall be king after me, and he will sit on my throne in my place."

1 KINGS 1:30 NIV

Nearly everyone knows the story of David's failure with Bathsheba. Movies have been made about this scandalous story of lust and intrigue. When this man David—whom God called one "after my own heart" (Acts 13:22 NIV)—fell, he fell *hard*.

Yet God is in the business of rebuilding. Indeed, God is always "making everything new" (Revelation 21:5 NIV). In this case, David's repentance after his highly visible failure brings David a son, Solomon, whom the Lord loves. David, in fact, declares that Solomon will be the next king over Israel instead of his eldest son, Adonijah.

Do you remember a time in your own life when you failed, publicly and visibly? A time when you felt caught, dirty, sinful beyond repair? Be encouraged by David's story and the birth of Solomon. Remember, God takes the brokenness of our lives and, when we repent, He makes beautiful things. Like a medieval craftsman, God takes the shattered glass of our lives and makes the pieces into a stained-glass window as beautiful—and as reflective of His light—as any that ever hung in a stately European cathedral.

A TEMPLATE FOR GOD'S MEN

When the time drew near for David to die, he gave a charge to Solomon his son. "I am about to go the way of all the earth," he said. "So be strong, act like a man, and observe what the LORD your God requires: Walk in obedience to him, and keep his decrees and commands, his laws and regulations, as written in the Law of Moses. Do this so that you may prosper in all you do and wherever you go and that the LORD may keep his promise to me: 'If your descendants watch how they live, and if they walk faithfully before me with all their heart and soul, you will never fail to have a successor on the throne of Israel.'"

1 KINGS 2:1–4 NIV

Today's scripture reading is a little longer than usual. That's because it gives us as Christian men an important template to follow in our own lives.

Take note of the components of David's charge to Solomon: first, encouragement to be strong and take personal responsibility; second, a call to follow after God's ways; third, a promise of prosperity and success if the first and second exhortations are followed; finally, an appeal to look at God's promises via his legacy.

Men, these are critical components of your personal legacy. The older you get, the more influence you have, whether or not you have children. Follow David's lead: testify to God's work in your life and share the encouragement you've received from God with the next generation.

WISDOM FOR THE ASKING

God gave Solomon wisdom and very great insight, and a breadth
of understanding as measureless as the sand on the seashore.
1 KINGS 4:29 NIV

In an earlier reading, we found that God loved Solomon. When he became king after his father, David, died, God appeared to Solomon with an enticing proposition: "At Gibeon the LORD appeared to Solomon during the night in a dream, and God said, 'Ask for whatever you want me to give you'" (1 Kings 3:5 NIV).

Everyone dreams of being given the chance, just once in life, to ask for whatever we want. Whether through a lottery ticket or from a genie in a bottle, we all long for that chance to have the proverbial "three wishes" that will allow us to fulfill all of our dreams.

Prudently, the newly ascended King Solomon asks for wisdom. Pleased with this request, God delivers with astounding generosity.

Wouldn't it be amazing to have the same opportunity to be as wise as Solomon?

The truth is, you have it. Read Jesus' words to His disciples, and to us, in John 14:26 (NIV): "But the Advocate, the Holy Spirit, whom the Father will send in my name, will teach you all things and will remind you of everything I have said to you."

Jesus' Spirit inhabits those who believe. When we're looking for wisdom, we need look no further than God's Word, sincerely praying for the Spirit's direction and guidance. Solomon's wisdom was legendary; with the Spirit's help, yours can be as well.

INSPIRED PEOPLE INSPIRE PEOPLE

[Hezekiah] encouraged them with these words: "Be strong and courageous. Do not be afraid or discouraged because of the king of Assyria and the vast army with him, for there is a greater power with us than with him. With him is only the arm of flesh, but with us is the LORD our God to help us and to fight our battles." And the people gained confidence from what Hezekiah the king of Judah said.

2 CHRONICLES 32:6–8 NIV

King Hezekiah stands in front of the people of Judah as they stare down an imminent siege from the terrifying Assyrian army, a force known for their murderous, grisly, and shocking terror tactics. Assyria's King Sennacherib does his best to terrorize Hezekiah; temporarily, the plan works.

Read what happens next:

> *King Hezekiah and the prophet Isaiah son of Amoz cried out in prayer to heaven about this. And the LORD sent an angel, who annihilated all the fighting men and the commanders and officers in the camp of the Assyrian king. So he withdrew to his own land in disgrace.... So the LORD saved Hezekiah and the people of Jerusalem from the hand of Sennacherib... He took care of them on every side.*
>
> (2 Chronicles 32:20–22 NIV)

Inspired people inspire people.

Hezekiah, trusting only in God's deliverance, was able to inspire an entire city despite a seemingly hopeless situation. As we've seen throughout this month, God heard and answered in an overwhelming way.

It's another story of God's action to encourage us today in our own lives.

ISAIAH'S VISION OF GOD'S GLORY

In the year that King Uzziah died, I saw the Lord, high and exalted,
seated on a throne; and the train of his robe filled the temple. . . .
"Woe to me!" I cried. "I am ruined! For I am a man of unclean lips,
and I live among a people of unclean lips, and my eyes
have seen the King, the LORD Almighty."
ISAIAH 6:1, 5 NIV

In the last two days of this month, we'll look at God's encouragement in the Bible as He revealed Himself to two of the Bible's authors.

The prophet Isaiah, who in our last reading prayed for Jerusalem's deliverance from the king of Assyria, in this passage receives a vision of God Himself, high and exalted and sitting on His throne. At the sight of it, Isaiah is terrified at God's majesty and power.

We know Isaiah as Israel's greatest prophet; Christians understand that God revealed to Isaiah more about God's Messiah than perhaps any other prophet. Indeed, in the very next chapter we find Isaiah's first prophecy about the Christ: "The virgin will conceive and give birth to a son, and will call him Immanuel" (Isaiah 7:14 NIV).

We who follow the Messiah to whom Isaiah pointed have a greater "vision" than the prophet Isaiah could have possibly imagined. We have the totality of the scriptures—the full story of God's intricate and purpose-filled plan to redeem all of humanity, begun in Genesis and ending in Revelation—whenever we hold a Bible in our hands.

God, revealed. How amazing is that?

Halloween

REASSURANCE

Among the lampstands was someone like a son of man, dressed in a robe reaching down to his feet and with a golden sash around his chest. . . . His voice was like the sound of rushing waters. In his right hand he held seven stars, and coming out of his mouth was a sharp, double-edged sword. His face was like the sun shining in all its brilliance. When I saw him, I fell at his feet as though dead.
REVELATION 1:13, 15–17 NIV

Here we see a triumphant vision of the resurrected Christ. Like Isaiah, John's reaction to this glorious vision was dramatic and immediate.

But Jesus didn't want to leave John, or us, with an intimidating vision of His power. Rather, He reached down reassuringly to touch John, and delivered an incredible word of encouragement:

> *"Do not be afraid. I am the First and the Last. I am the Living One; I was dead, and now look, I am alive for ever and ever! And I hold the keys of death and Hades."*
> (Revelation 1:17–18 NIV)

Jesus, both now and forever, is firmly in control of what happens in our lives and in our world. He sees everything, and nothing surprises Him. He can be trusted, because He is forever all-seeing and all-powerful.

Have you seen Jesus' glory as revealed in the scriptures? Be amazed. Be encouraged. Devote your life to Him, and wait faithfully and patiently for God to work His will—designed just for you, before the beginning of time—in your life.

A BEAUTIFUL THING

*A woman came with an alabaster jar of very expensive perfume,
made of pure nard. She broke the jar and poured the perfume on his
head. Some of those present were saying indignantly to one another,
"Why this waste of perfume? It could have been sold for more than a
year's wages and the money given to the poor." And they rebuked her
harshly. "Leave her alone," said Jesus. "Why are you bothering her?
She has done a beautiful thing to me. The poor you will always have
with you, and you can help them any time you want. But you will
not always have me. She did what she could. She poured perfume
on my body beforehand to prepare for my burial."*

MARK 14:3–8 NIV

It is not possible to "waste" anything on Christ if we are motivated by love.
It's not a waste to give up things of value, or our time, or our hopes for the
future if He is the One to whom we offer them. Others may scorn our gifts
as impractical or impulsive, but Christ sees them as beautiful. Anointing a
body that is still alive seems like nonsense, but it's the reason we know of
her today (Mark 14:9).

We don't need to have great resources to do beautiful things, either.
This woman did not occupy an important or powerful station in life, but as
Jesus points out, she did what she could for Him. And she did it when the
opportunity came, without hesitation and at the cost of scorn and criticism.
May we all have the love and courage of that woman.

A PEOPLE FOR HIMSELF

"For the sake of his great name the Lord will not reject his people,
because the Lord was pleased to make you his own."
1 Samuel 12:22 niv

God has been on a mission since Adam and Eve departed from His will: to gather back to Himself a people of His own—a willing people, eager to be with Him and do His will. But it's been a rough journey for our Father. He hasn't always gotten His way, so to speak. Being a Father committed to our free will, He has done everything to encourage us to respond to Him. Paul described it to the Greek philosophers this way:

> *"From one man he made all the nations, that they should inhabit the whole earth; and he marked out their appointed times in history and the boundaries of their lands. God did this so that they would seek him and perhaps reach out for him and find him, though he is not far from any one of us."* (Acts 17:26–27)

God is so persistent in having a people for Himself that he sacrificed His only begotten Son to make His desire a reality. "[Jesus] gave himself for us to redeem us from all wickedness and to purify for himself a people that are his very own, eager to do what is good" (Titus 2:14 niv).

Ultimately, a people belonging to God and pleasing to Him will be like Him, eager to do good works and to see others join His family.

EMPTY JARS

Yet you, LORD, are our Father. We are the clay,
you are the potter; we are all the work of your hand.
ISAIAH 64:8 NIV

It's the most natural thing in the world to think we own ourselves, to think that we are the reason we exist. It's the story of human history once mankind "did not think it worthwhile to retain the knowledge of God" (Romans 1:28 NIV). It's an ignorance that has become part of our DNA. But it's not the truth, and God our Father does not want us to struggle under the burden of trying to be fulfilled without Him.

Man was designed to be filled, but not by anything we can devise on our own. A potter makes vessels empty for a purpose. That design feature is what drives man. But it's a vain pursuit without God, as King Solomon—who tested everything to fill the void—declares: "'Meaningless! Meaningless!' says the Teacher. 'Everything is meaningless!'" (Ecclesiastes 12:8 NIV).

The flesh and the world offer the promise of filling the emptiness inside, but it will always leave us "hardened by sin's deceitfulness" (Hebrews 3:13 NIV). Even good things, apart from God, leave us ultimately unfulfilled. At best, a life of a good, successful, decent man is a life of revolving distractions, if it's done without the Potter's purpose. As St. Augustine put it so well, "You have made us for yourself, and our hearts are restless, until they can find rest in you."

Only in God, our Father—God, our Potter—will we ever find the filling we were designed for.

EVERY DAY A BATTLE FIELD

So I say, walk by the Spirit, and you will not gratify the desires of the flesh. For the flesh desires what is contrary to the Spirit, and the Spirit what is contrary to the flesh. They are in conflict with each other, so that you are not to do whatever you want.

GALATIANS 5:16–17 NIV

For the follower of Christ, there is no day without a battle. Some days it rages harder than others, but there's never a truce that lasts between the Spirit and the flesh. They are opposed to each other by their very nature. One is life and peace, the other death (Romans 8:6). From one we will inherit eternal life, from the other only corruption (Galatians 6:8). No wonder they are always in conflict!

We are born into this conflict when we become God's child. So how do we prepare ourselves for this conflict? The Galatians had fallen back into keeping the law, which never did have the power to win this battle. The flesh is always stronger than rules and regulations. The only thing that wins against desire is a stronger desire. To avoid siding with the flesh—which can be a powerful lure at times—means cultivating a *stronger* desire to walk with the Spirit. Amos 3:3 (MSG) poses the simple question, "Do two people walk hand in hand if they aren't going to the same place?" Walking by the Spirit means we are in agreement, going in the same direction, hand in hand, growing a greater desire for the things of the Spirit every day.

FACING THE FUTURE

"I will give you every place where you set your foot.... No one will be able to stand against you... I will never leave you nor forsake you.... Be strong and courageous. Do not be afraid; do not be discouraged, for the LORD your God will be with you wherever you go."
JOSHUA 1:3, 5, 9 NIV

Joshua at eighty, with all his life experiences and training, should have been more than prepared to lead the Israelites into the Promised Land, right?

Born into slavery in an empire over a thousand years old before Moses entered the picture, Joshua witnessed the struggle with Pharaoh firsthand, since he "had been Moses' aide since youth" (Numbers 11:28 NIV). He marched out of Egypt through the Red Sea, drank water from the rock, ate manna from heaven, led the first army of Israel, heard Moses read the Ten Commandments, and saw the first tabernacle constructed. At forty, he and eleven others spied on the land of Canaan, but then had to endure the next forty years wandering in the desert with those too fearful to take hold of God's promise. He and Caleb were the only ones over the age of twenty who did not die during that time (Numbers 14:29, 26:65), making them the oldest men in Israel.

So why the big pep talk? Because we are nothing without the presence and the promises of God. No history or résumé can give courage like His presence. We can do nothing without Him, no matter how much we've already achieved with Him.

FROM THE MESS, VALUE

Where no oxen are, the trough is clean;
but much increase comes by the strength of an ox.
PROVERBS 14:4 NKJV

Oxen are messy creatures. But there's no way to take advantage of their strength without having to watch where you step. If you want to produce something of value, you're going to have to deal with the mess it causes.

The work world can be quite messy. It's risky to run a business—people don't always do what you expect, customers demand more than you can provide, and every week you have to clean up something that hits the fan.

Marriage, for all its delights, can generate piles of debris. Sacrificing individual dreams, working through conflict, dealing with in-laws, negotiating finances, serving even when you would prefer to be served—all these make for a messy "trough." For those who persevere, the rewards are well worth it.

Having kids may be literally and figuratively the messiest choice of all. But most parents would tell you they'd do it all over again.

The principle in this verse is that nothing of value comes without work, consequences, and risk. Laziness and fear are our only obstacles. In the parable of the talents (Matthew 25:14–30), two servants risk the money entrusted to them and earn more, while one simply buries it in the ground. He pleads fear; his master calls him a "wicked and lazy servant" (Matthew 25:26 NKJV).

God wants us to work at whatever He's put into our lives, not fearing the consequences, but focusing on creating something of value. He wouldn't assign it if He didn't have a reason.

LET'S MAKE A DEAL

*"For the kingdom of heaven is like a landowner who went out early
in the morning to hire workers for his vineyard. He agreed to pay
them a denarius for the day and sent them into his vineyard."*
MATTHEW 20:1–2 NIV

A contract binds two parties to an agreement, each being obligated to the other as long as each upholds his end. In this parable, the workers hired early agreed to a denarius, and considered themselves lucky to be hired for a full day. Later, the landowner hires others, but instead of a contract, he promises: "'You also go and work in my vineyard, and I will pay you whatever is right.'" (Matthew 20:4 NIV). Finally, with only one hour left to work, he finds a group of workers whom no one has hired. To these, he simply says: "'You also go and work in my vineyard'" (Matthew 20:7 NIV).

When the foreman pays the workers, the ones who worked for just one hour, surprisingly, receive a full day's pay! The early workers' complaint sounds justified: "'These who were hired last worked only one hour, and you have made them equal to us who have borne the burden of the work and the heat of the day'" (Matthew 20:12 NIV). But the landowner reminds them of the contract they happily made that morning.

The first workers were given a legally binding guarantee; the second group received just a promise; the final ones could only hope in landowner's goodness. Each was rewarded in proportion to the faith it took to go into that vineyard.

LISTENING IS A DANGEROUS ACTIVITY

*Herod feared John [the Baptist] and protected him, knowing him
to be a righteous and holy man. When Herod heard John,
he was greatly puzzled; yet he liked to listen to him.*

MARK 6:20 NIV

John the Baptist was the first prophet to come along after what has been called the "Four Hundred Silent Years" in Israel's history. During the time between the last prophet of the Old Testament, Malachi, and the ministry of John, no prophets spoke to the people to remind them of God's law and His commandments.

So when John the Baptist showed up, looking and acting like the greatest prophet in Israel's history (Mark 1:6), preaching "'in the spirit and power of Elijah'" (Luke 1:17 NIV), people flocked to him. He became something of a religious celebrity, so much so that even tax collectors and soldiers came to ask his advice (Luke 3:12–14). John didn't hold back his message of repentance even with Herod the tetrarch, publically rebuking him for adultery. That of course landed John in prison and ultimately cost him his life (Matthew 14:6–12).

Herod made the worst mistake a person can when it comes to hearing the Good News—he treated it like entertainment. He listened without changing. Jesus said bluntly of those people: "There is a judge for the one who rejects me and does not accept my words; the very words I have spoken will condemn them at the last day" (John 12:48 NIV).

Listening is dangerous business, *if* we don't intend to apply what we hear from God. The very words themselves will testify against us.

MYSTERY TURNED MESSAGE

The mystery that has been kept hidden for ages and generations, but is now disclosed to the Lord's people. To them God has chosen to make known among the Gentiles the glorious riches of this mystery, which is Christ in you, the hope of glory.

COLOSSIANS 1:26–27 NIV

In the Old Testament, God used prophets to reveal mysteries for His purpose. When Daniel interpreted Nebuchadnezzar's dream, the king fell on his face, confessing, "'Surely your God is the God of gods and the Lord of kings and a revealer of mysteries'" (Daniel 2:47 NIV). Then Daniel was placed in authority over most of Babylon. God reveals mysteries in His own time and His own way—for our benefit and for His own glory.

When the time was right to reveal the mystery of salvation through grace, however, He did not rely on a prophet.

> *But when the set time had fully come, God sent his Son, born of a woman, born under the law, to redeem those under the law, that we might receive adoption to sonship. Because you are his sons, God sent the Spirit of his Son into our hearts, the Spirit who calls out, "Abba, Father."*
> (Galatians 4:4-6 NIV)

The mystery of mysteries—Christ living in us—had to be delivered face to face. Jesus revealed it the very night He would pay the price to see it happen: "At that day you will know that I am in My Father, and you in Me, and I in you" (John 14:20 NKJV). In us, Christ turned the mystery of the ages into the message for the world.

NO FORMULAS

In the course of time Cain brought some of the fruits of the soil as an offering to the LORD. And Abel also brought an offering—fat portions from some of the firstborn of his flock. The LORD looked with favor on Abel and his offering, but on Cain and his offering he did not look with favor. So Cain was very angry, and his face was downcast.

GENESIS 4:3–5 NIV

God doesn't need our "stuff," being the Creator. But the exercise of sacrificing is the exercise of priorities, of the condition of our hearts, and the hope for a closer walk with our Father. Abel approached God in faith (Hebrews 11:4) and was commended. He offered "firstborn" and "fat portions" because he reverenced God. But Cain offered his sacrifice reluctantly, not with a whole heart; he offered it under obligation, not gratitude. This kind of offering is the beginning of a dead religion built on formulas and equations. We offer a sacrifice to fulfill a requirement, and in turn we expect to get blessings. God is not interested in a "working" relationship with us, and He's certainly not going to be obligated by anything we do.

God wants us to experience His freedom—the freedom to be close to Him. Cain's "face was downcast" when his formulaic approach failed—in other words, he couldn't look God in the eye. If we insist on formulas rather than a sincere and open heart toward God, we risk going the way of Cain, angry with our Creator, turning away to the sin that is "'crouching at [our] door'" (Genesis 4:7 NIV).

OVERTHINKING AND UNDER-PRAYING

Do not be anxious about anything, but in every situation,
by prayer and petition, with thanksgiving, present your requests to
God. And the peace of God, which transcends all understanding,
will guard your hearts and your minds in Christ Jesus.
PHILIPPIANS 4:6–7 NIV

The Bible is full of stories of some very intelligent men. Joseph was described as discerning and wise (Genesis 41:39); of Daniel and his three companions it's recorded that "God gave [them] knowledge and understanding of all kinds of literature and learning" (Daniel 1:17 NIV); to Solomon was granted "wisdom and very great insight, and a breadth of understanding as measureless as the sand on the seashore" (1 Kings 4:29). In their days, these men were renowned for their intellect, and God used all of them to accomplish His will. But their real strength came from knowing the source of their gifts and the absolute necessity of meeting God in prayer.

Prayer does not replace knowledge, wisdom, or discernment—it transcends it. Prayer is borrowing the power of thought that we cannot generate. It's inviting the God of all wisdom to participate in whatever has captured our attention. He delights in trading His peace for the anxiety that has us running in mental circles. Thinking by itself will not get us out of every situation, but He "is able to do immeasurably more than all we ask or imagine" (Ephesians 3:20 NIV).

Let us always ask for wisdom (James 1:5) remembering that we are exercising the highest wisdom by coming to God in prayer.

PUT YOUR GUARD UP

Then he returned to his disciples and found them sleeping.
"Couldn't you men keep watch with me for one hour?" he asked Peter.
"Watch and pray so that you will not fall into temptation.
The spirit is willing, but the flesh is weak."
MATTHEW 26:40–41 NIV

Any man in midlife or older who lifts weights, runs, or pursues any athletic pastime learns one lesson quickly—the heart may be in it, but the body can't always pull it off. It's also true of other areas of our lives. We mean to spend more time with our families, but work keeps us preoccupied. We need to lose weight, but just can't seem to say no when the burgers are hot off the grill. We plan to get up earlier to meet with our Father in His Word, but something always steals that time from us.

Thankfully, Jesus is always gracious with our weaknesses. He knows we want to do better, but that we will need help:

> *"And I will ask the Father, and he will give you another*
> *advocate to help you and be with you forever."*
> (John 14:16 NIV)

Even in His admonition to watch and pray, He promises to help us:

> *In the same way, the Spirit helps us in our weakness. We do*
> *not know what we ought to pray for, but the Spirit himself*
> *intercedes for us through wordless groans.*
> (Romans 8:26 NIV)

With His promises of help, we can watch and pray with confidence that He will supply the strength we do not possess within ourselves.

SEEING OURSELVES RIGHTLY

For he knows how we are formed, he remembers that we are dust.
PSALM 103:14 NIV

As our creator, God never needs to be reminded what we are. He knows that we were made from the dust of the earth (Genesis 2:7), that we are "jars of clay" (2 Corinthians 4:7 NIV), a mere "mist that appears for a little while and then vanishes" (James 4:14 NIV). God knows our time is short and our power limited even if we forget.

And we regularly forget. It's easy to think too highly of ourselves and depend on our own strength in a way that "dust" simply wasn't designed for. Pride may tell us we're invincible and powerful, but God knows the truth. Thankfully, He does not look on our frailty with contempt. Instead, He is moved with a Father's compassion when He sees our vulnerability (Psalm 103:13–14). And as a good Father, He patiently disciplines us for our benefit:

> *Moreover, we have all had human fathers who disciplined us and we respected them for it. How much more should we submit to the Father of spirits and live!*
> (Hebrews 12:9 NIV)

God can't afford to have His children taken in by a false sense of strength and power and miss what He has for us. While we may spend our time making great plans, God spends His time making great sons. Whenever the two are in conflict, He will always choose our character over our success. Let us ask Him to open our eyes to our own limitations, not disdaining what we see but allowing it to keep us leaning on Him.

THE BREATH OF LIFE

*Then the LORD God formed a man from the dust of the ground
and breathed into his nostrils the breath of life,
and the man became a living being.*

GENESIS 2:7 NIV

Genesis 1 beautifully describes the origination of everything from a formless, dark void culminating in the creation of man, made in God's likeness and given the purpose of his existence: to use his God-given qualities to complete the picture God had begun painting (Genesis 1:28).

But there's one important element to man's creation that makes him unique: God breathed life into him to make him a "living being [literally, *soul*]." And interestingly, this breath of life was into his "nostrils" rather than his mouth. The natural position of the mouth is closed, but the natural state of the nostrils is open. We "swim" through air, surrounded by our next breaths; oxygen even circulates inside our bodies through the bloodstream, reaching every part of us. There is an inescapable connection and dependence on the God who made us.

In the most literal sense, our natural state of being is one of constant connection to God. Adam was designed to stay in connection with God in order to carry out his mission. Of course, willful disobedience ruined that plan. But hope returns with the promise of the Holy Spirit.

*And with that he breathed on them and said, "Receive the
Holy Spirit."*
(John 20:22 NIV)

In Christ, our connection to God through the Holy Spirit is as real, as essential, and as satisfying as the next breath we take.

THE SPIRIT OF ADOPTION

The Spirit you received does not make you slaves, so that you live in fear again; rather, the Spirit you received brought about your adoption to sonship. And by him we cry, "Abba, Father."

ROMANS 8:15 NIV

There's nothing more honest than a cry of the heart, one that comes from so deep within that nothing can stop it. That's the powerful affection the Spirit in us has for God the Father.

Of being adopted as sons of God, theologian J.I. Packer notes, "To be right with God the judge is a great thing, but to be loved and cared for by God the father is greater" (*Knowing God*, p.186–188). Being adopted goes beyond being forgiven, even beyond being made righteous. Adoption brings us into a warm family relationship: "Our fellowship is with the Father and with his Son, Jesus Christ" (1 John 1:3 NIV).

Adoption also bestows on us some specific privileges. First, we are granted immediate, unhindered access to God. "In him and through faith in him we may approach God with freedom and confidence" (Ephesians 3:12 NIV). Nothing can stop us from coming close to our Father. Second, as members of the family we get to share in His name. "'Therefore go and make disciples of all nations, baptizing them in the name of the Father and of the Son and of the Holy Spirit'" (Matthew 28:19 NIV). And third, adoption guarantees an inheritance from a Father "who has qualified you to share in the inheritance of his holy people in the kingdom of light" (Colossians 1:12 NIV).

Praise God that He adopted us!

THE FACE OF WISDOM

*The wisdom that comes from heaven is first of all pure;
then peace-loving, considerate, submissive, full of mercy
and good fruit, impartial and sincere.*

JAMES 3:17 NIV

A lot of information these days claims to be "wisdom." How do we recognize what is truly of God? James gives us an eight-point checklist to navigate the many voices that claim to be speaking wisdom. If any voice fails on one of these points, it's not wisdom from heaven:

1) *Pure.* Wisdom from above is never compromised by sin or contradicts the truth of the Gospel.

2) *Peace-loving.* True wisdom seeks peace, and does not value stirring up unnecessary conflict.

3) *Considerate.* Godly wisdom is not harsh or divisive, but gentle and thoughtful.

4) *Submissive.* Wisdom from heaven is not stubborn, obstinate, or narrow-minded, but open to reason as long as truth is not compromised.

5) *Full of mercy.* True wisdom is gracious to the ignorant, lost, and guilty, ready to forgive and encourage.

6) *Full of good fruit.* Wisdom from above produces real results, inwardly and outwardly in the lives of those who practice it.

7) *Impartial.* Real wisdom is not swayed by people; it doesn't harbor biases or take sides because of group affiliation. It remains true to itself.

8) *Sincere.* Authentic wisdom is frank, open to all, and has no agenda besides the truth of God.

Whatever claims to be good advice or wise counsel but does not pass James's checklist is not of God and cannot help us to live wisely before Him.

FRAMEWORK FOR FREEDOM

See to it that no one takes you captive through hollow and deceptive philosophy, which depends on human tradition and the elemental spiritual forces of this world rather than on Christ.

COLOSSIANS 2:8 NIV

Spiritual captivity comes through a mind-set or belief that's influenced by any philosophy that originates from this world rather than from God. It may be built on outright deception, cultural bias, false assumptions, or even good intentions that don't line up with the character of Christ. Worldly thinking is anything that promises deliverance without Christ, anything that creates hope without the Messiah, anything that points to a future without the One who created it.

This world has its evangelists looking for converts. We are to be on our guard so that we are not "spoiled," as the King James Version would say.

The framework for our freedom is described in the rest of Colossians 2:

- 2:9—We can know the Father because Christ embodies Him fully.
- 2:10—Christ fills us, not this world, and He is the final authority.
- 2:11—Christ marks us as His own by releasing us from the power of the flesh.
- 2:12—Christ buried our old identity and gave us a new one in Himself.
- 2:13-14—God created a "togetherness" with Christ that assures our forgiveness and our permanent release from the debt that the law has the right to demand.
- 2:15—Christ disarmed any authority or power, worldly or spiritual, that stands in opposition to His resurrected life.

THE GOSPEL'S COMPETITION

"But the worries of this life, the deceitfulness of wealth and the desires for other things come in and choke the word, making it unfruitful."
MARK 4:19 NIV

Receiving the word sown by Christ is just the beginning; His goal is to have it grow and become fruitful. But the world pulls against us, sometimes in not-so-obvious ways—like weeds that spring up in a garden a few at a time until it's overgrown.

The worries of this life: Getting the right job, finding a wife, buying a house, raising kids, planning for retirement. These can be blessings from God, but they can also engross us to the point that we grow cold in pursuing Christ.

The deceitfulness of wealth: A comfortable life, a nicer house, a more prestigious job, luxuries, and fashionable possessions. "Whoever loves money never has enough; whoever loves wealth is never satisfied with their income. This too is meaningless" (Ecclesiastes 5:10 NIV). Money itself isn't the problem; it's the false promises money makes. If we get on the treadmill of riches, we'll stop running the race we were designed for.

The desires for other things: Success, influence, entertainment, political power, immorality, fame. These idols are just as false as the ones that ensnared ancient Israel when Joshua declared, "'Choose for yourselves this day whom you will serve. . . But as for me and my household, we will serve the LORD'" (Joshua 24:15 NIV).

A seed that sprouts is a good start, but fruitfulness is the goal. We need to be alert to the weeds that choke the fruit God wants to produce in our lives.

THE HEART OF FORGIVENESS

*Therefore, as God's chosen people, holy and dearly loved,
clothe yourselves with compassion, kindness, humility,
gentleness and patience. Bear with each other and forgive one another
if any of you has a grievance against someone. Forgive as the
Lord forgave you. And over all these virtues put on love,
which binds them all together in perfect unity.*

Colossians 3:12–14 NIV

The heart has long been the metaphor for the deepest parts of a man's emotions, thoughts, and attitudes. In addition to the Bible, the ancient Greeks and Egyptians credited the heart as the seat of our mind and thoughts, and therefore our actions.

Today we can extend that metaphor with what we know about the heart from science. The heart is essentially a pump for the blood, and the blood is a vehicle for oxygen to be taken to every point of the body. Without this pumping of oxygen, the body dies. Perhaps this is why the Bible declares "the blood is the life" of all flesh (Deuteronomy 12:23 NIV).

Importantly, the point of a pump isn't to receive something, but to *push* it along. The heart wouldn't be functioning according to its design if it kept freshly oxygenated blood to itself. In the same way, if we receive forgiveness from the Lord without pushing it along, then our spiritual heart isn't functioning according to its design. A healthy Christian heart is characterized by compassion, kindness, humility, gentleness, and patience; it bears with the shortcomings and offenses of others. The only way to "hear" the beat of that heart is to witness forgiveness in action.

THE LIKENESS OF GOD

But God disciplines us for our good,
in order that we may share in his holiness.
HEBREWS 12:10 NIV

Holiness is God's nature and His fondest hope for His children. But the concept of holiness is almost always mired with misconceptions: holiness means no more fun, holiness is too hard to attain, holiness is a lot of work, holiness is boring, holiness means becoming "too religious."

Holiness is actually freedom. Nothing about it is boring or restrictive *when we are walking in it*. The psalmist described the joy of shared holiness well:

> *You make known to me the path of life; you will fill me with joy*
> *in your presence, with eternal pleasures at your right hand.*
> (Psalm 16:11 NIV)

And holiness is the only way for us to experience the Lord.

> *Make every effort to live in peace with everyone and to be*
> *holy; without holiness no one will see the Lord.*
> (Hebrews 12:14 NIV)

Of course, when we deny our new nature in Christ (2 Peter 1:4) and are living according to the flesh, valuing things that God says are worthless, then holiness will most certainly seem burdensome. That's because, even for believers, "the mind governed by the flesh is hostile to God" (Romans 8:7 NIV). When we feel that holiness is growing heavy, we should check our thought life, because "the mind governed by the Spirit is life and peace" (Romans 8:6 NIV).

Let us be on the watch for the discipline God promises so that we embrace it and grow in His likeness. Holiness is our birthright, and He is committed to seeing it in us.

SHARPENING SUCCESS

If the ax is dull, and one does not sharpen the edge,
then he must use more strength; but wisdom brings success.
ECCLESIASTES 10:10 NKJV

If you've ever tried to cut down a tree with an ax instead of a chainsaw, you know how much work it can be. And if you've ever tried to do it with a *dull* ax, you know it's almost impossible. Common sense tells us that it's better to take the time to sharpen the ax beforehand; otherwise you'll just wear yourself out.

What does this proverb have to say to us today? What areas of life have us exhausted from exerting more and more effort for very little return? Where do we need wisdom to succeed?

Does my work leave me worn out? Do I need more education or training to see results? Am I in the right job to start with?

In relationships, am I constantly frustrated? Does sharpening the ax mean becoming a better listener? Being more patient? Controlling my temper?

What does success look like in my personal life? What goals have I had for years with no real results? Losing weight? Getting on a budget? Sharing my faith?

The challenge of this proverb is to identify where we are exhausting ourselves, and to take the time to seek God's wisdom in sharpening the ax for success. Thankfully, He promises to give to those who ask:

> *If any of you lacks wisdom, you should ask God, who gives gen-*
> *erously to all without finding fault, and it will be given to you.*
> (James 1:5 NIV)

THE TRUE BATTLE

What causes fights and quarrels among you?
Don't they come from your desires that battle within you?
JAMES 4:1 NIV

The inner life of a man is the real life of a man. Proverb 23:7 (NKJV) puts it this way: "For as he thinks in his heart, so is he." The heart—or inner life—will determine everything that we do and say over time since from it comes our value system. That's why we are warned: "Above all else, guard your heart, for everything you do flows from it" (Proverbs 4:23 NIV).

One of the clear promises of scripture is that the inner life of a man will always come out:

> *A good man brings good things out of the good stored up in his heart, and an evil man brings evil things out of the evil stored up in his heart. For the mouth speaks what the heart is full of.*
> (Luke 6:45 NIV)

When we experience conflict with others—especially sincere believers—we may be allowing the inner turmoil of our own hearts to express itself in those relationships. Other people may not be "the problem." We may be engaging in the wrong battle. The real battle is saying no to our own desires and wants, and humbling ourselves to serve.

> *Do nothing out of selfish ambition or vain conceit. Rather, in humility value others above yourselves, not looking to your own interests but each of you to the interests of the others.*
> (Philippians 2:3-4)

Thanksgiving Day

CULTIVATING GRATITUDE

*"Those who sacrifice thank offerings honor me,
and to the blameless I will show my salvation."*
PSALM 50:23 NIV

If there was ever a cure for being "hardened by sin's deceitfulness" (Hebrews 3:13 NIV) in a man's life, it's offering thanks to God. It's so easy to let the worries and distractions of this life pull us away from the things that matter; they make us forgetful of the blessings we've received and are daily living in. It takes humility to admit it and direct action to reverse it. And no action softens the heart and encourages the spirit like offering thanks to God.

The scriptures often use the word *sacrifice* in context of thanksgiving. The first instances of sacrificing an offering to God were Cain and Abel. Abel did it well, with a genuinely thankful heart, and Cain did not. The objects offered are not what God receives, but rather the gratitude itself. Consider Jesus' comments to one of ten lepers He had healed:

> *He threw himself at Jesus' feet and thanked him—and he was a Samaritan.*
> *Jesus asked, "Were not all ten cleansed? Where are the other nine? Has no one returned to give praise to God except this foreigner?"*
> (Luke 17:16–18 NIV)

Thanksgiving opens up the relationship God Himself wants. Not giving thanks is the symptom of those who have abandoned truth, as Romans 1:21 (NIV) says, "For although they knew God, they neither glorified him as God nor gave thanks to him, but their thinking became futile and their foolish hearts were darkened."

BREAD FROM HEAVEN

*"You are looking for me, not because you saw the signs I performed
but because you ate the loaves and had your fill". . . . So they asked
him, "What sign then will you give that we may see it and believe you?
What will you do? Our ancestors ate the manna in the wilderness;
as it is written: 'He gave them bread from heaven to eat.'"*
JOHN 6:26, 30–31 NIV

It's easier to acknowledge Jesus when we've just experienced His power—
when our stomachs are full. But our interest in Him often fades as quickly
as a good meal.

The five thousand knew a prophet was among them when the baskets
of food were being passed around (John 6:14). But as soon as they were
hungry again, the gift rather than the Giver became their focus. Though
Jesus points this fact out to them, they "cleverly" try to get Him to prove
Himself again by providing a daily supply of bread the way Moses had.
Wouldn't that be great? No more work, no going hungry, just collect free
bread every day. But they missed the point of the manna. They hungered
for an easy solution to this life's hardships, not Christ filling their souls. So
they demanded free bread in exchange for their belief in a Messiah.

Isn't it easy to fall into the trap of trading faith for favors? But it's like
being hired to follow—*as long as I'm being paid, I'm on God's side.* Let us
all strive not to seek God to be filled only for a day when He offers so
much more.

THE VALUE OF BETRAYAL

"Because the patriarchs were jealous of Joseph, they sold him as a slave into Egypt. But God was with him and rescued him from all his troubles. He gave Joseph wisdom and enabled him to gain the goodwill of Pharaoh king of Egypt. So Pharaoh made him ruler over Egypt and all his palace."
ACTS 7:9–10 NIV

Betrayal isn't usually part of the recommended route to success. But in Joseph's case it was essential. His brothers hated him because he was their father Israel's favorite (Genesis 37:4). Matters only got worse when he began having dreams of the future in which they all bowed down to him. They considered killing him (Genesis 37:18), then finally settled on selling him into slavery. Of course, in the end, Joseph rescues his entire family from famine because he's been put in charge of all Egypt by Pharaoh.

Betrayal was part of God's plan for Joseph. In His hands, the hardest experiences in life can be tools for His use. Disappointment can clarify our expectations by stripping away false hopes. Tragedy can work its painful service to show us the reality of a world that isn't our home. Pain, as C. S. Lewis once wrote, can be "God's megaphone" to cut through the world and the flesh's noise and temptations.

Joseph remained faithful to God during his afflictions until God's timing was complete and he became the savior, literally, of Israel and the twelve tribes that would come from his brothers and himself. He was a foreshadowing of Jesus, who also endured betrayal as part of God's will, in order to save His people eternally.

TRUE RIGHTEOUSNESS

*"For I tell you that unless your righteousness surpasses that
of the Pharisees and the teachers of the law, you will
certainly not enter the kingdom of heaven."*
MATTHEW 5:20 NIV

The Pharisees and scribes believed they "earned" righteousness by strictly following the Mosaic law. And, as if that weren't hard enough, they added other rules and traditions—even though sometimes they contradicted the law. Jesus rebuked them about this: "'You have a fine way of setting aside the commands of God in order to observe your own traditions!'" (Mark 7:9 NIV).

However, before Jesus exposed these groups as hypocrites, they were the top of the line in Jewish righteousness. They were learned, powerful, and influential. They ran the Sanhedrin, passing judgment on all aspects of life. Paul even makes reference to his past as a Pharisee to underscore his religious "pedigree":

> *Circumcised on the eighth day, of the people of Israel, of
> the tribe of Benjamin, a Hebrew of Hebrews; in regard to the
> law, a Pharisee; as for zeal, persecuting the church; as for
> righteousness based on the law, faultless.*
> (Philippians 3:5-6 NIV)

The Pharisees were an intimidating bunch. There must have been many Jews who said, "If only the law wasn't so hard, we could follow it, too!" But Jesus wasn't sympathetic to that argument. The law, Jesus stressed, doesn't change. It's supposed to be hard—in fact, it's impossible if you go beyond outward practices to include the heart's attitudes and intentions. The Pharisees missed this, working instead for a counterfeit righteousness. Only Christ fulfilled the law completely; only He can offer us true righteousness.

WHOLEHEARTEDLY HIS

[Amaziah] did what was right in the eyes of the Lord,
but not wholeheartedly.
2 Chronicles 25:2 niv

Religion may ask, "Are you in or are you out?" But God asks, *How far in are you?* His interest is in an active, real relationship. It's the difference between a wedding and a marriage.

Before the wedding, a man is "out" but afterward, he is "in." And once he's married, the question is, "How married is he?" Really married, or just a little married? Which does his wife expect?

Everything God has done in history is to have His people be "really in"—wholeheartedly with Him. It's possible to do what is right in His eyes, but not in a way that demonstrates a real relationship with Him. Following the rules is never enough for a father. Character and heart matter more.

No one ever impressed his wife, his boss, his commanding officer, his dad, or anyone else with a halfhearted effort. Why should we expect God to be happy when we just go through the motions? We certainly don't resemble our Father, "who did not spare his own Son, but gave him up for us all" (Romans 8:32 niv) when we hold back in doing His will.

The good news is that in Christ, we are given a whole heart to be His:

> *"'I will give them a heart to know me, that I am the Lord.*
> *They will be my people, and I will be their God, for they will*
> *return to me with all their heart.'"*
> (Jeremiah 24:7 niv)

WORDS THAT BURN

They asked each other, "Were not our hearts burning within us while he talked with us on the road and opened the Scriptures to us?"
LUKE 24:32 NIV

On the very day of Jesus' resurrection, two of His followers left Jerusalem for the nearby town of Emmaus. They were overwhelmed by the loss of their leader at the hands of the Romans just a few days earlier, and disturbed by some women who reported that His body had disappeared from the well-guarded tomb. Then the resurrected Christ joins them on their two-hour journey, though "they were kept from recognizing him" (Luke 24:16 NIV). They pour out their anguish and disappointment to Jesus, who gently rebukes their lack of faith (Luke 24:25), and generously opens the scripture to them.

> *And beginning with Moses and all the Prophets, he explained to them what was said in all the Scriptures concerning himself.*
> (Luke 24:27 NIV)

Imagine the opportunity! Having the Author and Subject of the sacred writings explain everything about how they point to His coming, His suffering, and His resurrection. But even then, they didn't perceive the full truth of things. It wasn't until Christ revealed Himself by breaking bread with them that their eyes were spiritually opened and His teaching became as alive as He was (Luke 24:30–31).

Today we can walk the road to Emmaus whenever we rely on the Holy Spirit to reveal more to us:

> *"But the Advocate, the Holy Spirit, whom the Father will send in my name, will teach you all things and will remind you of everything I have said to you."*
> (John 14:26 NIV)

WORSHIP LIKE A MAN

Wearing a linen ephod, David was dancing before the LORD
with all his might, while he and all Israel were bringing up
the ark of the LORD with shouts and the sound of trumpets.
2 SAMUEL 6:14–15 NIV

Masculinity is made complete in worship. Where else can a man open himself so completely without fear of failure, without pretending to be strong or competent or in control? Where else can a man be so honest without fear of being taken advantage of? Where else can a man look into the face of the most Real Man of all?

To worship as a man means to disdain what others think of your openness. The Complete Jewish Bible says David "danced and spun around with abandon." When his wife, Michal, daughter of Saul, rebuked him for this enthusiastic public display, he responded:

> "It was before the LORD, who chose me rather than your
> father or anyone from his house when he appointed me ruler
> over the LORD's people Israel—I will celebrate before the
> LORD."
> (2 Samuel 6:21 NIV)

Basically, David didn't give a rip what people thought of him when he was worshipping. David cared only for God's opinion. As a king, a warrior, and a shepherd, he had faced death from man and beast, so public opinion wasn't about to scare him away from worshipping with all his might.

Humbling yourself in worship, confessing, singing, crying, dancing with wild abandon before your Maker, your Redeemer, your Eternal Example is to return to masculinity, not to relinquish it.

YOUR WILL BE DONE

He was near Jerusalem and the people thought
that the kingdom of God was going to appear at once.
LUKE 19:11 NIV

When God starts to lead, it's easy to get out ahead of Him. The *idea* of His will can become the object of our hopes. In other words, we can begin to love our expectations of God's will to the point that we stop following Him to see where His will actually takes us.

The disciples often got ahead of things, sometimes missing Jesus' will spectacularly:

> *[The Samaritans] did not receive Him, because His face was*
> *set for the journey to Jerusalem. And when His disciples*
> *James and John saw this, they said, "Lord, do You want us*
> *to command fire to come down from heaven and consume*
> *them, just as Elijah did?" But He turned and rebuked them,*
> *and said, "You do not know what manner of spirit you are of.*
> *For the Son of Man did not come to destroy men's lives but*
> *to save them."*
> (Luke 9:53–56 NKJV)

Talk about being on the wrong page! Clearly they hadn't been paying attention to Christ during their time together and had come up with a plan pretty much opposite of His.

We can learn from the disciples' worldly mind-set and apply Paul's sound advice so that we stay in step with God's unfolding will for our lives:

> *And do not be conformed to this world, but be transformed*
> *by the renewing of your mind, that you may prove what is*
> *that good and acceptable and perfect will of God.*
> (Romans 12:2 NKJV)

WHO JESUS CHRIST IS IN US

For it pleased the Father that in Him all the fullness should dwell,
and by Him to reconcile all things to Himself, by Him,
whether things on earth or things in heaven,
having made peace through the blood of His cross.
COLOSSIANS 1:19–20 NKJV

In a classic *Peanuts* cartoon, Charlie Brown hears that Snoopy is writing a book of theology, and tells him, "I hope you have a good title." Snoopy lifts his hands off the typewriter, closes his eyes, and thinks to himself, *I have the perfect title*. He then types, "Has It Ever Occurred to You That You Might Be Wrong?"

True, we probably haven't thought of even 10 percent of the questions we should be asking, let alone answering, biblically, intellectually, and experientially. Still, we have learned and experienced so much that is true. Truths we can't review too often!

Truly transforming? Reviewing the dozens of "who I am in Christ" statements compiled and popularized by Neil T. Anderson, and more than doubled in size by others. Untold millions have experienced spiritual healing, health, and hope by reading them.

What would happen, however, if we turned the equation around? Specifically, what would happen in our heart and life if we began affirming what's true about "who Jesus Christ is in me"?

When we ponder "who Jesus Christ is in me," what immediately comes to mind? We can thank the Lord daily for His sovereignty (greatness), providence (goodness), holiness (glory), love (graciousness), and mystery (God alone knows).

In the coming days, let's continue to consider majestic truths about our Lord and Savior.

JESUS CHRIST OFFERS FORETASTES OF HEAVEN

"Go back and report to John what you have seen and heard:
The blind receive sight, the lame walk, those who have leprosy
are cleansed, the deaf hear, the dead are raised,
and the good news is proclaimed to the poor."
LUKE 7:22 NIV

Two thousand years ago, Jesus Christ's earthly ministry gave the men, women, youth, and children around Him amazing foretastes of what is eternal for each of His followers. Those foretastes cover a wide horizon. To name but a few: seeing individuals raised from the dead, seeing other individuals healed spiritually, seeing still others healed physically, seeing yet other persons healed psychologically.

Let's not make the mistake, however, of thinking that wonderful foretastes of heaven aren't *ours* to experience *today*. As followers of Jesus Christ, our sins past, present, and future are already all forgiven, yet we experience it anew each time we confess our sins. Immediately afterward, we want to slow down and savor that specific experience of being forgiven. If we do, we enjoy a delicious foretaste of heaven.

Even though our salvation is all-encompassing, it doesn't mean we don't sin—any more than it means we never get sick, never suffer trials, never wrestle with temptation, never fail, never fall, never fear cancer, and never end up dying. Aren't these means, while on this planet, helping us to continue longing for heaven?

What we don't want to miss is the critical need to slow down and savor each specific foretaste experience this side of eternity. In a real sense, these are Jesus Christ's rich and valuable gifts to us.

ADVENT BEGINS WITH JESUS CHRIST

God, who at various times and in various ways spoke in time past to the fathers by the prophets, has in these last days spoken to us by His Son.
HEBREWS 1:1–2 NKJV

During the first few days of Advent, let's consider what the opening verses of the New Testament letter to the Hebrews tell us about our majestic Lord and Savior. After all, Hebrews is a passionate appeal urging readers to see a bigger vision of Jesus Christ—and then worship and live accordingly.

In the opening verses, though, the writer of Hebrews doesn't say "Jesus Christ." He waits until partway through chapter 2 before mentioning "Jesus" by name, partway through chapter 3 before using the name "Christ," and all the way to chapter 10 before combining the two names together. Usage of *Jesus, Christ,* and *Jesus Christ* is much more prevalent in the latter chapters of Hebrews. From the get-go, however, the writer's preferred name for Jesus Christ is the "Son" of God, as we see in today's scripture passage.

Does it matter which English words we do, and do not, use to speak of Jesus Christ?

And, does it matter how biblically accurate and true those words are?

A. W. Tozer said: "Much of our difficulty. . .stems from our unwillingness to take God as He is and adjust our lives accordingly." Do you agree or disagree?

What's more, how do you think a bigger vision of Jesus Christ could change how you worship and live?

ADVENT BEGINS AND ENDS WITH JESUS CHRIST

In the past God spoke to our ancestors
through the prophets at many times and in various ways.
HEBREWS 1:1 NIV

The book of Hebrews begins as dramatically as a missile launch. Let's look again at Hebrews 1:1, phrase by phrase. *In the past* refers to the millennia between Adam and Malachi. *God spoke* makes it clear we need to listen! *To our ancestors* refers to the leaders of the ancient Israelite nation. *Through the prophets* refers to the Old Testament writers. *At many times* understates God's hundreds of revelations over thousands of years. *And in various ways* makes it clear God doesn't have only one or two methods of communicating with humanity. Instead, the Lord is pleased to use a wide variety of means:

- Through personal appearances and angels
- Through visions and dreams
- With lightning and fire
- With the voice of a trumpet and a quiet inner voice
- Using dictation and dialogue
- By using laws, institutions, ceremonies, sacrifices
- By issuing warnings and exhortations
- By using types, parables, and proverbs
- By using psalms, laments, histories, sermons, prophecies, and direct oracles
- By the perseverance of godly men and women, despite severe persecutions no ordinary human beings could endure
- By enacting incredible miracles, mysterious signs, bizarre symbolic acts, and feats of strength

Which of these means did Jesus Christ, God's Son, use during His first Advent? And why do they still matter today?

JESUS CHRIST IS GREATER

But in these last days he [God the Father] has spoken to us
by his Son, whom he appointed heir of all things.
HEBREWS 1:2 NIV

The more we worship Jesus Christ with our heart, soul, strength, and mind, the greater He will become in our eyes.

C. S. Lewis portrays the growing Christian's experience of an ever-enlarging Jesus Christ in book 2 of *The Chronicles of Narnia*. One of the four children, Lucy, sees the lion Aslan—a Christ figure in the series—shining white and huge in the moonlight:

> "Welcome, child," he said.
> "Aslan," said Lucy, "you're bigger."
> "That is because you are older, little one," answered he.
> "Not because you are?"
> "I am not. But every year you grow, you will find me bigger."

In Hebrews 1:2-3, our Lord and Savior Jesus Christ is honored in four distinct ways *in relation to God the Father*. Today, we will consider the first two ways.

1. As the unique Son of God. This is something that never could be said of angels or other created beings. By putting our faith and trust in Jesus Christ, we become children of God, His sons, part of His family. Then again, Jesus Christ alone is God the Son.

2. As the heir of God. God has "appointed [Jesus Christ the] heir of all things." All things means *we* are part of His inheritance, *now and forever*. For some incredible reason, the Lord values and treasures us. And why is that true? Because He has invited us to join His forever family.

No wonder we should worship and sing His praises!

JESUS CHRIST IS FULLY GOD

*The Son is the radiance of God's glory
and the exact representation of his being.*

HEBREWS 1:3 NIV

During this season, we remember the first Advent of Jesus Christ. Only God could script something so unexpected, so radical.

No, this isn't an earthly king wearing common clothes to secretly visit his people. Instead, this is God Himself entering fully into humanity—supernaturally conceived, naturally formed in His earthly mother's womb, and humbly born into the most austere of circumstances.

In Hebrews 1:2–3, God the Son, Jesus Christ, is honored in four different ways *in relation to God the Father*. Today, we will consider the third and fourth ways.

3. As the manifestation of God. The phrase "the radiance of God's glory" speaks of a flood of resplendent light. The word *radiance* means an outshining, not a reflection. The moon reflects light; the sun radiates it—and so does God the Son.

As the brilliance of the sun is inseparable from the sun itself, so the Son's radiance is inseparable from Deity. No wonder the Nicene Creed describes Jesus Christ as "God of God, Light of Light, Very God of Very God." In Jesus, we see God Himself.

4. As the ultimate revealer of God. The phrase "the exact representation of his being" reiterates the fact that Jesus Christ is fully God—equal to and yet distinct from God the Father and God the Holy Spirit. Scripture calls us to worship Jesus accordingly.

One encounter with God's Son is enough to change someone. . .instantly, forever. What has been your most meaningful experience with Jesus Christ? What was your response?

JESUS CHRIST, CREATOR AND SUSTAINER

In the past God spoke to our ancestors through the prophets at many times and in various ways, but in these last days he has spoken to us by his Son, whom he appointed heir of all things, and through whom also he made the universe. The Son is the radiance of God's glory and the exact representation of his being, sustaining all things by his powerful word.

HEBREWS 1:1–3 NIV

We can never honor Jesus Christ too much. The past two days we saw how Jesus Christ is honored four distinct ways *in relation to God.* Today and tomorrow, we see four more ways Jesus Christ is honored *in relation to all things.*

1. As the creator of the universe. This isn't a new idea. The fact that Jesus Christ is the creator of all things is taught in John 1:3, Colossians 1:16, and other scriptures. The implication is clear: *We* are part of Jesus Christ's creation. No wonder *He values us!*

Sometimes, though, we have a hard time feeling a sense of personal self-worth. Such worth isn't something we strive to obtain. Instead, it's something God has breathed into us from the moment He began creating us.

2. As the sustainer of the universe. The phrase "sustaining all things by his powerful word" means we are sustained not by our own strength but by Jesus Christ. We experience that strengthening as we read the Bible, meditate on it, read devotionally, pray with God, worship Him alone and with others, spend time with other growing Christian men, love our neighbors, and share our faith with them.

JESUS CHRIST, SAVIOR AND LORD

After he [Jesus Christ] had provided purification for sins,
he sat down at the right hand of the Majesty in heaven.
HEBREWS 1:3 NIV

In relation to all things, Jesus Christ is honored four ways. Today, let's consider the third and fourth.

3. As the Savior of the universe. Romans 8:20–21, Colossians 1:19–20, and other scriptures tell us that Jesus intends to redeem creation itself. The phrase "had provided purification for sins" speaks more particularly of the fact that we are purified, washed, redeemed, and being sanctified because of Jesus Christ's death on the cross.

4. As the Lord of the universe. The phrase "he sat down at the right hand of the Majesty in heaven" spoke powerfully to the original readers, because they knew that priests never sat down. Jesus could sit down, however, because His priestly work of redemption was complete. He is now supremely honored in heaven.

What's more, in His position of authority, Christ intercedes with the Father on our behalf. It's quite astounding to realize that even when we don't feel we can pray, Jesus never stops praying for us.

The healing method of the writer of Hebrews is to lift the Son higher and higher. He is sure that the eloquence of Jesus Christ's person is the most practical thing on earth. Indeed, Jesus, understood and exalted, eloquently informs every area of life.

Does your life sometimes feel stressful and perhaps even overwhelming? If so, the essential answer to each of life's problems is. . .what? *Who Jesus Christ is*—in you. Not in theory. Not in "theology." But—*in you!*

JESUS CHRIST WILL ALWAYS BE FULLY HUMAN

*For this reason he had to be made like them, fully human in every way,
in order that he might become a merciful and faithful high priest in
service to God, and that he might make atonement for the sins of
the people. Because he himself suffered when he was tempted,
he is able to help those who are being tempted.*

HEBREWS 2:17–18 NIV

As we talk with friends about Jesus Christ, particularly this season of the year, mistakes are bound to happen. According to leading pollsters, it's quite astounding how many misconceptions people have about the Bible, about God, and specifically about Jesus Christ.

The one mistake we don't want to make is assuming our friends understand that Jesus Christ is eternal. As God's Son, Jesus has existed for all of eternity past. There is no point at which Jesus Christ didn't exist.

Yet many speak as if Jesus came alive and was created at the point of conception in the virgin Mary's womb. That point simply represents when He went from being fully God to being fully God *and human*.

It sometimes can be hard to imagine Jesus spending nine months "trapped" before birth, let alone spending years "trapped" as an infant, toddler, child, older child, young man, and full-fledged adult before starting His public ministry at age thirty.

Yet Jesus Christ didn't become *barely human*. Instead, He became, is, and for all eternity will be *fully God and fully human*.

Our scripture today mentions three reasons Jesus had become "fully human in every way." They're great reasons to thank Him again today.

HOW WE BRING JOY TO THE LORD

Therefore by Him let us continually offer the sacrifice of praise to God, that is, the fruit of our lips, giving thanks to His name. But do not forget to do good and to share, for with such sacrifices God is well pleased.
HEBREWS 13:15–16 NKJV

Unlike the original cast of characters in the Holy Lands two thousand years ago, we know that the greatest story ever told doesn't begin, let alone end, with Christmas.

The story of Jesus Christ, as God's eternal Son, has *no beginning*.

The story of Jesus Christ, as fully God *and fully human*, begins with His conception and birth, which we celebrate during Advent and Christmas. Three months later, we celebrate the focal point of His earthly life and ministry during Passion, Good Friday, Easter Resurrection Sunday, and His Ascension six weeks later.

And how do we celebrate these decidedly Christian holidays? We do so by praising and thanking God the Father, God the Son, and God the Holy Spirit. We also do so by doing good and sharing with others, "for with such sacrifices God is well pleased."

Put another way, our words praising who Jesus Christ is in us, and our words and actions toward family and friends around us, make the Trinity happy!

So, it's okay to decorate our homes, make delicious foods, assemble gifts, offer hospitality, and then give thanks to the Lord before one and all during Christianity's most important holidays.

After all, actions speak loudest with words. Like the original cast two thousand years ago, let's offer both this joy-filled Advent season.

THE ANGEL GABRIEL SAID WHAT?

"I am Gabriel! I stand in the very presence of God.
It was he who sent me to bring you this good news!"
LUKE 1:19 NLT

Gabriel is arguably one of the most important angels. In the Christmas story, Gabriel speaks to Zechariah and his much younger relative, the virgin Mary. Many of us know the differences between the two stories, but it's easy to miss the similarities.

- To both, Gabriel says, "Do not be afraid" (Luke 1:13, 30 NKJV). Make no mistake: Gabriel was no fat, cute little cherub. So, let's dial in the right picture now so we're not terrified when we meet him in glory.
- To both, Gabriel says God is pleased with him or her. How strange that we find it hard to believe *God is happy*—let alone *with us.* Again, let's get the right picture. What a difference it makes!

God's Good News:
- To both, Gabriel says a miraculous conception will bring about the birth of a "great" son. The first will become great "before the Lord" (Luke 1:15 ESV). The second is great because He's "the Son of the Most High" (Luke 1:32 ESV).
- Gabriel declares God's chosen name for each boy and speaks of the Holy Spirit's role in each before birth. The Holy Spirit filled John in Elizabeth's womb. Greater? The Holy Spirit superintended the very conception of Jesus.
- Gabriel says God's good news will happen as promised. How strange that we find it hard to believe that 1) every word God says is true, and 2) with Him nothing is impossible!

Hanukkah begins at sundown

ZECHARIAH SAID WHAT?

To everyone's surprise he wrote, "His name is John."
Instantly Zechariah could speak again, and he began praising
God. Awe fell upon the whole neighborhood, and the news of
what had happened spread throughout the Judean hills.
LUKE 1:63–65 NLT

When Zechariah finds himself in the presence of the angel Gabriel, he speaks words of *dis*belief—only to be told he will be unable to speak another word for nine long months.

When he can speak again, eight days after his son's birth, Zechariah is filled with the Holy Spirit and is anything but at a loss for words. In a well-written, oft-rehearsed, and divinely inspired prophecy, Zechariah declares seven enduring truths. We do well to remember them.

1.   The Lord God has visited and redeemed His people.
2.   As promised, God has sent a mighty Savior from David's royal line.
3.   Zechariah's little newborn son, John, one day would be called the prophet of the Most High, preparing the way for the Lord Jesus.
4.   His son, John, will tell people how to find salvation through the forgiveness of sins.
5.   The Savior, Jesus, is the morning star from heaven, bringing the light of salvation.
6.   The Savior will give light to the oppressed and those near death, guiding them to the path of peace.
7.   Now we can serve God without fear, in holiness and righteousness, for as long as we live!

ELIZABETH SAID WHAT?

When Zechariah's week of service in the Temple was over,
he returned home. Soon afterward his wife, Elizabeth,
became pregnant and went into seclusion for five months.
LUKE 1:23–24 NLT

The third character in the Christmas accounts is Zechariah's wife, Elizabeth.

Like Zechariah, Elizabeth is 1) from the priestly line of Aaron, 2) righteous and just in God's eyes, and 3) careful to obey God's commandments.

Despite all this, Elizabeth bore the stigma of being childless, which in that culture was assumed to signify a lack of God's blessing and favor. So, you can imagine how frustrated she was when Zechariah couldn't tell her what happened in the Temple. Thankfully, he was a good writer!

When we hear Elizabeth speak the first time, *it's one of the world's shortest soliloquies:* "'How kind the Lord is! . . . He has taken away my disgrace of having no children'" (Luke 1:25 NLT).

When we hear Elizabeth speak a second time, *it's the most astonishing greeting any Jewish woman could have given another:* "'God has blessed you [Mary] above all women, and your child is blessed. Why am I so honored, that the mother of my Lord should visit me? When I heard your greeting, the baby in my womb jumped for joy. You are blessed because you believed that the Lord would do what he said'" (Luke 1:42–45 NLT).

When we hear Elizabeth speak a third time, *it's one of the ancient world's most emphatic statements by a Jewish woman:* "No! His name is John!" (Luke 1:60 NLT).

Let's always cherish these powerful words within the Christmas story.

THE VIRGIN MARY SAID WHAT?

*"For the Mighty One is holy, and he has done great things for me.
He shows mercy from generation to generation to all who fear him."*
LUKE 1:49–50 NLT

A century ago, Oswald Chambers wrote, "Faith is hanging on very stubbornly to the belief that things are not really as they seem." That's apropos when we come to Mary's central place in the Christmas story.

With Gabriel:
"Mary asked the angel, 'But how can this happen? I am a virgin'" (Luke 1:34 NLT).
"Mary responded, 'I am the Lord's servant. May everything you have said about me come true'" (Luke 1:38 NLT).

With Elizabeth:
After Elizabeth's astonishing greeting, Mary responds with a beautiful, scripture-filled song of praise called the Magnificat (Luke 1:46-55).

With Joseph:
Neither Matthew nor Luke record anything Mary said to Joseph. What's the point? He already knew "things are not really as they seem." We can only begin to imagine her relief when Joseph did as the Lord instructed him.

With the shepherds:
"All who heard the shepherds' story were astonished, but Mary kept all these things in her heart and thought about them often" (Luke 2:18-19 NLT).

Whether it's a high calling or difficult chore the Lord gives us, are we ready to respond like Mary?

ZECHARIAH AND ELIZABETH'S FRIENDS SAID WHAT?

*When it was time for Elizabeth's baby to be born, she gave birth
to a son. And when her neighbors and relatives heard that the Lord
had been very merciful to her, everyone rejoiced with her.*
LUKE 1:57–58 NLT

We sometimes forget that Mary and Joseph's relatives, friends, community leaders, and neighbors couldn't understand what was happening in their lives. The same was true of Zechariah and Elizabeth's neighbors.

The social pressures were so great that Elizabeth felt embarrassed and ashamed of her barrenness. Then, when she finally conceives a child in old age, she goes into seclusion for five months, and then spends three months with young Mary. They mutually build up each other's faith and ponder God's staggering plans for their sons.

Snickering about Elizabeth during her final months of pregnancy gave way to rejoicing when her baby was born healthy. When everyone gathered a week later for the Jewish circumcision ceremony, however, Elizabeth boldly confronted the older men trying to name the baby after his father. "No!" she exclaimed. "His name is John!" (Luke 1:60 NLT).

Their shock when Zechariah wrote, "His name is John," was only superseded by Zechariah praising God aloud for all He had done. Only then could he speak about his miraculous encounter with Gabriel.

Luke goes on to say, "Awe fell upon the whole neighborhood, and the news of what had happened spread throughout the Judean hills. Everyone who heard about it reflected on these events and asked, 'What will this child turn out to be?'" (Luke 1:65-66 NLT).

The forerunner of Jesus, of course!

THE ANGEL OF THE LORD SAID WHAT?

That night there were shepherds staying in the fields nearby,
guarding their flocks of sheep. Suddenly, an angel of the Lord
appeared among them, and the radiance of the Lord's glory
surrounded them. They were terrified, but the angel reassured them.
LUKE 2:8–10 NLT

"Don't be afraid!" the angel told the shepherds. "I bring you good news that will bring great joy to all people" (Luke 2:10 NLT). So great that Luke, himself a Gentile, would be asked of God to write the longest and most detailed of the four Gospel accounts. And what was the great news? That on the first Christmas, two thousand years ago, God became one of us.

Of course, that's only part of the greatest story ever told. By itself, Christmas is astounding, almost unbelievable. But it's not miraculous enough.

In scripture, the "good news that will bring great joy to all people" is never understood in terms of Christmas alone. The angel immediately goes on to say, "'The Savior—yes, the Messiah, the Lord—has been born today in Bethlehem, the city of David!'" (Luke 2:11 NLT).

In other words, the Good News is always to be understood in terms of Christmas *and* Good Friday *and* Easter. We see this not only in the Gospels, but throughout the New Testament.

God's greatest gift wasn't simply sending His Son, but sending Him to live among us, die for us, and rise again. . .to offer us the forgiveness of sins, redemption, and adoption into His family forever.

May we never grow too old to contemplate such glad tidings of great joy!

JOSEPH SAID WHAT?

This is how Jesus the Messiah was born. His mother, Mary, was engaged to be married to Joseph. But before the marriage took place, while she was still a virgin, she became pregnant through the power of the Holy Spirit. Joseph, her fiancé, was a good man and did not want to disgrace her publicly, so he decided to break the engagement quietly.

MATTHEW 1:18–19 NLT

What do we know about Joseph? He lived in Nazareth of Galilee. He worked as a carpenter. He was a good, godly man. His fiancée was godly young Mary. He liked to do things "quietly." More remarkable? An angel of the Lord spoke to him in dreams not once or twice, but four times.

The first time, the angel told him not to fear God's miraculous plan to visit earth through His Son already conceived by the Holy Spirit in Mary.

Perhaps a few months later, shortly after the visit of the magi, the angel told Joseph to get up immediately and flee to Egypt with Mary and Jesus.

Perhaps a year later, the angel appears to Joseph in a third dream, telling him to return to Israel. In a companion dream a short time later, Joseph is told to take Mary and Jesus farther north back to Galilee. In the end, they return to their hometown, Nazareth.

So, what do we know about Joseph? He is a man of action, immediately getting up in the middle of the night to obey God. More remarkable? Scripture doesn't record a single word Joseph said.

What matters most is being a good, godly man of action!

THE ANGEL CHOIR SAID WHAT?

And suddenly there was with the angel a multitude of the heavenly host praising God, and saying, Glory to God in the highest, and on earth peace, good will toward men.
LUKE 2:13–14 KJV

So profound were the events of the first Christmas that one angel of the Lord wasn't enough. As soon as the angel finishes his announcement of "good tiding of great joy" to the shepherds of Bethlehem, the lights go up and a choir of hundreds—perhaps thousands—of angels celebrate in song. In words immortalized by Linus each year during the TV special, *A Charlie Brown Christmas*, Luke tells us:

> And there were in the same country shepherds abiding in the field, keeping watch over their flock by night. And, lo, the angel of the Lord came upon them, and the glory of the Lord shone round about them: and they were sore afraid.
>
> And the angel said unto them, Fear not: for, behold, I bring you good tidings of great joy, which shall be to all people. For unto you is born this day in the city of David a Saviour, which is Christ the Lord. And this shall be a sign unto you; Ye shall find the babe wrapped in swaddling clothes, lying in a manger.
>
> And suddenly there was with the angel a multitude of the heavenly host praising God, and saying, Glory to God in the highest, and on earth peace, good will toward men.
> (Luke 2:8–14 KJV)

Glory to God, indeed!

THE SHEPHERDS SAID WHAT?

When the angels had returned to heaven, the shepherds said to each other,
"Let's go to Bethlehem! Let's see this thing that has happened,
which the Lord has told us about."

LUKE 2:15 NLT

God had visited the fields of Bethlehem with singing before. A thousand years earlier, His Spirit inspired a shepherd to sing dozens of songs of praise (including psalms in our Bibles today). Of course, every Israelite also knew that particular shepherd eventually left the fields and went on to become Israel's greatest king.

No one had such hopes, however, for these shepherds. Much more important people—King David's descendants—filled the rooms of Bethlehem's inns.

Yet it was not to any of the VIPs that God sent His angel and the armies of heaven to announce the birth of the Savior, the Son of David. Instead, God displayed His extraordinary concert and light show to a group of shepherds—and invited them to see the Messiah so many others had been waiting for.

Although initially awed and stunned by the breathtaking message of the angels, the shepherds immediately ran to see the baby, swaddled in cloth and snuggled in the hay, just as the angel said. This baby fulfilled every godly Israelite's greatest hopes and answered every God-fearing Gentile's deepest longings.

The shepherds couldn't stick around all night, of course. As they headed back to the hills and their sleeping sheep, scripture tells us they told the miraculous news to everyone they met. Sadly, they probably were mocked. After all, who would believe a bunch of *shepherds*?

It mattered not if others believed. They *knew*.

SIMEON SAID WHAT?

At that time there was a man in Jerusalem named Simeon.
He was righteous and devout and was eagerly
waiting for the Messiah. . .
LUKE 2:25 NLT

". . . to come and rescue Israel. The Holy Spirit was upon him and had revealed to him that he would not die until he had seen the Lord's Messiah.

> *That day the Spirit led him to the Temple. So when Mary and Joseph came to present the baby Jesus to the Lord as the law required, Simeon was there.*
> *He took the child in his arms and praised God, saying, 'Sovereign Lord, now let your servant die in peace, as you have promised. I have seen your salvation, which you have prepared for all people. He is a light to reveal God to the nations, and he is the glory of your people Israel!'*
> *Jesus' parents were amazed at what was being said about him. Then Simeon blessed them, and he said to Mary, the baby's mother, 'This child is destined to cause many in Israel to fall, but he will be a joy to many others. He has been sent as a sign from God, but many will oppose him. As a result, the deepest thoughts of many hearts will be revealed. And a sword will pierce your very soul'"*
> (Luke 2:27–35 NLT).

Like Simeon, we can wake up each day looking forward to the promise of Jesus' coming again. Unlike Simeon, however, we don't know when.

We may or may not see Jesus Christ's return in our lifetime.

It's so hard to wait.

First Day of Winter

ANNA SAID WHAT?

Anna, a prophet, was also there in the Temple. She was the daughter
of Phanuel from the tribe of Asher, and she was very old.
Her husband died when they had been married only seven years.
Then she lived as a widow to the age of eighty-four.

LUKE 2:36–37 NLT

Like Simeon, Anna was quite elderly, but she wasn't waiting around to die. Instead, every day she woke up with the expectation that today could be the day she had dreamed about for decades.

> She never left the Temple but stayed there day and night,
> worshiping God with fasting and prayer.
> (Luke 2:37 NLT)

Unlike Simeon, who had God's promise that he would not die until he saw the Lord's Messiah, Anna had no such guarantee. Like many others, however, she knew the time of the Messiah's coming was near. While she waited, she lived righteously and devoutly with all her heart.

When Mary and Joseph entered the temple with the newborn Jesus in their arms, they looked like any other devout couple fulfilling their duty to God. Then again, to an old woman led by the Spirit, the family stood out as if in a spotlight. The small child and his parents were welcomed to God's house as no family had ever been greeted before.

> She talked about the child to everyone who had been
> waiting expectantly for God to rescue Jerusalem.
> (Luke 2:38 NLT)

Imagine how Anna must have praised God and shared the good news! May we do the same.

THE MAGI SAID WHAT?

About that time some wise men from eastern lands arrived in
Jerusalem, asking, "Where is the newborn king of the Jews?"
MATTHEW 2:1–2 NLT

Why did the magi risk everything? These wise men had become holy fools—desperate, compelled, and finally obsessed. In the end, they traveled a thousand miles or more, probably in a small camel train, only to stop in Jerusalem to ask, "Where is the newborn king of the Jews?" King Herod was deeply disturbed when they asked this

(Matthew 2:3 NLT).

These men may have come from a prestigious city of the ancient Medes, Persians, or Chaldeans. Braving extreme heat, sandstorms, and the constant threat of thieves, these magi traveled for months through foreign lands to the far west—to within a day of the great Mediterranean Sea.

Then Herod called for a private meeting with the wise men.
(Matthew 2:7 NLT)

Why then their intense dedication to find Jesus Christ? Somehow, they knew that God in heaven had sent His Son to earth. They felt driven to welcome this child and to present Him with exquisite gifts of great wealth.

After this interview the wise men went. . .to Bethlehem.
(Matthew 2:9 NLT)

Why such persistence and risk? What in the world did they hope to gain?

They returned to their own country by another route, for
God had warned them.
(Matthew 2:12 NLT)

Like the magi, you and I have a terrible, haunting choice to make. Are we willing to risk it all? For what?

KING HEROD SAID WHAT?

*Then he told them,
"Go to Bethlehem and search carefully for the child."*
MATTHEW 2:8 NLT

What is Christmas without a little drama? For children, the plethora of casting options includes sheep and camels. For adults, the choices narrow a bit, and some parts admittedly have become more favored than others.

Which part would you prefer to play? Zechariah? Joseph? A shepherd? A wise man?

No, we reject such options and by default find ourselves living in ease and plenty, like King Herod, who feigned reverence for the one born King of the Jews, yet was driven by the cold calculus that a slaughter of the innocents now might, possibly, someday save his own neck.

Yes, with such a clear-cut calculus, we, too, are more than eager to raise our hands and voices, saying, "Pick me! I want to play the part of King Herod." Yes, it's us. True, we won't take their lives ourselves, but we'll demand that today's international refugees die somewhere else, offstage, if only to ensure that we still get to take the final bow.

After all, King Herod has the best of all lines: "Go to Bethlehem and search carefully for the child. And when you find him, come back and tell me so that I can go and worship him, too!" (Matthew 2:8 NLT).

If today's refugees are going to die, Charles Dickens was right: They had best hurry up and do it and decrease the world's excess refugee population.

Of course, this is satirical. Yet some accept such cold reasoning as gospel truth. After all, what is Christmas without a little drama?

Christmas Eve

THE CHIEF PRIESTS AND SCRIBES SAID WHAT?

He called a meeting of the leading priests and teachers of religious law and asked, "Where is the Messiah supposed to be born?" "In Bethlehem in Judea," they said, "for this is what the prophet wrote: 'And you, O Bethlehem in the land of Judah, are not least among the ruling cities of Judah, for a ruler will come from you who will be the shepherd for my people Israel.'"

MATTHEW 2:4–6 NLT

How radical is the idea behind Christmas? The religious leaders at the time scoffed at the shepherds' report. They couldn't imagine God, Creator and Sustainer of the universe, humbling Himself to visit earth. Yet the scriptures clearly predicted this—and they knew it! Isaiah alone had made two dozen specific prophecies fulfilled seven centuries later by Jesus, the Christ.

- being born of a virgin, being called "Immanuel" (7:14)
- being anointed with the Spirit (11:2, 61:1), start of his public ministry (61:1–2), starting in Galilee (9:1–2)
- poverty (53:2), meekness (42:2), tenderness, compassion (40:11, 42:3), innocence (53:9)
- working miracles (35:5–6)
- being rejected (63:3), being a stumbling block (8:14), being hated (49:7)
- suffering for others (53:4–6, 12), patience, silence amidst suffering (53:7)
- appearance marred (52:14, 53:3), being spit on, scourged (50:6), being numbered with criminals (53:12), praying for His murderers (53:12)
- death (53:12), being buried with the rich (53:9), resurrection (26:19), being the "chief cornerstone" (28:16)

Unlike the religious leaders of old, let's actively affirm our belief in Jesus, the Christ!

TIME WITH FAMILY AND FRIENDS ON CHRISTMAS DAY

And while they were there, the time came for her baby to be born.
She gave birth to her first child, a son. She wrapped him
snugly in strips of cloth and laid him in a manger,
because there was no lodging available for them.
LUKE 2:6–7 NLT

What a wonderful day it is! As you share Christmas with loved ones and friends, you may want to read a favorite devotional from the past week or two. You also may want to ask a few good-natured questions to spark lively and warmhearted conversations.

What is one of your favorite foods at Christmastime?
What is one of your favorite beverages at Christmastime?

What is one of the aromas you enjoy the most at Christmastime?
What is one of the sights you enjoy the most at Christmastime?

What is one of your favorite songs to hear at Christmastime?
What is one of your favorite classic Christmas hymns?

What is one of your favorite Christmas memories as a child?
What is one of your favorite Christmas memories as an adult?

How much snow does it take to make it a favorite Christmas for you?
What else does it take to make it a favorite Christmas for you?

If you could go anywhere at Christmastime, where would you go?
If you could go anywhere this coming year, where would you go?

What is one of the best or most unusual gifts you have ever given?
What is one of the best or most unusual gifts you have ever received?

Ask each in love!

SEEING LIFE AS JESUS CHRIST SEES IT

Jesus wept.
JOHN 11:35 KJV

Did you enjoy Christmas with family and friends? During this wonderful season, we often like to read great literature, watch a great movie, or hear a great story—and be deeply moved.

Yet what moves us?

Among other things, point of view (POV) strongly affects how we're moved.

To the very finite, limited extent that a story's POV reflects God's POV, we can be moved to a new appreciation of Jesus Christ's unlimited POV in our lives.

POV can be omniscient or all-knowing. It doesn't mean the narrator tells us everything he or she knows. In fact, the best narrators tell us only what we need to know. During His public ministry, Jesus certainly didn't say everything He knew. In fact, most times He refused to answer the direct questions darting His way. He did that on purpose!

POV can be omnipotent or all-powerful. In most stories, the narrator isn't directly making this or that happen. Then again, that sometimes happens. Outside of the days of Moses, the days of Elijah and Elisha, and the days of Jesus Christ and the apostles, God doesn't directly speak to individuals, cast down plagues, blind armies, and bend the laws of nature. Or, does He?

POV can be omnipresent or all-present. Among other places, this is seen in movies with rapidly changing points of view, particularly during epic battle scenes.

Again, any story's POV is only a small inkling of the Lord's unlimited POV. So, don't get too carried away! Still, look for this the next time you sit down to enjoy a great story.

WHY WE DON'T NEED TO FEAR THE FUTURE

"Don't let your hearts be troubled."
JOHN 14:1 NLT

Outside of the Bible, no other sacred writings contain accurate, specific, detailed prophecies of future events. After all, only God can say what's going to happen! In 125 words, here's what we learn from biblical prophecy.

> *We should never be surprised by the phenomenal (albeit short-lived) success of evil, Satan-inspired men. Until the climax of history, many evil men will triumph for a time. The twentieth century was no exception. There's no reason to believe the twenty-first century will be an exception either. But we never need fear that evil will triumph completely. Why not? Because God controls the day they ascend to power and the day of their downfall. This will be true of even the most wicked, Satan-inspired man of all, the Antichrist. In the end, God will crush His enemies. Of that we can be sure! No matter what happens this century, we need to keep the end of God's story clearly in view—and never lose faith.*

After calling His first disciples, Jesus takes them to Capernaum, where an unseen war became visible momentarily. When a demon-possessed man tries to tell Jesus what to do, He immediate rebukes the evil spirit and tells *him* what to do. To everyone's astonishment, the demon has to obey what Jesus says.

The reality is we all have to obey Jesus. We may shake and scream. We may try to tell Jesus what to do. But in the end, *we* have to obey Him. The question isn't, "Is Jesus Lord of your life?" The question is, "Have you acknowledged that fact?"

THE FIRST WAY WE BECOME WHOLE MEN

And Jesus grew in wisdom and stature,
and in favor with God and men.
LUKE 2:52 NIV

We live in a broken world. . .full of broken promises, broken dreams, broken lives. Nothing seems "all together" anymore. In the midst of such shatteredness, however, God invites us to experience wholeness. Wholeness in our own life and in our relationships.

As a result, growth as whole persons is anything but optional. We see this most concisely in the Bible's description of Jesus as a teenager (quoted above). Though Jesus was the perfect Son of God, He experienced apparent personal growth in four ways.

It is vital that we do the same! As we countdown to 2018, let's consider each way—from the most tangible to the most spiritual.

PHYSICALLY ("and stature")

We need proper exercise physically. How? By playing ball. Golfing. Walking. Jogging. By riding a stationary bike. By working out with light weights. By exercising regularly. . .and feeling better as a result.

We need proper rest physically. How? By not pushing too hard all the time. By getting enough sleep. By taking take a nap if needed (even professional athletes do this when necessary). By being consistent in our sleeping patterns (inconsistency makes us even more tired—think "jet lag").

We need proper nourishment physically. How? By eating three well-planned meals daily. By eating plenty of whole grains, vegetables, fruits, and proteins. By enjoying desserts and junk food once in a while, not as a steady diet.

In everything, let's give thanks to God for blessing us with the joys that come from good exercise, sleep, and eating!

THE SECOND WAY WE BECOME WHOLE MEN

Now that we know what we have—Jesus, this great High Priest with ready access to God—let's not let it slip through our fingers. We don't have a priest who is out of touch with our reality. He's been through weakness and testing, experienced it all—all but the sin. So let's walk right up to him and get what he is so ready to give. Take the mercy, accept the help.
HEBREWS 4:14–16 MSG

Though Jesus was the perfect Son of God, He experienced apparent personal growth. This enabled Him to relate fully with others. The same can be true for us. . .

SOCIALLY ("and man," Luke 2:52 NIV)

We need proper exercise socially. How? By cultivating existing friendships. By sharing a meal with new friends from church. By offering practical assistance to a neighbor. By being a listening ear. By keeping in touch with family. By praying for others by name.

We need proper rest socially. How? By taking breaks. By enjoying the great outdoors. By jettisoning any compulsive need to be with others all the time. By appreciating downtime before an appointment. By listening to a favorite mix of music. By meditating on God's Word. By taking extended time to worship and pray privately.

We need proper nourishment socially. How? By not viewing all friendships the same. By discerning who our good friends and our closest friends are. By cultivating deep friendships. By inviting trusted friends to speak into our lives with truth and grace. In turn, by actively encouraging our best friend to become the man God wants him to be.

THE THIRD WAY WE BECOME WHOLE MEN

May God himself, the God of peace, sanctify you through and through.
May your whole spirit, soul and body be kept blameless at the coming of
our Lord Jesus Christ. The one who calls you is faithful, and he will do it.
1 THESSALONIANS 5:23–24 NIV

How good that God invites us to experience personal growth and wholeness four ways. The past two days we've looked at good health physically and socially. Today, let's look at a third way. . .

PSYCHOLOGICALLY ("in wisdom," Luke 2:52 NIV)

We need proper exercise volitionally. How? By our choices. In particular, by consistently exercising our will for good. Each of us faces the problem of "choice overload." Daily we are faced with too many choices. Not only must we decide preferences between viable options, but we also must make healthy moral judgments, especially in so-called gray areas.

We need proper rest emotionally. How? By getting a refreshing night's sleep. By spending time with a godly friend. By reading an edifying book. By listening to uplifting music. By spending quality quiet time with the Lord. By slowing down (if we've been pushing too hard). By doing more (if we've been too lax). By actively seeking to balance life's demands. By making specific plans for another vacation, even if it's simply a quick getaway.

We need proper nourishment intellectually. How? Actually, scripture has a lot to say! By renewing our mind (Romans 12:1–2). By cultivating a discerning mind (Hebrews 5:14). By nurturing an enlightened mind (1 Corinthians 2:12). By protecting our mind (Philippians 4:8). And, by occupying our mind with Christ (Ephesians 4:13).

New Year's Eve

THE FOURTH WAY WE BECOME WHOLE MEN

Everyone who heard about it reflected on these events and asked,
"What will this child turn out to be?" For the hand of the Lord
was surely upon him in a special way. . . . John grew up
and became strong in spirit. And he lived in the wilderness
until he began his public ministry to Israel.

Luke 1:66, 80 NLT

Happy New Year's Eve! Thankfully, there's still time to keep growing stronger physically, socially, psychologically and. . .

SPIRITUALLY ("with God," Luke 2:52 NIV)

We need proper exercise spiritually. How? By getting on our knees. By depending on God to meet our needs. By coming alongside a friend who's struggling in his faith. By investing in the life of a friend who isn't a Christian yet.

We need proper rest spiritually. How? If a particular spiritual discipline feels "dry," by taking a short break from it and selecting two or three "rest" verses to memorize and claim as our own. Favorites include: "Be still before the LORD and wait patiently for him" (Psalm 37:7 NIV); "Truly my soul silently waits for God; from Him comes my salvation" (Psalm 62:1 NKJV); and "Those who live in the shelter of the Most High will find rest in the shadow of the Almighty" (Psalm 91:1 NLT).

We need proper nourishment spiritually. How? By reading scripture wholeheartedly, asking God to speak to you. By meeting with a small group that loves God and its members. By attending services at a vibrant local church each Sunday. By inviting a wise, gracious older believer to mentor you. And, finally, by reading edifying Christian books.

CONTRIBUTORS

Rev. Robin Burkhart, PhD, has served for more than thirty years as a pastor, author, educator, and denominational leader. His varied background includes ministry in Latin and South America, the Caribbean, Europe, Africa, and the People's Republic of China. He is the father of three adult children and five grandchildren. His readings can be found in the month of April.

Ed Cyzewski is the author of *A Christian Survival Guide: A Lifeline to Faith and Growth* and *Coffeehouse Theology: Reflecting on God in Everyday Life,* and is the coauthor of *The Good News of Revelation* and *Unfollowers: Unlikely Lessons on Faith from Those Who Doubted Jesus.* He writes about prayer and imperfectly following Jesus at www.edcyzewski.com. His readings can be found in the month of May.

Glenn A. Hascall is an accomplished writer with credits in more than one hundred books. He is a broadcast veteran and voice actor and is actively involved in writing and producing radio dramas. His readings can be found in the month of March and July.

Jess MacCallum is president of Professional Printers, Inc. in Columbia, South Carolina. He has authored three books—two on marriage, and one on raising daughters—and has twice been featured on "Family Life Today with Dr. Dennis Rainey." He also works with two leadership organizations as an executive coach, and is a regular contributor to HealthyLeaders.com. Jess has been married for 28 years, and has three grown children. His readings can be found in the month of November.

Chuck Miller lives in Sylvania Township, Ohio. He worked for fourteen years as a high school English, journalism, and Bible teacher in the public schools of Lexington, Kentucky, and then at Toledo Christian Schools. He worked as a hospital chaplain—nights and weekends, the "disaster shift"—for seven years, and currently works in the surgical instrument department of that hospital and as a freelance writer of devotions and poetry. Some of his devotional work and poetry can be found on his website, BardofChrist.net. He's been married for forty-two years; his four-year-old grandson Preston (aka "Pres-Tron"!) is the joy of his life. His readings can be found in the month of September.

David Sanford serves on the leadership team at Corban University, which is consistently ranked by *US News Best Colleges* as one of Top 10 colleges in the West. Among his many credits, David has served as executive editor of *Holy Bible: Mosaic*, general editor of the popular *Handbook on Thriving as an Adoptive Family*, coauthor of the bestselling *God Is Relevant*, and author of *If God Disappears*. Better yet? David is husband to Renée, dad to five, and grandpa to nine (and one in heaven). His readings can be found in the month of December.

Ed Strauss is a freelance writer in British Columbia. He has authored or coauthored more than fifty books for children, tweens, and adults. His readings can be found in the months of January and August.

Tracy M. Sumner is a freelance author, writer, and editor in Beaverton, Oregon. An avid outdoorsman, he enjoys fly-fishing on world-class Oregon waters. His readings can be found in the month of June.

Mike Vander Klipp is a professional editor and writer who works in the Zondervan Bible Division of HarperCollins Christian Publishing. He and his writer/editor wife live with their teenagers, the cats, and the dog in Grand Rapids, Michigan. His readings can be found in the month of October.

Lee Warren is published in such varied venues as Discipleship Journal, Sports Spectrum, Yahoo! Sports, Crosswalk.com, and ChristianityToday.com. He is also the author of the book *Finishing Well: Living with the End in Mind* (A Devotional), and he writes regular features for The Pathway newspaper and Living Light News. Lee makes his home in Omaha, Nebraska. His readings can be found in the month of February.

SCRIPTURE INDEX

84:12 July 29
90:12 March 12
91:1 August 8
92:12 April 9
95:2 August 21
103:14 November 13
118:24 March 26
119:9–11 July 21
119:165 June 7
127:3 March 6
138:8 July 3
145:8–9 May 20

Proverbs
3:4 July 20
3:11–12 January 26
3:27–28 September 9
4:18 January 1
5:3–4 February 10
10:9 July 8
11:13 June 20
13:11 January 12
13:12 January 9
14:4 November 6
14:23 January 4
15:23 January 21
16:3 January 2
17:9 August 12
17:22 August 10
18:15 February 13

18:24 August 6
20:7 June 21
22:1 June 24; July 13
22:29 February 1
27:2 June 1
27:17 March 28
29:23 July 27

Ecclesiastes
3:1, 4 January 17
9:10 January 19
10:10 November 21

Isaiah
1:18 June 22
6:1, 5 October 30
38:1 September 10
42:6–7 May 7
55:8–9 July 15
64:8 November 3

Jeremiah
9:23–24 June 11
10:23 March 31
15:16 May 25
29:11 July 23
33:2–3 May 24

Ezekiel
2:4–5 May 22

1 Peter
1:1 February 18
3:15 January 22
4:3 February 4
4:10 March 16
4:12-13 May 27
5:8 April 27
5:10 April 28

1 John
2:1 June 17
3:1 July 24
3:14 February 19
3:21-22 September 7
4:10 July 16
4:18 August 17

3 John
1:5-6 May 21

Jude
1:22-23 June 29

Revelation
1:13, 15-17 October 31
3:11 August 14

Love Sports and the Outdoors?
Check Out...

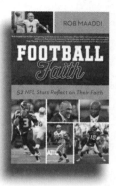

Football Faith by Rob Maaddi

Football Faith will inspire and encourage readers in their faith journey, as 52 NFL players share their stories and how they are chasing the success that only comes from being God's man and following His plan. Featuring personal stories from Russell Wilson, Aaron Rodgers, Colin Kaepernick, Deion Sanders, and dozens more—plus with a foreword from Coach Joe Gibbs.

Paperback / 978-1-63409-222-7 / $16.99

The Man Minute by Jason Cruise

Every "Man Minute" devotional is designed to be read in sixty seconds, yet a man will carry the insights he gleans into a lifelong journey of spiritual manhood. *The Man Minute* is packaged alongside a DVD featuring hunts—each couched in spiritual truths—with some of the most recognized hunters on the planet.

Hardback / 978-1-63058-718-5 / $16.99